Deaf in Delhi

DEAF IN DELHI

A Memoir

MADAN VASISHTA

GALLAUDET UNIVERSITY PRESS
Washington, D.C.

Deaf Lives
A Series Edited by Brenda Jo Brueggemann

Gallaudet University Press
Washington, D.C. 20002
http://gupress.gallaudet.edu

ISBN 1-56368-284-2

Library of Congress Cataloging-in-Publication Data

Vasishta, Madan, 1941–
    Deaf in Delhi : a memoir / Madan Vasishta.
    p. cm.
    Includes bibliographical references and index.
    ISBN 1-56368-284-2 (alk. paper)
    1. Vasishta, Madan, 1941– 2. Deaf—India—Delhi—Biography. I. Title.

HV2865.D45V38 2006
362.4′2092—dc22
[B]
                                                            2005055214

CONTENTS

Pt #1

Pt. #2

To my parents,
Hakim Rai and Sandhya Devi,
for their love and faith in me

ACKNOWLEDGMENTS

Yes, I wrote this book, but I probably wouldn't have without the encouragement of many people in my life. Much love and thanks to my wife Nirmala, for her patience and support;

> to my two children, Dheeraj and Neerja, for being enthusiastic about this project, reading drafts, and giving me honest input, some of which I even incorporated;
>
> to Cathryn Carroll, for making me believe that I could write;
>
> to Brenda Brueggemann, my editor, for combining cheerleading with editing;
>
> to Christine Torres, Brenda's assistant, for carrying on Brenda's work;
>
> to Annette Posell for reading the whole manuscript;
>
> to Eugene Bergman, friend and philosopher, for pushing me when needed;
>
> to my brother-in-law, R. L. Joshi, for telling me, "you've got to write it!"

There are many others who suffered through reading parts of various drafts and who encouraged me to write this memoir. The list is long and I cannot include them here, but I am thankful to all.

Deaf in Delhi

Madan Vasishta's Family Tree

GENERATION TWO   GENERATION THREE

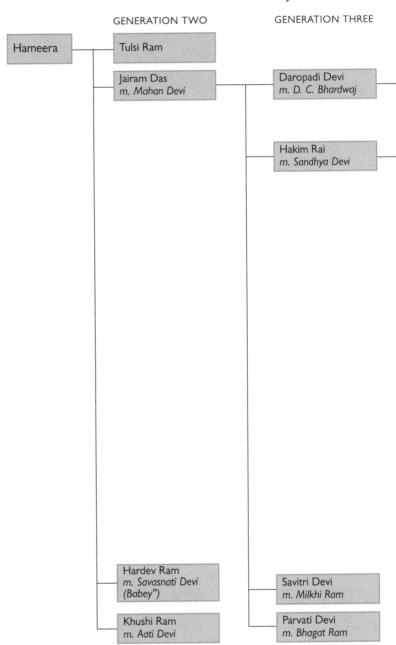

Hameera

Tulsi Ram

Jairam Das
m. Mahan Devi

Daropadi Devi
m. D. C. Bhardwaj

Hakim Rai
m. Sandhya Devi

Hardev Ram
m. Savasnati Devi
(Babey")

Savitri Devi
m. Milkhi Ram

Khushi Ram
m. Aati Devi

Parvati Devi
m. Bhagat Ram

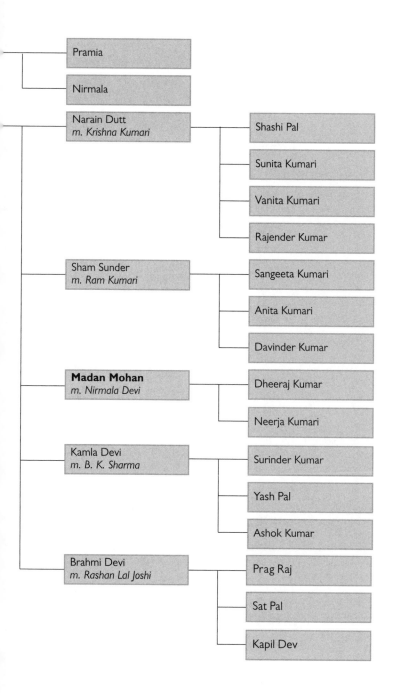

1

Silent Morning

IN THE EARLY MORNING HOURS OF JANUARY
5, 1952, my life changed forevermore. I was a few weeks short of turning
eleven and had been sick with the mumps and typhoid for two weeks.
But that night, I went to bed feeling a bit better and thought I would go
to school the next morning. During the night, I woke up with a strange
feeling. I shivered in the cold of the pitch-dark room I shared with my
mother and Sham, my elder brother. I knew something was not right,
but I had no idea what it could be. My head was full of very loud noises,
as if I were standing in a major railroad station. I heard blaring whistles,
people yelling, and trains thudding along the tracks. This noise had
awakened me, or so I thought. I stared hard inside the room and saw
nothing but darkness.

I felt frightened.

"Bhabhi," I called.

Bhabhi, which means "elder brother's wife," was my mother. I called
her Bhabhi, as did everyone in our joint family. Bhabhi did not answer.
Growing more frightened by the minute, I said her name again, louder
this time, with all the strength my fever-ravaged body could muster.

"Bhabhi!"

Still there was no answer. The darkness became scarier.

I was about to yell again, when I saw a flicker of light. My mother
had struck a match and was lighting the hurricane lamp. She closed the
chimney over the wick and, holding the hurricane lamp high in her hand,
stepped toward me and started to talk. That is, I saw her lips move, but
there was no sound.

My fear deepened.

"Why are you not using your voice?" I began screaming.

My mother, her face bewildered, kept moving her lips without using any voice. My heart pounded and my head hurt. My hands found my face and I felt it wet with tears.

Suddenly, I understood.

"Oh, Bhabhi, I cannot hear!" I began to sob uncontrollably, and my mother began to cry too. She sat next to my bed and her face blurred before me as her lips kept moving.

She must have called Babey, her elder sister who was married to my father's uncle. Babey had come into the room and was also staring at me, her heavily wrinkled face filled with bewilderment, sorrow, and disbelief. Then I saw my father, whom we called *Babuji,* appear.

"Babuji!"

I had a lot of faith in my father and wanted him to cure me right then. He did nothing, however. He just stood there transfixed—shocked and grim, stoical and silent—behind the two weeping women. I was disappointed. Another face joined the onlookers. It was Narain, my eldest brother, whom I called Bhai Narain or Bhaiji. I saw him confer with my father, go away, and then return after a few minutes with a notebook and a pen. Narain scribbled on it determinedly and held it out to me.

I still remember the Urdu text verbatim. "Madan ji," he wrote. "Cannot you hear? Do not worry. It is three a.m. As soon as it is light, we will call the doctor and have him treat you. You will be fine soon."

I read the message and relief flooded over me. His mention of doctors, fixing my hearing, the coming morning—all gave me hope. Great hope. I stopped crying while my mother dried my eyes. I looked at the faces gathered around me, and the faces looked back at me. Their lips kept moving. They were talking to each other without using any sound. Tired and overwhelmed, I fell back asleep.

When I woke again, it was light. Babuji was talking with Vaid Naranjan, his friend and our family doctor. *Vaid* means an ayurvedic doctor. Such doctors follow the ancient Hindu practices in ayurvedic medicine, and Vaid Naranjan was known for his expertise. He was like an uncle to all of us.

He smiled at me. I was glad to see him. He was going to cure me!

"What is up?" he asked me, making the gesture with his hand that everyone in Northern India uses—an open palm with the thumb facing you at chest level, which swiveled inwardly accompanied by raised eyebrows and a questioning look. I found myself crying again at the realization of the catastrophe that had befallen me. I said, "I cannot hear." Then I added, "I have very loud noises in my head." Vaid Naranjan gestured to me to be calm and began to feel my pulse and forehead. I still had a high fever and a splitting headache. Vaid Naranjan talked to my father and stood up.

"You shall be okay," he gestured. Babuji walked over and patted my forehead, and the two men stepped away from me, conferring with voices I could not hear.

I stared at the ceiling and tried to understand the loud sounds in my head. The noise was so loud that I could not hear other people talk. I wondered how I could make that noise go away. I tried, but I could not. However, in this effort, I learned that I could change that noise as I wished. The railroad noise changed to someone talking loudly. Then I made it sound like a movie song that I liked. This knowledge made me smile.

Suddenly, I noticed faces at the door: my elder brother Sham, my cousin Ramesh, and another cousin Vishwa. They wore clean clothes and shoes, and their hair was combed. Book satchels hung on their shoulders. I knew they were going to school after two weeks of winter break. The realization that I was not going was painful. I looked away from them to hide my tears. They did not say anything; they just stared.

Until today, they were talking to me and playing with me. Today, they just looked and did not dare even to enter the room. They did not even wave their hands; and neither did I. We looked at each other across a gulf that none of us understood, and then I was alone.

They had been my companions since I was born. We went to school, played soccer and other sports, went to the well to bring water; we did almost everything together. Now they were going out on their own, leaving me behind. On that day, I understood that I would be traveling a different path.

2

Panic

I WAS DEAF.

I could not hear. I could not understand people. Birds did not chirp, cows did not moo, the wind did not howl, stray village dogs did not bark!

It was total silence, but it was not!

The noise in my head continued unabated and, having nothing to do, I played with this pesky noise. I had an orchestra playing in there. I tried to get the noise out of my head with the belief that once I got rid of it, I would be able to hear. I decided that this noise was blocking out all the other sounds. My efforts kept my mind from thinking too deeply about my condition.

The weakened condition of my body was even worse than the noise in my head. After one month of high fever, I could not get up from bed. Bhabhi and Sham or another relative would help me get up when I needed to relieve myself. It was very embarrassing as I had to sit on a bowl placed in a corner of the room. I would sit on it and relieve myself while they looked away to give me a false sense of privacy. The stench made me sick, but Sham and Bhabhi never mentioned it. They would carry the bowl outside, keeping it at arm's length, and throw the contents in the gorge outside the cluster of houses where we lived.

During the day, they would put a cot outside in the sun and carry me to it. There I would lie under quilts, savoring the warmth of the January sun and hiding my face from the village women who gathered in front of our house daily to swap gossip. I would not look at them when they tried to talk to me. My deafness embarrassed me. They would patiently come and try to get my attention. I learned to shut them out just by looking away. If you can hear, you cannot ignore people trying to get your attention; if you are deaf, it is easy—just look away! I realized there were benefits to being deaf!

4

But the idea of being deaf petrified me. I shuddered at the terms *bola* in Punjabi, *behra* in Urdu, and *vadhir* in Hindi. All these are extremely offensive and derogatory words to describe someone who is not really a human. I had never known a deaf person in my life; however, I had seen one. Thinking about him while lying in the warm January sun in Gagret made me wish I could hide under the quilt until I disappeared.

The only deaf person in our village was an old man who was also mentally retarded. He had no name. Every one called him bola. Both his legs were bent and he walked funny. He couldn't talk; instead he sounded like a dog in pain. He wore torn clothes that were almost never washed. Other members of his family dressed much better than him. His elder brother, based on the talk in the village, got the old man's share of land and made him work like a slave on their farm.

We boys used to make fun of him. We would stop him and make him put down the sack in which he carried grass he had cut with the scythe he always carried. We would make obscene gestures, and he would laugh and copy us. We would roll on the ground laughing at his signs for masturbating or having sex with someone. He would laugh with us. Sometimes, he would get mad at us and make horrible sounds that would scare us, and we would run away.

Now I was bola.

Lying sick in my bed, I thought more and more about that old deaf man. I imagined growing up and being like him. I thought about being ridiculed by young kids and wearing torn clothes. I would hide my head in the quilt and cry silently at this bleak and miserable vision of my future.

I had always been a very good student. Ramesh and I were always at the top of our class. Teachers had always spoken glowingly about me. I had gotten used to them saying, "He is going to be a doctor or a lawyer." This was significant because Gagret was a farming village, and few boys there finished the eighth grade. Babuji was one of Gagret's first men to finish high school. There I was, a boy from Gagret who was going to be a doctor!

The fall from the dream of being the first doctor from the village to being the village idiot shocked and depressed me. I was also unable to speak to anyone about my condition. My friends were at school and my cousins were afraid of being around me. Ramesh, Sham, and Vishwa would sometimes stop by after school, but they would talk with each other and give yes-or-no answers to my questions about school (What was being taught? How was this or that kid?).

My deafness affected my interactions with others. I would start talking to people when they were in the middle of a sentence or talking to someone else. Everyone was patient about it, but I could detect some hidden annoyance at these rude interruptions. I also began speaking too softly or too loudly. Hearing people increase or lower the volume of their voice in order to be heard and depending on background noise. I noticed people looking at me in surprise when I spoke very loudly in a quiet room or ignoring me when I spoke in a normal voice in a noisy atmosphere. Either way, it was frustrating.

My optimistic nature, however, helped me stay in good humor. I imagined waking up one morning fully hearing, just like I had woken up fully deaf. This possibility gave me a playful idea. When I regained my hearing, I would keep it a secret. That way I could eavesdrop on all the conversations around me. Of course, I thought, I would have to keep a poker face and not laugh if someone said something funny. I thought about pretending to be deaf for the rest of my life. However, I had to change that plan because I could no longer attend school until I was hearing again.

The morning I was going to wake up hearing, however, never came.

3

Looking for a Cure

ON THE MORNING I WOKE UP DEAF, VAID NARANJAN left about twenty hand-rolled homeopathic pills for me to take. I swallowed one pill, which Bhabhi gave me with warm water, and waited. Bhabhi stood there with the glass in her hand, her face expectant and questioning.

"I do not hear anything!" I said disappointedly.

She put the glass down, brought her mouth close to my left ear, and I felt some warm air. I shook my head in despair. The pill did not work!

Bhabhi moved her open palm up and down in front of her—a gesture for patience. I agreed reluctantly, remembering that homeopathic medicines took time to take effect. In the past, whenever we were sick, we had to swallow Vaid Naranjan's pills or powdered medication. They always took several days to take effect.

Soon though, the pills were gone without any improvement in my hearing. Vaid Naranjan must have told Babuji about his inability to cure me as plans were made to take me to Hoshiarpur, the nearest city, sixteen miles away.

Babuji told me of this plan one night. He wrote in Urdu on his left palm with the index finger of his right hand.

"We are going to Hoshiarpur tomorrow!" he traced, while I peered at his moving index finger.

"Who is there?" I asked, hoping it might mean new hope for me.

"There is a doctor. He is good. He might help."

The next morning, I was dressed in several layers of warm clothes for the trip. I was still weak and walked between Ramesh and Sham, holding them for support. We had to stop several times for me to rest between our home and the bazaar where the bus stand was located. I was upset at my weakness. I was also embarrassed; as we passed houses,

Front row: Bhua Parvati (Bhua means that she's my father's sister), Bhabhi, Babey, Bhua Savitri. Back row: Sister Brahmi, Sister-in-law Karishna, Sister-in-law Ram Kumari (Sham's wife), Sister Kamla. Taken in 1964.

faces in doors appeared to look at me. Young children not old enough to go to school clung to their mothers, who covered their faces behind veils because of Babuji's age. As they stared, I told myself, they are looking at the bola, the one and only.

Sham and Ramesh went to school after escorting me to the bus stand. The Hoshiarpur bus was to leave at 9:00 in the morning, but did not show up until around 9:45. Like all things in India at that time, buses did not follow the schedule. No one complained, and being late or early was taken for granted.

The sixteen-mile trip from Gagret to Hoshiarpur took forty-five minutes even though most of the road was paved. The winding road required the bus to go as slow as five miles an hour. The passengers fell on each other at each steep S-shaped turn, despite hanging on to seat backs and window bars. Babuji held me to keep me steady. He tried to write something on his palm but I looked away. I did not want anyone on the bus to know I was deaf. However, everyone knew Babuji, and he had to explain to them why we were going to Hoshiarpur and from what kind of sickness the little boy was suffering.

Every time I looked up, I saw inquisitive faces staring at me, nodding their heads in sympathy or bewilderment. I ignored their eyes, looking instead at the ceiling or the floor or the back of the seat ahead of me. I wished I could become invisible.

Narain, who was attending college at Hoshiarpur, met us at the bus stand. Always a neat dresser, he stood apart from everyone else. I was proud that he was my brother. The people around us looked at Narain, not at me. That was just fine with me. "Wait," I said to myself. "As soon as I get my hearing back and grow up, I will dress better than Narain when I go to medical college."

We took a bicycle rickshaw to the doctor with Narain following us on his bicycle. The doctor examined me—thermometer, pulse, tongue, ears—and then took out a tuning fork. I had never seen a tuning fork before. He hit it on the corner of his desk and then brought the forked metal close to my ears. I did not hear anything. He kept changing tuning forks and asking if I could hear. No. No. No. I shook my head.

The doctor talked to Babuji and wrote down a prescription. We returned to Gagret that evening. I was tired but also very proud of making the trip. Travel to and from Gagret in 1952 was a major event. I told exaggerated stories about riding the bus, meeting with Narain, and riding the cycle rickshaw. I made fun of the doctor and his tuning forks.

"He thinks those *chimtas* could cure my deafness," I mocked and laughed. Ramesh, Sham, and Vishwa did not think I was funny. They just looked at each other.

The Hoshiarpur doctor had prescribed some pills. I took them diligently with warm water three times a day, and everyone in the family periodically checked my hearing. Sometimes, Ramesh or other younger boys would scream really loud in my ears. That would make Bhabhi put her fingers in her ears. She would get mad at them. I did not hear them scream, but did feel a rush of warm air and sometimes a slight pain in my eardrum. The yelling in my ear became a fun activity for the boys, and I did not stop them since I liked attention, just like any other kid.

When the pills from Hoshiarpur ran out and there was no improvement in my hearing, Babuji decided to go to Amritsar, the largest city in the state of Punjab, about seventy miles from Gagret. Unbeknownst to me, he was getting advice about all kinds of wonderful doctors from everyone he talked to about his son's deafness. According to the people he spoke to, great doctors who could cure any sickness resided in every city in India. He decided on Dr. Tulsi Das in Amritsar; he was renowned all over the state for his medical expertise.

Vishwa's mother, whom we called Vishwa's Bhabhi, had a sister living in Amritsar. When she learned that we were going to Amritsar, she decided that she would go with us. Women did not travel alone, therefore, our visit to Amritsar provided Vishwa's Bhabhi an opportunity to make the trip.

We packed two bedding sets in a holdall and our clothes in a suitcase. Vishwa's Bhabhi had only a small bundle of clothes, which she carried herself.

The seventy-mile trip to Amritsar took four hours. We had to change buses twice, at Hoshiarpur and at Jalandhar. At each bus stop, we had to wait for half an hour. The buses that ran this route were larger and more comfortable than the bus that took us to and from Hoshiarpur. I had never been to Amritsar and was excited about the trip to a new city.

Because of the presence of my father, Vishwa's Bhabhi was veiled. According to cultural protocol, they could not directly talk to each other. When Babuji had to say something to her, he would address the empty air ahead of him. When she needed to tell something to Babuji, she would talk to me with her back to Babuji. Vishwa's Bhabhi, like almost all Indian women at that time had never been taught to read or write. Therefore our communication efforts were a bit erratic and an adventure in themselves. She was a good mimic and would move her lips exaggeratedly so I could understand her. The combination of gesture and mouthing would give me a clue as to what she wanted me to say to Babuji. However, it was clear that I misunderstood her more often than not. She had to put her hand on my mouth when I misunderstood her, and she wiggled her index finger vigorously to tell me I was wrong.

We got off at the bus stand in Amritsar, and Vishwa's Bhabhi gave me a small piece of paper with an address on it, which I passed on to Babuji. He put on his reading glasses and hailed a tonga. A tonga is a two-wheeled buggy pulled by a horse. Vishwa's Bhabhi and I sat in the back, the holdall at our feet. Babuji sat in front with the driver.

Streets in most Indian cities are surrounded by mazes of alleys and side alleys. Vishwa's Bhabhi's sister and her husband lived in one of these alleys. Babuji read the address to the tongawalla (the tonga driver), who simply moved his head from side to side. This head gesture, used by everyone in India, has an ambiguous meaning. It could mean anything from, "I know" to "I do not know, but we will find out."

The tongawalla obviously did not want to admit he did not know where to go. He lashed the horse hard with his whip, and we moved as fast as the starving nag could move. After going about half a mile, the tongawalla stopped to ask for directions. One teashop vendor pointed in a general direction and mumbled something, which the tongawalla pretended to understand. After an hour and trying four different, and conflicting, directions, we were able to find Vishwa's Bhabhi's sister's house.

It was a one-room affair with the kitchen in one corner and the bed in another. Of course, we could not stay there. It was not because the room would not hold five people, but because we did not know the hosts well enough. Babuji talked with Vidhia, Vishwa's Bhabhi's brother-in-law, and they both went out after lunch. There was an inn a couple of blocks from their place wherein we could get rooms.

After lunch, Babuji, Vidhia, and I marched single file behind a coolie who carried our holdall and suitcase to the inn, which was a huge, dark building. We got a room for two *annas* daily (roughly three cents) since the inn was built by a philanthropist for pilgrims coming to visit a nearby temple.

In the room were two bare cots made of bamboo and jute. After Vidhia left, Babuji opened the holdall and spread *dhurries*, or blankets, on the two cots; we both took a nap or tried to look like we were asleep. But we were both awake. I took a furtive look at him. He was staring at the ceiling, his face grim. That was when I realized that while I was rolling in self-pity, Babuji was suffering also. I thought about Bhabhi. I had seen her cry often. My deafness was a family tragedy, not just my problem. This insight suddenly changed my outlook. I had people who shared my sorrow. Sorrow divided, as a Hindi song goes, is reduced sorrow.

In the afternoon, we summoned a cycle rickshaw. After asking several people for directions along the way, we found Dr. Tulsi Das's clinic, which was also his residence. It was a huge beige house standing in the center of a large garden with trees, flowers, and manicured lawns. A uniformed guard stood at the gate, which opened into a semicircular drive toward the house. We had to get off the rickshaw outside the gate as per the guard's order. We walked in and joined a crowd of about one hundred people standing or sitting on the large verandah of Dr. Tulsi Das's house. Babuji registered his name with the clerk sitting outside the office.

I sat on the floor of the verandah while Babuji smoked a cigarette and talked to other people. At 4 p.m. on the dot, Dr. Tulsi Das appeared in a fancy blue suit with a red tie. I had never seen such an elegant person. He waved at the crowd and talked to some people, like a leader working his constituency. After a few minutes of this, Dr. Tulsi Das went into his office.

The clerk called out names, and then patients and their relatives went inside. They would return within a few minutes with a small piece of paper in their hands. Dr. Tulsi Das must be very smart, I thought. It took him less than two minutes to decide what was wrong with each patient and then prescribe medication.

Our turn came, and we marched into Dr. Tulsi Das's shrine. He was sitting on a fancy chair with instruments on tables around him. Babuji bowed with his hands clasped in front of him and began to talk to the renowned doctor. The doctor began to examine my ears and then went through the tuning fork routine, which brought no response from me. Then the very smart doctor, who was known to be the best in Punjab, jotted down something on his prescription pad and gave it to Babuji. Babuji fumbled for his wallet and put a ten-*rupee* note in front of Dr. Das, who threw the note in a small box next to him. Ten rupees were Babuji's earnings for one day. Dr. Das made that much money in less than one minute. New people came in so we had to get out of the office fast.

It was too late to go back to Gagret, so Babuji decided we should stay the night at the inn. We were sitting there in the room on our cots and Babuji surprised me by writing on his palm: "Do you want to go see a movie?" Indian fathers are supposed to forbid their sons from ever going to the cinema or developing similar bad habits. Babuji, to the best of our knowledge, did not go to the cinema. Here he was asking me to go see a movie. I loved movies more than any other kid and yelled "yes" before he had finished tracing the million-rupee question on his palm.

Babuji, after asking a few shopkeepers about the nearest cinema hall and the movies they played, decided on one. There was a long line for purchasing tickets, and he joined the line at the end. I sat on a stone near the street and looked at people passing by and wondered if they knew I was deaf.

In my excitement to see the movie, I had forgotten that I would not be able to hear the dialogue and songs. *How will I understand the movie?* I was mulling this question over when Babuji walked up to me holding a small booklet. He had asked someone to hold his place in the line while he purchased this booklet for four annas that contained the movie's script and song lyrics. Song lyric pamphlets were commonly sold outside movie houses for people to take home and learn the songs. But dialogue! Who needed that? We had never seen dialogue books before. Babuji must have thought about this new problem and having heard the hawker yell, "dialogue and songbook for four annas," he purchased one and gave it to me.

It took half an hour for Babuji to purchase our tickets. By that time, I had read all the movie dialogue. I carried the booklet with great pride in one hand and held Babuji's finger in another as we entered the cinema hall. I had memorized the dialogue, and during the movie, I would whisper in Babuji's ears what the person on the screen was saying and would say next. This must have been distracting to him, but he let me do it; he was really happy that I could follow the movie's story so well.

The famous doctor had prescribed penicillin and one other medicine, whose name I do not remember, for me. After we returned home, Babuji hired a medical assistant who worked in the government hospital to trek to our home twice daily and give me a shot. For the next full month, I received those shots. The medical assistant, an old man, would arrive on time and open the bag that contained his equipment. He would turn on a small spirit lamp and boil a needle in a large spoon. After breaking the neck of a distilled water vial, he would siphon the liquid into his syringe and then shoot it into the vial containing penicillin powder. After shaking the little vial vigorously, he would siphon the mixture back into the syringe. I would bare my butt dutifully for the inevitable sting. In the beginning, Sham, Ramesh, and Vishwa showed some interest in this procedure, and I would have a lively audience discussing the process. I would sit proudly since I was the major player in it. They wanted the cute penicillin vials. I had hoarded the first few as I thought they belonged to me. However, after the fourth or fifth vial, I relented and began to proudly pass them out to each one of them. Sham, as the elder brother, got most of them. They used these vials for storing ink.

Despite all these shots, my hearing did not improve. At the end of the month, when all the penicillin vials were gone, Babuji thanked the medical assistant as he was about to leave and produced a ten-rupee note. The medical assistant made a show of not accepting the money, and Babuji had to force the note into his pocket. He still kept objecting even when the note was safely in his pocket. I compared Dr. Tulsi Das's five minutes of work with the medical assistant's work involving sixty trips to our house and 120 shots. They both had earned the same amount of money.

No other doctors visited me for a while. I was disappointed and kept asking Babuji daily if he had found another—better—doctor. He would shake his head sadly and scribble on his palm, "I am still trying."

4

Other Cures

WHILE BABUJI WAS CHECKING ON DOCTORS, *hakeems* (physicians who practiced a Greco-Persian form of medicine), and vaids, other members of the family were busy finding "better" cures.

My Bhua Parvati, Babuji's younger sister, was a very religious woman. Everything in the world, according to her, happened according to the pre-written will of Rama or Krishna or Vishnu or Shiva—the four major Hindu gods. Her faith in her gods was inimitable and unshakable. Her life itself was inimitable and full of faith, despite all the personal catastrophes she suffered and prevailed through.

Bhua Parvati was nine years Babuji's junior. Just like all the girls of her time, she did not receive any education—not even the three Rs. She could not read or sign her name, but she could count up to 1,000 and had a good concept of *lakh* (100,000) and *crore* (a billion).

She started to work in the kitchen before she started to crawl and did not stop until, close to age ninety, she was carried out for cremation. At the ripe old age of nine years, she was married to Bhagat Ram of Lohara village. Bhagat Ram was much older—twelve or thirteen. As was the custom at that time, the bride and groom never met each other during the four-day wedding ceremony. She did not know why she was dressed up in a red suit, wearing jewelry, with her hands and feet covered in red henna. Nor was she sure why she had to be veiled from all the people in Lohara, where she stayed for only one day. She was brought back to Gagret in a red cloth-covered palanquin carried on the shoulders of four young men. The very next day, she resumed her normal life—cooking, bringing water from the well, washing clothes, and cleaning the house. For her, the wedding ceremony was nothing more than a four-day vacation from work. Bhua Parvati was supposed to go to her husband's home when she was thirteen or fourteen and start her married life, but Bhagat

Ram died of some illness before that. Thus, Bhua Parvati became a widow before she was a teenager and before her marriage was consummated.

Widows did not, and still do not in most cases today, marry a second time. A woman's marriage, according to Hindu scriptures, was like a glass; once broken, it could not be put together or fixed. So Bhua Parvati never married again. As was required of a widow, she wore simple, white clothes and no jewelry or makeup, had her head shaved, and ate very simple and Spartan meals.

She had a house in Lohara, where she spent a total of about one month in a year. During the rest of the year, her home was our home, and she was everyone's aunt. Babuji loved and cared for her. Bhabhi was not very fond of her, but appreciated her since Bhua Parvati worked all day long and took care of everything. However, her real full-time job was spoiling her nephews and nieces, including me.

Bhua Parvati strongly believed that my deafness was caused by my lack of respect for various gods. I had read Ramayana and Mahabharta epics when I was only ten years old and was convinced that neither Rama nor Krishna were bona fide gods. Bhua Parvati used to cover her ears when I would try to argue my theory about the gods.

"That is sinful, young boy," She would scold me. "Lord Rama will hear you. Do not talk like that or He might punish you." Her fear was genuine, and that only encouraged me to push my theory about the gods even more. My deafness, according to Bhua Parvati's unshakable belief, was the result of my mocking of the gods. She wanted to make sure that I made amends for my transgression so I would be forgiven. She was as sure as the sun rises that I would regain my hearing if I asked for forgiveness.

My already weak faith in the gods was further shaken by this "punishment" meted out to me for no reason. I refused to pray and ask for forgiveness for a sin or crime that I had not committed. Bhua Parvati was not one to give in easily. She made plans and got support from Babuji, who did not think that my deafness was the result of some celestial punishment, but who also thought that a little religion would not hurt me. Thus, I was taken to a number of *sadhus*—holy men, temple priests, and those who claimed to have a direct line to gods.

The first was the Gurkha sadhu who lived in a cave next to a very old temple about half a mile from our home. We all called him Gurkha

Baba because he was from Nepal. (Gurkha is a city-state in Nepal.) He was a well-built young man who dressed only in a *langoti*, which closely resembles thong bikini underwear. Gurkha Baba's langoti was a thong tied around his waist, which held a two-inch-wide strip of cloth that went from front to back between his legs. His whole body was covered with white ash, as was the practice of many holy men in India. Even in winter, when the temperature went down to forty degrees and all of us wore woolen sweaters, Gurkha Baba walked around only in his langoti. His immunity to cold won people's respect for him as a man of God. I, along with other kids in the village, used to make fun of Gurkha Baba. No wonder he did not like me. The fact that he had worked as a cook for us in Delhi a couple of years back did not help the situation either. It was a strange coincidence that he ended up in our village, 250 miles from Delhi, while he was wandering as a sadhu.

Bhua Parvati brought Gurkha Baba to our home. He sat there in front of my bed, erect on a chair with his left foot crossed over his right knee, holding the *trishul* (a three-pronged spear that many sadhus carried as a symbol of Shiva) in his right hand. His eyes were very serious, and he did look very graceful—almost holy. No wonder Bhua Parvati and Bhabhi sat there looking at him with their hands clasped in abeyance. I knew if we were both alone, I would have made some smart remarks and he would have threatened me. Here, we were acting very civilized to each other, and I did not want to exasperate Bhua Parvati and Bhabhi.

Bhua motioned for me to touch his feet, which I did with an exaggerated motion. He blessed me, matching my exaggeration. While I lay there, Bhua and Bhabhi took turns explaining something to him while pointing toward me. Gurkha Baba listened with great earnestness and then closed his eyes and began to mumble something. Bhabhi and Bhua also closed their eyes in respect to the great saint's efforts to bless me. I tried my best to hide a smile, as I believed Gurkha Baba, behind his facade of prayers, must have been thinking, "serves the little brat right."

With the prayer over, Gurkha Baba dug his hand into the small cloth bag that hung from his shoulder. He produced a small packet made of old newspaper, unwrapped it, and took out some white ash between his thumb and index finger. Bhua Parvati stood up and hurriedly made me get both my palms open so I could receive the holy ash. He put a pinch of ash in my palm and applied some of it with his thumb to my forehead.

I did not want Bhua Parvati to give me further directions, so, knowing what was expected of me, I licked the ash from my palm and moved it around my tongue and swallowed it. Gurkha Baba gave the ash to both ladies and applied it to their foreheads. They both touched his feet with great respect and prayed with their eyes closed.

After he left, I got mad at Bhua Parvati and told her that Gurkha Baba was nothing but a thug, who was too lazy to work and was leading a nice life by fooling people. Both Bhabhi and Bhua Parvati were upset and asked me not to be sacrilegious. They pointed to my ears and toward Heaven, explaining that God will cure me.

"God does not need a Gurkha as a middle man to help me," I declared. "If God wants to make me hearing, he would do it without that faker." They got exasperated and I went to sleep.

Needless to say, I received some admonition from Babuji that night for being disrespectful to a holy man. I quietly read as he traced words on his palm and said, "OK!"

In Gagret, a son never disagrees with his father; he just obeys. I did.

The second sadhu I encountered was the Mahatma, or "great soul," of Andora, a small village, two miles from Gagret, across the Swan river. The Andora Temple was on a cliff right on the Swan's bank. The main temple was high with a white steeple topped by a red flag. The Mahatma of Andora was well known throughout the district. People from miles away came to worship there. They brought offerings—food grains, dals, fruit, milk, butter, and, of course, cash. Every time I visited there, I tried to figure out how much the temple earned in cash and the other items. My guess was it was hundreds of times more than a laborer would make and even more than what Dr. Tulsi Das made by writing prescriptions full-time. Each year, the Mahatma would go on two- or three-month-long pilgrimages. It was known that he had many disciples who invited him to bless their homes in faraway cities. I had a different theory: I believed he just went out to spend the money. Maybe he saw a lot of movies in cities where no one knew him. Maybe he had a lot of fun spending the money and came back to his ascetic life after having a ball. Not many people agreed with me.

The Mahatma of Andora, being a holy man of higher stature, did not make house calls. So, there was no alternative but for us to visit him. Since there was no bus service to Andora, the trip had to wait until I was strong enough to walk two miles each way. Bhua Parvati, of course, had to go. Sham, Ramesh, and a few other kids made up the entourage. I walked slowly and kept chattering and making snide remarks about the Mahatma. But soon I had to stop since no one seemed to share my view. Sham was religious and strongly believed in holy men. Ramesh and the others believed at various levels and did not want to speak out.

The Mahatma himself greeted us very warmly at the temple. He knew Bhua Parvati as a generous donor, therefore, he gave her the red-carpet treatment. After we had touched his feet and received his blessings, we sat down on the cold marble floor of the temple. Bhua Parvati talked to the Mahatma while Sham and the other kids sat very solemnly listening to her. I looked at the various statues of gods dressed in clothes. Their eyes were lifelike. I looked into their eyes and tried to communicate with them.

The Mahatma applied sandalwood paste to our foreheads—a fancier stuff than the Gurkha Baba's ash. He also gave us fruit and sweetmeats. The Mahatma ran an upscale establishment. We ate lunch at the *langar* (open kitchen), which the temple provided daily, and headed back home. Sham, at the bidding of Bhua Parvati, told me that the Mahatma had blessed me so I would be able to hear soon.

"When?" I asked.

"Soon." Sham interpreted Bhua Parvati's speech into tracings on his palms. "As soon as God wants you to hear."

So that is what the smart mahatma had told her. It was an open-ended and broad answer—anytime between now and whenever. I wanted to comment on this totally ambiguous and nebulous prophecy, but kept quiet. I knew my opinion in that group would not be valued and that Bhua Parvati's firm belief that my deafness was caused by my mocking everything religious would only be strengthened. I had no intention of increasing her conviction.

Bhua Parvati next took me to faith healers who professed to have connections with ghosts, goblins and lost souls. The sadhus and mahatmas I had visited previously at least practiced from temples and had some kind of legitimacy. These faith healers, however, used old tombs, broken-

down temples, or their own houses to run their trade. I visited several
of these, but will describe only one experience to illustrate their modus
operandi.

These faith healers usually got into this business of healing abruptly.
A good and honest farmer, carpenter, or blacksmith would wake up one
morning and go into a trance. Sitting on the floor with legs crossed and
most of the weight on both palms, he would start moving his head in a
jerky circular motion with his eyes closed and face in deep concentration.
Then suddenly, strange people would start talking through him. He would
make prophecies or curse people. Some of the prophesies would come
true, and then word would spread from village to village through the very
effective grapevine that so and so had become a *siddh,* an enlightened one.

I did go to some of these just so I could visit places. One of the trips
still stands out in my memory.

I loved to watch movies, and the nearest cinema house was in Hoshiarpur. I could not, of course, just ask Babuji to go to Hoshiarpur for
such an activity because watching movies was frowned upon. My cousin
Ramesh and I hit upon a plan.

Two years after I became deaf, we learned that a siddh was plying
his trade in Bheekuwal, a village not far from Hoshiarpur. Ramesh and
I slowly and craftily began to sow the seeds for making the trip. I talked
to Bhabhi about going to see this saint who had become famous for
curing people. Ramesh casually mentioned it to Babuji one evening and
volunteered his services to escort me there. A week later, I made the
proposal to Babuji for taking a walking trip to Bheekuwal to see this
siddh. Babuji was surprised and also pleased with my interest and increasing belief in siddhs. I suspected, however, that he saw through our conspir-
acy. He knew Ramesh well enough; he also knew that when we two got
together, we could not be trusted. Still, he decided to approve our trip
and made arrangements with someone to care for the cattle on the day
we would be gone.

The next morning at 4 a.m., we woke, packed meals of chapatis and
mango pickle in a piece of cloth, and set out for the long trip. We did
not have a map and were not sure how far Bheekuwal was from Hoshiarpur. We walked, or rather ran, in the warm June morning fragrant
from pine trees. We were very excited about the movie we were going

to see. We had no water and no change of clothes. All we had with us were the chapatis and clothes we wore. We carried our shoes in our hands; walking barefoot was easier and less tiring. Soon it became hot and we were thirsty. The sandy dust became hot under our feet. The temperatures in June in India go into three digits, and I began to wonder if I was being punished for lying to my father.

We managed to get drinks of lukewarm water in the villages we passed. People would pour water out of a jug, and we would take turns gulping it from our tightly cupped palms. Then we would ask for directions to Bheekuwal. Most of the people who gave us directions had never been there, but had heard the name of the village because of the siddh. We followed the general direction and felt fortunate we were not lost.

By noon, we knew that Bheekuwal was not next to Hoshiarpur; it was seven miles to the east. We kept walking as fast as we could and asked for directions whenever we passed anyone. We arrived in Bheekuwal in the afternoon after walking twenty-three miles.

It must have been over one hundred degrees at that time. We were hungry and tired and both had splitting headaches from hunger; we had been in too much of a hurry to stop and eat our chapatis. We came upon a huge crowd of people who had come for the blessing. It was apparent that this siddh did not provide individual service; he blessed people en masse. His disciple passed out ash that was supposedly blessed by him.

Ramesh asked me to sit on a rock in the hot shade of a mud house while he checked around. Since we had walked twenty-three miles in the hot sun for this, we needed to get some ash. He managed to get some and wrapped it in a piece of old newspaper.

We were crestfallen when we learned that Hoshiarpur was seven miles away. We had just enough money for the cinema and food for the evening. We decided that we would skimp on dinner and spend some money on a tonga since walking seven miles would require about two hours, and we didn't want to miss the movie. The seven-mile trip took a little over one hour by tonga pulled by a nag. We both dozed in the semi-shade of the tonga roof.

There were two cinema houses in Hoshiarpur. We saw movies at both cinemas. The fact that both cinema houses were hot, crowded, and smoke-filled did not bother us. Indian movies are full of songs and dances.

Ramesh, of course, sang along with the actors on the screen and was told repeatedly to shut up by other viewers. He would borrow my program to read the song lyrics and return it to me so I could follow the movie.

After seeing the movies, we bought some chapatis and dal from a roadside tandoor. Then we started walking toward Gagret. After walking for about five miles, we became too tired to travel any farther. We found a brick platform built around a *peepal* (fig leaf) tree and lay down in the dust. Before we knew it, we were asleep and did not wake up until next morning. Our bodies were sore as we arrived home around noon the next day. We gave ash to Bhua Parvati who touched it with her forehead and gave pinches of it to everyone in the family. She touched my head to show her affection and patted Ramesh on his back for taking me to the holy siddh.

5

Home Remedies

THE "TREATMENT" FOR MY DEAFNESS DID
not stop with the holy men and miracle workers. There were other "remedies" that ranged from harmless fun to pure physical discomfort bordering
on torture. I submitted to these hoping against hope that something might
work or just because I had nothing to do or did not want to insult the
person perpetrating the torment, as they all wished well.

My eldest sister Brahmi was a firm believer in home remedies and
considered doctors and other licensed practitioners as nothing more than
adventurers looking to take your money. It was ironic that her family
later produced no less than five doctors. Of course, she always ignored
their advice, saying "you go give medical advice to people who are stupid
enough to pay you."

Sister Brahmi learned from an older lady how deafness can be cured
by steam from milk. She had to, of course, invent her own system for
introducing steam from boiling milk into my ears. A makeshift arrangement with consultation from other ladies was made.

Milk in villages is cooked slowly to form a thick layer of *malai,* which
becomes the base for making butter. A large black pot called a *dudhunu*
is used for first boiling and later simmering the milk. Sister Brahmi positioned the dudhunu on the burning coals in a *launda* (a large bowl used
for feeding cattle) under my cot. After moving the dhurrie and bed sheet
aside from above the twine mesh which was knitted to form the "mattress"
in the cot, she made a small hole in the yarn that formed the support for
the bed.

After establishing this setup for her operation, she positioned my head
over the hole in the yarn—right above the steaming dudhunu. She blew
at the coals to increase the boiling and steam poured from the dudhunu.

The warm steam felt good on my cold ears at first, but soon it became uncomfortable. People gathered to see the miracle happen, and their presence did not help to reduce my discomfort. I would pull my ear away from the hole in the yarn each time the steam became uncomfortably hot. The kids and ladies gathered around would encourage me to keep my ear there in order to make the steam do its magic. I tried to oblige them but it was really hot. Then I would be asked to change side so the other ear could be subjected to the torture.

After each treatment, which lasted about half an hour, everyone standing or sitting around me would take turns yelling into my ears to see whether or not my hearing had improved. It was not the most scientific audiometric test, and my responses varied. Sometimes, I was convinced that I could hear better mostly because of the volume of the "tester's" voice or the distance of the speaker's mouth from my ear. There would be an expression of delight, hand-clapping by ladies, and jumping by the kids each time I professed to hear better. Plans to decrease the time between treatments, increase the treatment time, and make the heat produce more steam were discussed and implemented. This went on for the whole month on a daily basis and ended abruptly when Sister Brahmi had to return to Kuriala, the village where her in-laws lived. Additionally, the inconsistency of my response to the audiological tests indicated that either my deafness was fluctuating or the benefits were short-term.

Needless to say, I was relieved when this ended, as I was sure after the first treatment that it did not help at all. However, I loved my sister and knew she genuinely believed in the possibility of me being cured by the steam. I did not have any other activities with which to entertain myself either.

My grand uncle, Hardev Ram, was a really nice guy. He was a retired railway clerk and spent most of his time reading newspapers and visiting various shops in the bazaar. His remaining time was spent puffing on his hookah and staring into space. He was friendly with everyone, and people loved and respected him. His only flaw was his habit of yelling at Babey, his wife, over her cooking. He would go on and on about how bad her cooking was from the time he sat down for his meal to the time he went out. This daily tirade was a meal ritual that did not faze Babey, who perhaps had stopped paying attention to his culinary criticism a long time ago.

Baba Hardev Ram had an idea. Whether this idea was his or planted in his mind by someone else is not clear. He asked Bhabhi to let me walk with him to the well on his way to the bazaar. No one explained the purpose of this trip, and I willing went; I did not have any pressing engagements.

We walked single file to the well with Baba Hardev Ram smiling at me each time he looked back. We arrived, took our shoes off, and climbed the five two-foot-high stairs to the platform of the well. Baba Hardev Ram leaned on the wooden derrick and said something to the well. He moved back and pointed at me and then down at the well and said something which I could not understand. He did not have much patience for tracing his message on his palm. He would start to write something and then start talking and simply keep moving his finger in the air. This form of communication did not work well with me and I tried to smile while I misunderstood what he wanted me to do.

After a few attempts at communication, I learned that he wanted me to yell something to the well. I was shy at first and then obliged. I yelled a few times and Baba Hardev Ram looked pleased and expectant. He asked me if I could hear myself. I shook my head vigorously. I was not sure whether this was yet another audiometric test or a treatment. Perhaps my uncle thought that hearing my echo might cure my deafness. After a few tries, Baba Hardev Ram gave up and we descended the well stairs. He pointed me toward where our home was and continued on his way to the bazaar.

The next "treatment" was more elaborate. This was arranged by my other grand uncle, Baba Khushi Ram. Baba Khushi Ram lived in the inn that our family had built for free use by passing travelers and visiting wedding parties. He had a room with a kitchen to himself there. There is a story that he got mad at his wife, Chhoti Daad (Grand Aunt) Aati, when he was still young and swore never to talk to her again. He was one stubborn old coot and kept his word. He lived alone in the inn and visited our home only for weddings and funerals, and then too, he would only stay in the male part of the sprawling house. There are various stories about why he got mad at Chhoti Daad Aati, but none are clear. He was so mad at her that he rarely talked to his three sons born of their union.

Baba Khushi Ram abhorred everyone in the village. He yelled obscenities at them at the drop of a hat. I had heard stories about how hard-working he was. He was an old man into his seventies when I became deaf. He may have been a tall man once, but in his old age, he had a hunched back and looked small.

He liked Babuji very much and talked to him in an amiable way. Anything Babuji said was fine with him. If one of his sons wanted to ask him something, he was sure to disagree and declare them "having gone to take a leak when God was passing out intelligence." If Babuji proposed the same thing, he would go gaga with praise over Babuji's "wonderful" idea and wished his sons had the same level of intelligence and savvy.

Baba Khushi Ram had strong likes and dislikes. If he did not like someone, anything that person did was wrong. Conversely, if he liked someone, even the simplest thing that person did was a masterpiece in Baba Khushi Ram's book. He was also totally illiterate as there were no schools in or around Gagret when he grew up.

Baba Khushi Ram took a fancy to a passing traveler who made a living by removing ear wax. This guy, known as Sain to people, spent a night in our inn and won Baba Khushi Ram's heart with his city slicker ways. Baba Khushi Ram invited him to stay in the inn as long as he wanted, giving him a large room with a smaller room for cooking. Sain cleaned people's ears for half a rupee and made enough money to buy food and opium. He would lace his tobacco with a bit of opium each night and then go into a swoon and talk about his adventures around the country. Sain claimed he was once a very rich man and married to a very beautiful woman. That woman ran away with a bad guy and stole all his money. Since then, according to Sain's opium-induced saga, he lost interest in money and was wandering the country just like any holy man.

I used to take lunch to Baba Khushi Ram at the same time as I did for Babuji. When Sain saw me and learned about my deafness, he told Baba Khushi Ram that he would like to cure me. And so the stage for a major drama was set.

Word spread around Gagret that the holy Sain knew how to cure deafness. It was the monsoon season, and the sleepy village of Gagret was snoring while heavy rains fell intermittently. Gagret had no cinema house or any other kind of entertainment. People, including me, did not even know about the existence of television. Radios were rare; only a few households could afford them. Thus, the main pastimes in Gagret were talking, making fun of each other, watching other people make fun of each other, and playing cards. Sain's announcement to cure me was equal to elephants walking through a city street announcing the arrival of a three-ring circus.

The day was set for the operation. Since time in Gagret meant little most of the year and nothing during the monsoons, no specific hour was set or announced. I went with Ramesh, Sham, and a few other kids, and took my place on a mat in the largest room in the inn. There were about thirty people sitting on cots or on the floor smoking hookahs, cigarettes, and bidis. Every man in Gagret smoked tobacco, and those who did not smoke were considered sissies.

Sain appeared to be impressed with this audience and did not seem to be in a hurry to start working on me. I was nervous as he had laid out a small red doll in front of me. I wondered what was in it, and visions of sharp knives and hot oil were making me uneasy.

Finally, Sain seemed to be satisfied with the number of people in attendance and, after replacing his hookah, stood up. He faced the crowd and raised his arms slowly towards the ceiling. His eyes were closed and he seemed very pensive. Everyone, including me, was looking at him expectantly. I was, however, more scared about the mysterious stuff in the doll.

Sain suddenly sat down and put his head in abeyance in front of the little doll. He lay there prone on the floor for a few seconds, then sat up and began to slowly undress the doll. We all looked scared and wondered what would emerge after the sari was taken off. I looked at people and saw some of the older boys whispering in each other's ears and smiling. I did not like that. Here I was waiting for a cure and these boys were thinking of something else!

Finally, the sari came off and revealed a set of ear cleaning scoops. It was a letdown for many, but some people seemed to be impressed with the respect Sain had shown for the tools of his trade.

To make the long story of that unending rain-sodden afternoon short, Sain slowly and dramatically cleaned both of my ears. Each time he would succeed in extracting a large lump of wax, he would show it to the wide-eyed audience and chant something. I was also given a peek of the cause of my deafness coming out of ears. The people were awed at the amount of wax that my ears had generated.

After what seemed like ages, he stopped as he seemed to have gotten all the wax out of my ears. He said something to one of the young men in attendance, who moved forward with an air of importance and yelled into my ear. I did not hear anything, but did feel his warm breath and also smelled raw onions from his lunch. I shook my head when Sain looked at me askance.

Sain was so upset about this failure that he stood up and stomped out of the room, taking the torn doll and his tools with him. I looked at Baba Khushi Ram. He was looking angrily at me as if it was my fault that Sain had failed in his effort.

Sain left Gagret the next day without saying goodbye to anyone.

6

Schooling

WHILE ALL THESE MEDICAL AND NOT-SO-MEDICAL treatments were being meted out to me, I was also studying. Since the discovery of my deafness, I no longer attended school. Each morning, I hoped that "tomorrow" I would be returning to school. This "tomorrow" somehow kept moving forward as days changed to weeks, months, and years.

I kept up with Ramesh and Vishwa, my classmates, by doing the homework the class was given. I read assigned chapters in Hindi, history, and geography on my own and asked Sham's help with arithmetic, algebra, and new vocabulary. It was not hard to keep up, but I missed sitting in the classroom, talking to friends, and playing with them during recess. The school I had attended was the National High School in Ambota, which was a good two miles from our home. The daily trek to and from the school had been fun. We chased each other, talked or sang movie songs, and made fun of other classmates and teachers. With the loss of my hearing, all this fun was taken away from me, and at times, I was very depressed.

The final examinations were scheduled for March as usual, and I did not want to miss them. Babuji tried to convince me that I was not strong enough to make the round-trip to Ambota and that I could make up the class a year later. The idea of being left behind in school was inconceivable to me, and I kept insisting that I was going to take the examination. Seeing how strongly I felt about it, he gave in. He talked to the headmaster of the school and made arrangements for me to take in the examination.

On the very first day of examinations, I knew things had changed. I could not speak to people like in the old days. Everyone was talking to each other and no one had the patience to communicate with me. As Sham, Ramesh, and I approached the school, we encountered other

29

students coming from different villages. They would either look askance at me or ask Sham something, who would give a nod, say a few words, or a lengthy explanation depending on the status of the student asking the question. He also told some curious boys to mind their own business by showing them his open palm, which indicated that he was going to slap them if they did not stop staring at me.

The students walked at a distance from me. They were curious but also a bit afraid of catching something. They also had more pressing and interesting issues like memorizing facts for their final examination and talking to each other. Most of the time, I was left alone. However, some students did manage to find opportunities to tease me when Sham and the others were not around. They would stand behind me and make all kinds of noises. I would know about this only when I would see them laughing and jumping around me.

My inability to hear was hilarious to them.

The teachers were more sympathetic. I had been a star student there and they remembered it. They would look at me and move their open palm from the down to the up position (gesturing the question "How are you?"), shake their heads, and move on.

As expected, I passed in all subjects, but I was very disappointed that I did not get first, second, or even third highest position in any subject. I used to get first place in languages, including English, which they had started to teach in the fifth grade. Ramesh, as usual, got first place in mathematics and science. I was worried that he would make fun of me, but was relieved when he did not even mention it.

I was in the seventh grade and the not-so-proud owner of Sham's used books. I had been using his old books since first grade, and it was always a problem for me. I wanted to be the older brother and get the shiny new books, but I was the baby in the family and was destined to make good use of hand-me-down clothes and books.

I continued to study the seventh-grade books at home with Sham's help. I was disappointed and frustrated. Ramesh had moved to Delhi to live with his parents, and Vishwa had very little interest in studying. Vishwa was not receptive when I asked him questions about school. He did not even want to tell me what homework we had. This was very frustrating. So, I decided to go at my own pace. I needed help with mathematics and Sham helped me solve new problems.

At the end of my second year as a deaf boy, no one talked about my taking the seventh-grade examination. I wanted to take it, but was worried about facing all those rowdy kids. The subject was not broached. Babuji read my mind and declared one evening that I was going to start on eighth-grade textbooks the following year, as soon as Sham moved up to the ninth grade. In my mind, I had passed all the subjects and felt that my being in the eighth grade was justified.

Needless to say, I had a lot of time on my hands. I studied when I wanted to and sat and looked into space other times. I thought about school mostly; it played a major role in my early childhood.

7

My Childhood Before Becoming Deaf

THANKS TO THE BRITISH RULE, THE ENGLISH word *school* is used in India instead of its Hindi equivalent, *pathshala*. I recall trying to decipher the sound of *school* when I was three or four years old and saw Narain and Sham go to school in the morning with book satchels on their shoulders and all scrubbed up for the day. I had no idea why they went to some place called school, but I wanted to go too. I approached Bhabhi when I was three years old.

"I want to go to school," I declared.

She laughed and hugged me with joy. "Next year," she assured me.

I wondered how long a year was. Each day I asked whether it was "next year" yet.

However, I was learning all the time. I still remember how I learned to tell the time. I was about four years old. Bhabhi asked my cousin Bimla to find out what time it was, so she could start making tea. I followed Bimla into the other room where the only alarm clock in our household sat proudly on the mantelpiece. Bimla yelled to Bhabhi, "Bhabhi, it is 3:45." I was impressed. How could she tell time by looking at those figures!

"Can you tell me how to read time?" I asked Bimla.

Bimla was one of my favorite cousins. She was always smiling and nice to us kids. She was also helpful. Anyone who needed help had just to ask her and she was there. She looked down at me, first wondering how she should respond to my request. Then she smiled broadly, took my hand, and walked with me to the mantelpiece.

"First you have to read those figures." She pointed at the numbers.

"I know how," I said and read the numbers aloud to her. She was mystified.

32

"Who taught you to read numbers?" she asked. I did not know, but could read them alright.

Bimla pointed at the short hand. "This is the hour hand. The longer hand is for minutes. It is a bit tricky."

She explained that the longer hand was worth five minutes as it moved from one number to another.

That was easy. After about five minutes of Bimla asking me questions, I knew I could tell time. She was very proud of her achievement.

"Madan can tell time," she announced as she made her grand entrance, dragging me by my hand into the room where Bhabhi and Ramesh's mother, who was also called Bhabhi, were sitting.

Bhabhi and Bhabhi just laughed and I hid behind Bimla.

"I think Ramesh can also tell time," said the other Bhabhi, Ramesh's mother.

"I do not think so," reported Bimla, "but I will teach him today."

"Madan wants to go to school," Bhabhi, my mother, told Bhabhi, Ramesh's mother.

"He first has to learn how to wipe his nose and ass," said Ramesh's mother who loved to tease us kids.

"I know how and you do not," I said, fighting back from behind Bimla's legs. She patted my back in encouragement.

This was my earliest memory of learning.

When Ramesh and I were admitted to kindergarten, we were about four years old. We learned the entire Urdu alphabet in one day while the other students were still on the first five letters. The following week, the headmaster of the school walked into the kindergarten classroom, looked at us both, talked to the teacher for a few minutes, and then told Ramesh and I to pack our satchels and follow him.

We were moved to the first grade.

I was impressed with the power that the headmaster had. I wanted to become one.

Our stay in the Rawalpindi school was a short one. It was 1947. I did not understand what was going on, but an atmosphere of fear was everywhere. I was told that the country was being divided. The British had agreed to grant independence to India; however, the Muslims demanded that they be granted a separate nation. India, thus, was divided into two countries—the Hindu-majority India and the Muslim-majority Pakistan. I did not know what a country was or how it could be divided. I imagined a huge piece of land being cut in half with a saw or perhaps an axe. I asked questions of everyone. "You will understand when you will grow up." That was the only answer I got.

We moved to Gagret when Ramesh and I were in the middle of second grade. Only Babuji remained in Rawalpindi. He would be going to a place called Delhi from there. His job was being given to a man who was Muslim and was coming from Delhi to Rawalpindi. "Their jobs were swapped by someone in a big office," Narain told Sham, Ramesh, and me. Narain, who was nine years older than Ramesh and me, and seven years older than Sham, knew everything in the world.

The school in Gagret was much smaller than the one in Rawalpindi. The Rawalpindi school was built of large stones with vines climbing its walls. The Gagret school was built of mud walls and tin roofs, and one class was held on a verandah.

I attended the Gagret primary school for part of the second grade and all of the third grade. There were about 130 students—all boys—in the four grades. We were taught by four male teachers. The fourth-grade teacher was also the headmaster of the school. He was known for his strictness and ability to walk very fast. He lived in another village four miles away. Each morning, he would show up sweating from head to toe after his extremely fast walk. We would stand outside waiting for him to pass us. We would clasp our hands and chant "namaste headmaster ji."* He never responded to our greeting and just walked by fast to his classroom. One of the funny boys would copy his walk after he was out of earshot and all of us would roll with laughter.

The school opened at 7:00 a.m. in the summer and 10:00 a.m. in the winter. The school had no clock, and none of the masters had a wristwatch. The arrival of our headmaster was usually the time when the school started. If he was late, we had more time in the morning to play. His arrival signaled that the bell was going to ring soon.

---

*Namaste is a general Hindu greeting, which literally means "I bow to you."

We lined up for class in the courtyard grouped by grade. The four teachers stood facing us. Three or four students with good voices would march to the front and stand between teachers. They would lead the morning prayer song, the words of which we all had memorized but did not understand.

After the prayer, we would stay in line and march like little soldiers to our respective classrooms. The teacher would follow us, and the long day of education would begin. We sat with our legs crossed, like in a yoga position, on three or four long rows of rolled-out mats on dusty floors.

Our teacher sat in a chair behind a small table. That was the only furniture in the classroom besides the mats we sat on. The only other item that made the room a classroom was the blackboard. There were no pictures or maps in our classroom. Only the fourth-grade classroom had a map. We were told that serious geography lessons were taught there.

On the table, the teacher had an inkpot with a nib pen that he dipped in ink after writing "present" or "absent" after our names in the register. The most important piece on the table, however, was the *danda*—the two-foot-long baton, shiny from several years of use—for disciplining students. We did not have any problem students in our classroom, or the entire school for that matter. Any disciplinary breach was taken care of swiftly right in the room with one or more whacks of the *maula baksh*, as Babuji called his own imaginary baton, which he was going to use on us, but never did. *Maula baksh* in Urdu means "God's blessing."

Usually a slap on the face, a painful twist to the ear, or a kick on the rump or back was sufficient. The danda was called into action for more serious breaches of the rules, which were neither written nor explained to us. The teacher invented and applied rules as he deemed necessary. He was "the law" in the classroom, and we were taught never to question him.

Another form of discipline was being a *murga,* or a rooster. The rooster pose required you to first stand up, put both hands between your thighs from behind, bend your head slowly, reach for your ears with both hands, and hold your earlobes between your thumb and forefinger. You had to keep your ass pointed to the sky or it would get kicked by the teacher. I think this is the most effective yoga asna (position), except it is not listed in any yoga book. You have to be very nimble to attain this position, and maintaining it requires stamina that only runners in marathon races possess. Needless to say, after a few minutes in this position, you would promise yourself to follow every rule in the book (or, rather, in the teacher's mind). At least I did, after my first and last rooster pose, which I had to take during the second grade.

The decision to use one or other forms of discipline depended on the teacher's personality, his mood at that time, and how he felt about the offending student. Except for a few students, and I was one of the lucky ones, all got a dose of one or the other form of this effective punishment. You got it if you did not do your homework, made mistakes in your reading or arithmetic problems, talked to the boy sitting ahead or behind you, or simply attracted the attention of the teacher at the wrong time for a wrong reason.

We had one to four textbooks depending on the grade we attended. In the first grade, we had an Urdu primer, which included the alphabet, some words, and numbers. In the second grade, we had state-approved books for Urdu, arithmetic, and geography. The civics books included history and government, which were added in the third grade.

We used a half-squat position when we did arithmetic problems or wrote on a small slate or a *takhti*, a rectangular wooden board, and used our upright knee as a "desk" to support our slate, takhti, or notebook.

The correct way to clean your slate was to use a wet rag, which none of us carried. The side of your palm came in handy for wiping slates. For more serious cleaning, we spat on the slate a few times before applying the palm. At home, though, we did use water and a rag.

After washing our takhti, we applied a thin layer of special white mud to it. Upon drying, it formed a thin white film on the wood and was ready for writing with the *qalam*, a pen fashioned from cane that was then dipped in black ink, which we mixed ourselves. The inkpots usually were any small squat bottles we could find. They almost never had a cap, so we had to carry them in our hand like a lamp to avoid spilling the ink.

For writing we used *takhthis*. These slates were made either of polished tin or real slate set in wooden frames and were about two feet long and one foot wide. The crayon we used was very hard, and usually one lasted a full year. You did not forget your crayon; this oversight would bring four or five lashes of the danda. Usually we covered for each other by breaking off a small piece of our crayon and handing it to the neglectful neighbor. It had a diamond-shaped handle for carrying it.

We were not allowed to use a regular pen with a steel nib or a notebook until the fifth grade. The takhti and takhthi, along with the sole crayon and the qalam, made up our whole arsenal of writing instruments. Washing the takhti and recoating it once or twice a day was routine.

When the teacher would walk in, the class monitor would yell, "Stand up!" in English. These were the first two English words, in addition to *school,* which we learned. We would all stand up and stay standing, erect, looking straight ahead, until the teacher said, "Betho," or sit down. He would then take the baton in his hand and hit his palm with it a few times, look outside, and ask us to open our books at a specific lesson. There would be a quick rustle of pages and books would be opened within seconds. He would read a sentence and we would repeat after him. At times, when he was bored, he would ask the class monitor to take over and lead reading. He would then bow forward to put his head on the table and take a short nap while we mumbled after the monitor.

Later, for practice, we would read a few lines at the teacher's bidding while he walked between the rows hitting his leg or shoe with his danda. If a student made a mistake in his reading, the teacher would break his stride, make a fast about-face, and hit the offending student with the danda once, twice, or several times, depending on his mood.

This would be followed by group reading. We would read aloud and the teacher would again walk between the rows listening to us. If he caught someone mispronouncing or skipping a word, he would call the offender's name, who would stand up as if he had just found a burning coal under him. The teacher would ask him to bring his open palm forward and whack, whack him two sharp ones.

"Now repeat after me," he would demand.

The next action depended on how much progress in pronunciation the teacher thought you had made. Usually, a couple of whacks were enough for improving one's pronunciation and vocabulary skills.

The Urdu lesson was followed by arithmetic. We learned various skills and memorized our multiplication tables. The writing, geography, and civics followed after the recess.

We would shoot out of the room when the recess bell rang and run at top speed, chasing each other until we reached some open space in the bazaar. There was no playground or specific recess area at the school. No teacher came to supervise us either. It was a free-for-all. We did not have any money to buy food, and none of us brought any food from home. We just pushed each other or played *kabaddi*, a form of tag, which did not require any equipment. The school did not have any play equipment or a playground. We did not even have a ball to play with. Once in a while, an enterprising student would bring a small ball made of rags. We would kick it around until all the rags came loose. It took about five minutes for this to happen, and the unlucky student who brought the rag ball would be in tears.

The bell would ring, signaling the end of recess. We would run back to our classroom, making sure we were there before the teacher arrived. The teacher was prompted to use his danda on students who arrived after he did.

We attended school six days a week, with Saturday being a half-day. The school year began in April and ended in March. We had six weeks of monsoon break in July and August and a week's break in December. No one knew anything about Christmas. This break was started by the British, and when they were on vacation, everyone was on vacation. The British left India in 1947, but the Christmas break remained. No one has anything against having a holiday!

I do not remember ever having problems learning in school. Ramesh and I were way ahead of all the other students in our class. We were alternatively appointed monitors and enjoyed this limelight. The two years in the Gagret school flew by without any major incident. Then we moved to Delhi because the riots that had followed after the Partition had calmed down and it was safe to go there. Since Babuji worked in Delhi, the family moved there as well.

Moving to Delhi, the capital of India and one of the largest cities in the country, was a dream come true for Sham and me. We were thrilled to be going to the city whose name we were hearing all the time. They had cinemas there, and people wore nicer clothes. There were trains and cars too. And red buses that took you from here to there, as well as rickshaws and tongas. There was nothing in Gagret, except for cows, water buffaloes, and village people.

We were also scared. The village kids were easier to deal with, and they were respectful to us because of our family's position there. In Delhi, no one knew us; we were among millions.

Babuji had a huge house allotted to him by the government's railways department where he worked. It had four bedrooms, a huge kitchen with an adjoining storage room, and servants' quarters in the back. The house had a large walled-in courtyard with a platform in the middle of it. This was a great place for sleeping in the summer and sitting in the sun during winters.

We were both admitted to school—me to the fourth grade and Sham to the fifth grade. I was in the primary school and he was in the high school; however, both the buildings housing the two schools joined each other in an E formation. We learned that due to the creation of Pakistan, the teaching of Urdu was being phased out. Urdu was considered the language of Muslims, and Hindi was the language of Hindus. Thus, Urdu had become the national language of Pakistan. We did not know how to write Hindi, but could speak and understand most of it.

Both Hindi and Urdu have the same grammatical structure. Hindi is written in Devnagari script, the one used by Sanskrit, and Urdu is written in Persian script. Words in Urdu are mainly derived from Persian and Arabic, and Hindi's words are derived largely from Sanskrit. Still, both languages share a lot of common words, especially linking verbs. Another language emerged as the result of interaction between Hindi and Urdu speakers. It uses common vocabulary and has no written form. The British called this language Hindustani and used it for oral communication but kept English as the official language.

We were both admitted to the Urdu sections at the school but were told that next year, the Urdu sections would be eliminated and we would have to join the Hindi sections. Somehow, it did not make any difference to us.

Our school was about a mile from our house, and we passed all kinds of stores on our way to and from it. It was so different than walking on cow paths through Gagret's fields. Our route to school was a mile full of interesting sights and sounds. We started on the bridge that crossed over the railway tracks. The sidewalk on the bridge was crowded with all kinds of vendors—barbers plying their trade on a small dhurrie, hawkers selling everything from matches to sugarcanes to berries. The sidewalk broadened after the bridge, and we walked past shops that lined both sides of the street.

This was a Muslim area, and a large number of butcher shops had thriving businesses. Seeing a hanging carcass of a goat made us sick. We were very strict vegetarians and had only heard stories about people who ate eggs and meat. We viewed people who ate eggs and meat the same as most people viewed cannibals. The idea that someone would kill and eat an animal was hard for us to believe. Here, on our way to school, we had to believe that.

In between the butcher shops were small restaurants, tea stalls, tailors, cobblers, and condiment stores. They were of less interest to us. What interested us were the snake oil salesmen who would attract small crowds around them in the afternoons.

These salesmen sold oils and lotions that came in small bottles, and they would use a live snake or iguana to get the attention of people. The salesmen would talk incessantly about the many ailments that their salves could cure. A drop of the oil could make a weak man strong, improve the digestion system, make women fertile, and improve memory. At times, the salesman would tell the kids to go away, as what he was selling was not for them. I understood the reason: They used dirty language at times. They would also talk about people being *namard*, or impotent, and how a drop from one of their bottles could cure it. They did not want us children to hear such stuff. Actually, in my opinion, they did not care. They didn't want us around because we never had the money to buy the panacea extracted from a snake or lizard.

My class was composed of seventy or so students. Some of them were called refugees. "I am a refugee" was a proud statement made by these students. They came from well-off families that had acquired sizeable properties and businesses in Delhi in exchange for what they had left in Pakistan. Later, I read a lot of stories of the suffering of these refugees; however, those I met in my class had a very different lot.

Our teacher was named Harbans Lal. I do not remember him ever once getting around to teaching us anything. It took him half an hour just to take the roll call. He would call out a name and the corresponding child would stand up and yell, "Yessir!"

Yessir was one word to us. We never used the word *yes* in English class.

Mr. Lal would look up from his register, holding his pen in his right hand, and stare at the student as if he had never seen him before. After half a minute or more, when he was satisfied, he would mark his register and yell the next student's name. This was the signal for the standing student to drop back on the mat while another student screamed, "Yessir!"

After he had heard seventy *yessirs,* he would close his register and count the number of absentees. I do not remember missing even one day of class, but noticed that five or six students were missing on a daily basis. They would bring an "application for absence" written by their parents the day they returned to school. Mr. Lal would read this application with great aplomb and would always make a comment to embarrass the student.

"Bring your father to the classroom tomorrow," he would say with a sneer. "He might learn how to write Urdu properly."

If the application was in English, he would pretend to read it for a long time. We all knew he did not know English and would smile at his efforts. His comments about the English applications were always the same.

"Your father writes good English," he would also sometimes say, looking at a student with obvious respect.

I decided that if I ever had to be absent, I would ask Babuji to write the application in English. However, it was unnecessary planning on my part, as Babuji always wrote official letters in English and I was never absent from school.

The student with the English application would sit down and whisper "*Madar chod!*" to his neighbors, which is a common Punjabi/Hindi/Urdu expression declaring that the speaker has an extremely close relationship with the mother of the offending person. "It was my elder brother who wrote the application. He cannot read English." We would laugh silently with him.

During this marathon roll call, all of us would be sitting on our mats whispering to our neighbors about movies, our families, and what we were going to do during recess. A few boys would sing songs from movies and emulate movie stars. The words *love, pining in love, effects of spring on feelings of love, broken hearts,* and *first meeting,* among numerous

others, were common in these songs. I learned much vocabulary through
movie songs while the roll was being called and punctuated with loud
"yessirs."

After the roll call, Mr. Lal would close the register with great ceremony
and open the Urdu textbook. He would pick a student to read a few
lines and then ask another to follow up. Because the roll call took so
long, less than half of the class would have the opportunity to participate
in this exercise in language instruction. The rest of the class, especially
the students sitting in the farthest part of the room from Mr. Lal, were
deprived of this great exercise.

Eventually the bell would ring, interrupting our language instruction,
and we would all drop our books and shoot out of the classroom, pushing
each other and kicking the books that lay on the mats.

Sham and I got one anna as daily pocket allowance. We would buy
food from vendors selling things like toffee, chickpea curry, mango pulp,
or fried vegetable snacks like *pakodas* and samosas. I'd eat my snack as
I walked around and talked to friends.

The anna I got was never enough to buy anything substantial. Some
kids brought as many as four or even eight annas to school. But then,
some kids did not bring any money to school at all. These kids usually
stood looking at those who would buy these luxuries, hoping someone
would share with them. I never did. What I bought with my anna was
a lot less than I desired. Sharing was out of the question.

The remaining school day went by as lazily as the morning session.
We did mathematics, civics, and geography exercises. Kids sitting in the
front rows participated, and those sitting in the back talked to each other
or played marbles. Harbans Lal, unlike most teachers, did not take naps.
He did not teach much either.

During our second year in Delhi, I moved into the high school as a
fifth-grader. I was looking forward to sitting on benches and using desks,
but due to the influx of refugees from Pakistan, our class was held on a
verandah, and we had no desks. We had a different teacher for each
subject, and each of them was very interesting.

Hindi was taught by a soft-spoken pundit. He would scrawl the Hindi
alphabet on the blackboard and had us copy it. We were expected to
memorize it the next day and be prepared to read the Hindi text. He got
angry at us for our failure to master the alphabet within a day.

"You are Hindus and know Urdu, but cannot read Hindi. That is a shame," he would remind us.

The only memory I have of my fifth-grade experience is that I did attend it. Babuji retired at the age of fifty-three, and we moved back to Gagret. The mandatory retirement age was fifty-five at that time, but Babuji had saved up enough vacation time to retire two years earlier with full salary. We liked to live in the city, but there was no choice as the house we lived in had been allotted to the person who replaced Babuji. Once again, we were back in Gagret.

Mark Twain once warned children not to let their schooling interfere with their education. During my two years in Delhi, I did learn some things, but the real education I had there occurred outside the classroom. Meeting and associating with all those city boys gave multiple lessons in living on a daily basis. Sham and I learned to play city games and talk like city boys, but the most important thing I discovered in Delhi was going to the movies. It was love at first sight.

Since their introduction, movies have been the primary, if not the only, entertainment source for many Indian people. There were no cinema houses in villages, including Gagret; the villages did not have the critical mass to make building and running a cinema house profitable. Thus, I had not seen any movies until I went to Delhi in 1949.

In Indian culture, movies, unfortunately, were also considered the root cause of all evils; therefore, we children were not allowed to see them. Any adult who heard us singing a song from a movie was likely to scold us with epithets such as *badmash* (scoundrel) and *besharam* (shameless). Still, children did make up a sizeable proportion of any movie's audience. Indian cinema during the late 1940s and 1950s was still rather prudish even at its most ribald. A very strict Indian Censor Board did not allow any depictions of kissing on the cheek. The lovelorn hero was, at most, allowed to hold the hands of his paramour. The main attraction of a movie was its songs. A movie with good songs could run for more than twenty-five weeks and attain a "silver jubilee." The songs were usually full of double entendres and emphasized one's love, a broken heart, pining for love, or described a beloved's beauty. These were not the sort of songs that young impressionable children should hear! But the fact was that radios blared these songs round the clock, so everyone was familiar with them. I had memorized all the hit songs without once going to a cinema house. You did not really need to buy a ticket to be debauched!

Because my family frowned on my going to the movies, I only watched, maybe, ten movies during my two-year stay in Delhi. The first movie I saw was *Barsaat* (*The Monsoon*). It was a huge hit and was going into its "golden jubilee," having run for more than fifty weeks. My classmates talked about this movie and sang its songs, such as "*hawa main udta jaye, mera laal dopatta malmal ka*" (My red head scarf is waving in the wind) or "*jiya bequrar hai, chhai bahar hai*" (My heart is restless; the spring has sprung). How spring had sprung during the monsoon season was beyond anyone's understanding, but story lines in Indian movies did not follow any logic. The key was to insert ten to fifteen songs in a three-hour meaningless story and pray that at least one song would hit a chord with the audience. The story was almost always was the same: A good-looking hero with a heart of gold pursues a beautiful heroine who eventually falls in love with him, and a villain tries to foil their love. Into this triangle are woven other characters like friends of the hero and heroine who are always very funny and wise. The villain makes a lot of problems for the hero and heroine, resulting in a huge catastrophe. In the end, the hero vanquishes the villain, and the hero and heroine sing a song which shows they will live happily ever after.

At nine years old, I had yet to see my first movie. It was embarrassing for me when my classmates discussed the movies they had seen and all I could do was smile stupidly. Asking Babuji if I could watch a movie would have been analogous to asking his permission to commit a sacrilegious act. Babuji himself never went to the cinema. If he did, he did not tell us. Bhabhi did go once a year to see some religious cinema. It was not entertainment, but religious duty for her. Bhai Narain did go to cinema with his friends, but he was in his late teens.

I was a quiet kid and had the ability to blend in with the background in any room. In addition to Narain, Sham, our parents, and me, Jijaji B. K. Sharma,* our brother-in-law, lived with us. He was a regular cinema buff. He saw at least one movie a week. At that time, Parkash Chand, a very distant cousin of Bhabhi, also moved in with us. When Parkash

* Jijaji is Hindi for *sister's husband*

and Jijaji discussed the movies they had seen, I would listen with full attention and memorize details. I used these details at school to impress my friends. I told them I had seen this or that movie and would relate the story or excerpts that I had picked from Jijaji's and Parkash's earnest discussions. My friends were impressed as it seemed that I was watching more movies than anyone else.

But the desire to see a real movie gnawed at my heart. I made all kinds of plans, including stealing money for a ticket and sneaking out of the house for an afternoon. However, these plans were not practical. I had never stolen money before nor had I ever snuck out of our house. Actually, I was too chicken to break any rules. So, the dream of seeing a movie remained a dream for a while, but I knew I would get the opportunity sooner or later.

When Sister Brahmi visited us in Delhi, Sister Kamla, my other sister who was married to B. K. Sharma, told her that she must see the movie *Barsaat*. Both of them were in their twenties and married; however, custom dictated that two women did not go to the cinema by themselves. Sister Kamla talked to Shanti, Parkash's wife, and then they both talked to their husbands. I had listened to these conversations with great interest. They discussed getting permission from Bhabhi and also making sure Babuji did not learn about it. Finally, the issue was brought before Jijaji and Parkash by Sister Kamla and Shanti. They decided to go to the cinema the following Sunday, and Parkash, whose workplace was close to one of the cinema houses that was showing *Barsaat*, bought five tickets in advance as the show frequently sold out. The tickets were a great secret, and they did not realize I knew everything about the plan.

I still remember how, on the appointed day at 5:00 p.m., they all congregated and walked outside the gate to catch a tonga. I followed them from a safe distance. Just as they hailed the tonga and were getting into it, I ran and jumped onto the tonga seat.

"What are you doing here?" Jijaji asked. He was not happy.

"We are going to temple, you go back home and play," Parkash suggested. The ladies stayed quiet.

"No," I told him belligerently, "you are going to see *Barsaat* for the fifth time. I have not seen it even once." I ended my declaration with tears running down my cheeks. I knew my show of emotion would work on my two sisters as well as Shanti.

Sister Brahmi was the first to melt. "I will pay for Madan," she said. Sister Kamla and Shanti nodded their support.

"The question is not of money," said Jijaji. "It is the ticket. The cinema house is sold out. We got these tickets several days ago." Parkash nodded in agreement and added, "I got them through a friend whose cousin works there. Even he had a hard time getting these tickets."

They tried to cajole me and even tried to give me some money to buy sweetmeats. That was tempting; I loved sweetmeats, but I had a bigger cause and a loftier goal, so I refused. While they were discussing alternatives, I kept trying to produce more tears and wiped them away with elaborate movements. I knew the three ladies were softening.

Sister Kamla suggested that she stay home and I use her ticket. I liked the idea, but no one else agreed with her. Then Sister Brahmi said she was not much on cinema and should stay home. I liked her offer too, but everyone was against it since it was for her that the whole expedition had been organized.

The tongawallah also joined the discussion, suggesting that we try buying a ticket from the black market. It was getting late, so they decided to follow his advice and the tonga moved with me sitting on Sister Brahmi's lap. I was barefoot and wearing dirty shorts and a dirtier shirt. They were all dressed nicely for the cinema outing. I must have been a sight, but I did not care. I was the happiest kid in the world.

They did manage to buy a ticket for me from a black-market dealer for twice as much as they had paid for the other tickets. I sat alone in a nice chair and watched the black-and-white screen with people moving around and talking, singing, and dancing. The movie was three hours long, but it seemed to me to last only a few seconds.

On the way back, I was reminded about how expensive my ticket was. But I did not care. I had seen a movie! I had enjoyed the most popular movie songs right in the cinema and not from people who mumbled them in the street. I had a major experience and looked forward to telling my classmates about it the following day.

8

Working on the Farm

"I THINK," WROTE BABUJI ON HIS PALM ON the night of April 11, 1954, "You should herd cattle tomorrow." I remember the date and the message clearly even today; it was a bolt from the blue and hit me hard.

In Gagret, my family was considered rich or at least comfortable. However, being rich, like being tall, is relative. In the Gagret of the 1950s, my height of 5 feet 4 inches may not have attracted scouts from the National Basketball Association, but neither would I be of any interest to Barnum and Bailey's. My family was rich in Gagret, and I was fairly tall!

Because labor was cheap, we had servants to help with the household work and farmhands to till the land. We could eat all we want, but not everything we wanted. Our clothes and shoes were of better quality than that of other people in the village, but each of us had only one pair of shoes and four or five sets of clothes.

Perhaps we could have been better off financially if Babuji had not had an altruistic attitude. Helping other people in any way was in his blood. His drug store did not make any money despite doing a flourishing business, as payment for purchases was voluntary.

Our financial situation got worse when Babuji went into a business venture which went belly up. However, during all these financial crises, our lifestyle did not change. It took Babuji many years to get out of the hole, and by that time, I had moved to Delhi.

In the Gagret of 1950, no one owned a car or motorcycle. Our family owned eleven bicycles, and most of them used for work—carrying milk or selling vegetables, for example.

After returning from our time in Delhi, the villagers thought of us as *babus,* or city slickers. As babus, we did not perform the hard labor on our farm. We hired servants for that. The most we babus might do would

I am in the middle with my cousin Surender (left) and my
nephew Prag, May 1953.

be to draw water from the well and milk water buffaloes and cows, which
I already was doing. Now Babuji had the temerity to suggest that I should
also herd cattle.

"You mean take the cattle out to graze?" I asked just to make sure
I had not misunderstood.

He shook his head in a slow and painful "yes." I looked at his face
closely and knew the decision to send me out to work with the "common
people" must have been very agonizing for him. There must have been
several reasons. First, I was just sitting there at home doing nothing
except, to use the Gagret expression, "smell women's farts," which was
used to describe men who were no good. Second, it was hard to find a
cowherd, and hiring one cost money.

"I will go!" I declared like a martyr; I was feeling like one.

The next day, at 7:00 in the morning, I tied two chapatis and two
slices of mango pickle in the corner of my *parna*—the cotton cloth used
as a towel, sun bonnet, blanket, rug, and lunch bag—and headed for the
kudhi, our barn, where the farm servants lived along with the cattle. I
had to take the cattle to graze, as Babuji had asked me. I carried a six-

foot-long bamboo staff to help guide the cattle and felt very important as this was my first solo cattle herding experience.

I walked the length of the kudhi ground where all the cattle were tethered, counted them and classified them. Six oxen, two water buffaloes, three cows, and six calves of both genders and of various ages made up the herd. Putting my right hand on the top of the staff and my left at my waist, I decided to let the animals know who was boss.

"You are all going to behave or I am going to break this staff on your backs," I declared in an officious voice. My declaration had little or no effect on them. Some of them continued to cud and others gave me a quick look of boredom. Bagga, the white ox with huge horns, shook his head violently and snorted at me. I stepped a few feet back. Bagga was the largest ox in our household and he knew it. His nose was pierced when he was still a calf, and rope ran through his nostrils and was tied behind his horns. This rope helped control him. However, first you had to get close enough to him to get hold of the rope.

I slowly began to untie the cattle, starting with the calves. The hungry and thirsty cattle began to move toward the narrow, cobbled path. I untied all of them except for Bagga. As I came close to him, he shook his head in anger, his horns cutting the air like two swords. I got scared and retreated. This made Bagga restless as he wanted to join the rest on their trip to some green pasture and, of course, water.

"Look, if you want to eat, you've got to stand quiet," I admonished him, but I doubt he got my message. I was in a jam. All the cattle had left the yard, and here I was trying to untie Bagga who was getting more restless by the second. I looked around, helpless, and saw a neighbor's servant, Julfi, laughing and slapping his thigh in joy. Seeing a babu make an ass of himself is not a daily sight! I wanted to yell at him to remind him who was the servant, but then had an idea.

"Can you untie Bagga?" I asked him very politely.

Julfi shook his head and made a jerky motion with his head, meaning Bagga would gore him too. I asked him to please try. He walked over, stood by me, and looked at Bagga, who by now was jumping restlessly and, of course, must have been blaming me for his plight. Julfi took my staff from my hand and slowly advanced toward Bagga. He threaded the staff in Bagga's nose rope and jerked it up. That made Bagga jump higher, but also bray in pain. Julfi twisted the staff, forcing Bagga to move his head away. Then with a jerk, Julfi jumped and untied the clasp in the rope, which had Bagga tied to the wooden stake. As Julfi let go of Bagga's rope, the powerful ox jumped and thundered out of the yard.

And to think, herding cattle is considered the easiest job on the farm!

The main duty of a cowherd is to make sure that all the cattle stay together and graze in a specific area. You have to make sure that your wards do not wander into the fields of sugarcane, corn, wheat, or barley. For some reason, the cattle like to eat these crops much more than the grass that should be their main diet. Some of these cattle were meek and avoided going into restricted areas; however, most of them, especially Bagga and his younger brother Neela, considered it their birthright to go into these forbidden fields. They were sly and always ready to run into an adjoining field every time I looked away or was working on the other side of the grazing area. I would yell and run toward the bandit ox, waving my staff. They would grab a stalk or two, rip it out of the ground, and run away just before I arrived at the scene of the crime. They seemed to enjoy taunting me more than they enjoyed eating the succulent stalks of sugarcane they had stolen.

Standing in the three-digit heat with bare feet for ten hours can be tiring. Twice a day, I had to herd the animals to a pond about a mile away so they could drink the muddy water. By late afternoon, I was exhausted and red-eyed from watching the cattle in the 105-degree glare. I took them to the kudhi and tied them one by one, except for Bagga. I had to ask one of the servants to tie him. After it was safely tied, I gave him two sharp cuts of my staff to express my anger and displeasure at his behavior before heading home and calling it a day.

One problem with herding cattle, like with any other farm job, is that it must be done 365 days a year. There is no holiday or break—the cattle get hungry daily. The monotony of untying the cattle, taking them to one or the other grazing areas, and watching over them without a break, all day, all month, and all year, can get to anyone. I had no one to talk to since the other cowherds were illiterate and could not communicate with me. Whenever I got hold of a book, I brought it with me to read, but you could not read while herding without getting every farmer in the vicinity mad at you. Bagga and Neela knew that the book was their ticket for a luxury bite. Like most avid readers, when I read, I forgot the world around me, including Bagga and Neela and their propensity to get me in trouble.

The grazing day depended on the light. During summer, we grazed for eight to ten hours and in winter, the grazing days became shorter and shorter, a couple of hours on the way to or from the watering pond. As the summer progressed, the grazing fields dried up. During winters, we would feed the animals the dry grass which we had cut and stored in the attics of the kudhi.

In addition to herding cattle, I also had to cut grass from various meadows in the morning. Grass grew fast after the monsoon season, and there was plenty of it. I usually went with two other kids—Tirath and Antru—both brothers. We would walk one to four miles each way, depending on where the grass was ready to cut, use our scythes to cut a load, tie the grass in small bundles called *poolas,* and then tie those poolas into a large load held with two or three ropes fashioned out of grass. After that, we would help lift the grass loads onto each other's heads and start trotting toward the kudhi. The whole process took about two to four hours, depending on the distance. We had to jog and walk from three to eight miles—all before breakfast or even a cup of tea!

Then there were the shoes. Shoes of any kind in Gagret at that time were a luxury for most people. Shoes were worn only for weddings and special occasions. For the daily trudge from here to everywhere, people walked on bare feet. I, on the other hand, always had a pair of shoes and would get new ones when they gave in, which was every other month. I found it embarrassing, however, to wear shoes when everyone around me went with bare feet. So, to avoid this embarrassment, I too went with bare feet when I grazed cattle and cut grass. One incident still stands fresh in my memory.

It was January and bitterly cold in Gagret. Farm work slows down considerably during winters. One early morning, Tirath, Antru, and I decided to go to the Bainwala jungle to cut firewood. My mother insisted that I wear my shoes, but I hid them in the bushes outside our house when I went to join the brothers for the four-mile trek to the jungle. Soon my feet were frozen and began to burn. Tirath and Antru had a lot of experience walking barefoot, and the soles of their feet were one big callus; my feet were weak and soft from regular use of shoes. I felt like I was walking on burning coals, and they walked as if they had nice soft shoes. I did not want them to know how I was hurting, fearing their taunts about being a babu. We arrived in Bainwala, and luckily for me a couple of people there had built a small fire and were warming their feet and hands. I was so happy to see that, I made a beeline for the fire, but Tirath and Antru kept walking as they did not want other people to get hold of firewood before us. I walked by the fire, yearning for a few seconds of warmth, but the embarrassment of being called a babu kept me going. The cold, a couple of thorns that worked their way into my soles, and the pounding on the hard surface left my feet raw. I never hid my shoes in the bushes again.

For the next six years, I did all kinds of farm work and hated all of it with equal strength. I graduated from herding cattle and cutting grass to plowing, the main job. Plowing required the full attention of the plower. You held the wooden plow handle steady and made sure the plowing line you formed joined the earlier line so that dirt was fully turned over and no hard earth was left in between. At the same time, you had to yell at the oxen that pulled the plow and order them to make a left or a right turn. The order for a left turn in ox language, "Oxenese," was *"Aapaaair!"*—which they understood very well. The order for a right turn, which was very rare, was *"Aakutchh!"* To let them know they were slow and needed to increase their pace, the plower yelled *"Tainu mannuan"* and regular obscenities, which established the close relationship between the plower and the mothers and sisters of the oxen. I knew all these commands from the days when I was hearing and used them loudly for the benefit of everyone for miles around.

I have always wondered about Oxenese. Did the oxen really understand the lingo, or did they take clues from (a) the fact that the field had ended or the plow line from their earlier round had gone left or right at that point or (b) the fact that the plower had picked up the plow higher for the left or right turn? I also wondered why other teams of oxen within hearing distance did not also make a left turn after hearing my "Aapaair!" That would have been funny! Imagine all the pairs of oxen close by making a left turn in the middle of their fields. But it never happened, and I am more inclined to believe that the left and right turns the oxen made were controlled by other hints, not to mention the body language of the plower. As I look back, I think the oxen used the same strategy as us deaf people use while lipreading. We lipread using contextual clues like body language, facial expressions, and prior knowledge of the conversation's subject. However, there is one big difference. We lipread while facing the speaker; the oxen had their rumps to the plower!

As I said earlier, I hated every minute of working on the farm. How I managed to stay sane while working like that for more than six years is not a mystery. The greatest factor that helped me keep my sanity while yelling Oxenese and doing all the farm chores was my optimism. "Things will get better," I kept telling myself. I worked daily and dreamed about "something wonderful" happening one day that would catapult me into being a big man. I did not have a specific definition of what it meant to be a big man. It ranged from becoming a movie star to a major political leader to a high government official to a writer to a successful businessman to . . . whatever. I daydreamed about becoming someone very important while herding cattle and plowing fields alongside people who were very satisfied with their lives and would have laughed themselves silly had they learned about my big hopes and plans.

I dreamed of the faraway places that I read about—cities like Rio de Janeiro, Paris, London, New York, Moscow, and Rome. The bright city lights, big shiny cars, beautiful women, beaches, and powerful friends wandered in my head while oxen farted in my face to bring me down to earth. "Tainu mannuan," I would yell and give each ox a couple of lashes for good measure. Then I would return to Rio de Janeiro.

There was, however, one task I liked. Babuji did not have any income after retirement. The provident, or retirement, fund he received was equal to four years of his salary. It did not last for more than two years. The farm produced enough to feed the family, but we needed cash to pay the servants and buy clothes and other stuff. In 1953, after our visit to Delhi, Babuji bought four bags full of prescription drugs and general medicine and with that opened a small medical store in one of the buildings we owned. I was very proud of the store because it had a colorful sign proclaiming "Madan Medical Hall."

Babuji did not have a pharmacist's training but in Gagret; no one required that. People would bring prescriptions from the government hospital, and Babuji would count out pills or give them patent or generic medicine, including injections. The shop became more of an office and a meeting place for Babuji. The margin of profit was very small, and more than half of the clientele bought on credit. Selling on credit really meant giving things away for free as Babuji never asked people to pay their debts, and people conveniently "forgot" they had bought anything from our medical hall on credit.

I liked to sit in "my" shop and make the sale whenever I was there. Babuji saw how I enjoyed being a "salesman" and began to ask me to run the shop when he went to Hoshiarpur or Una for business. The servants would cover for me in the fields, or we would hire someone for a day while I sat in the store looking and feeling important. However, such assignments were rare—once or twice a month. Communication was not a problem since most the customers brought a written prescription. Others used mime to indicate that they had a stomachache or a headache.

Thus, life went on for me in a lane that was painfully slow while I daydreamed about jets and rockets and faraway cities.

9

Back to Study

FARMING FULL TIME DID NOT STOP MY EDUCATION, it just slowed it down. I had kept up with my "former classmates" until the eighth grade. At that time, I gave up and decided to study on my own pace, using Sham's hand-me-down textbooks. Why I was doing this was not clear to me. Neither algebra problems nor formulas nor geometrical theorems were helpful with my plowing or herding tasks. But learning and studying were in my blood; I just could not stop it.

One day, out of the blue, Sham asked, "Why don't you take the matriculation examination?" He was referring to the high school diploma examination.

"How could I do that?" I asked angrily. "I do not go to school. And since when did deaf people sit in those examinations?"

While I spurned Sham's idea, I began to think about it. Sham also talked to Babuji, who said, "It is up to Madan."

One night when Babuji was eating dinner and we were sitting waiting for him to finish, I declared, "I am going to take the high school diploma examination."

"Fine," he said, and the decision was made.

High school examinations were controlled by the university systems in each state. It did not matter which school you attended, you had to take the examination at a specific examination center. Students who were unable to attend school for whatever reason could take the examination as a "private candidate."

Early in October, I filled out an application form and went to Hoshiarpur to get myself photographed because three copies of the photograph were required to take the examination. Getting the photographs became a major project. I took a day off from farm work and rode the bus to Hoshiarpur where Sham was attending college. He met me at the bus stop and took me to his favorite photographer. After the photograph was taken, he took me to a restaurant and then to a movie. After the movie, he paraded me around, introducing me to his friends. He would show them the three copies of my photograph and then explain why they were necessary. His friends would stare wide-eyed at me and shake my hand vigorously as if I had just passed the high school examination.

It was decided that I would take the months of February and March off from farm work in order to study. The only responsibilities I had were cutting grass for the water buffalo, milking them, and drawing water from the well. I liked this fringe benefit of being a student. However, I did not spend all my new extra time on studying. I managed to use most of the time to read novels that I bought from a junk dealer in Hoshiarpur. Bhabhi did not know the difference between a novel and a textbook, and she got worried about my becoming blind, complaining to Babuji that the "boy was studying too hard."

"That is good for him," Babuji told her. "Why are you complaining?"

Bhabhi, being an obedient wife and full of respect for Babuji's knowledge, dropped the subject. Now I could read all kind of books without worrying about oxen running into a sugarcane field.

Still, I had to study also. I did not have any problem with algebra and geometry. I finished all the problems with little help. The problem was Sanskrit. In high school, the required subjects are Hindi, English, mathematics, geography, history and civics. In addition, one had to take either science or Sanskrit. I could not take science as I had no access to a laboratory, so it was decided that I would take Sanskrit.

Sanskrit is a complex language, and learning high school-level Sanskrit in three months was an uphill task. I had to memorize all the *gardaans*— grammatical inflections of verbs in three genders: masculine, feminine, and neutral. In the examination, one had to write these grammatical inflections for several verbs, translate a passage from Hindi to Sanskrit, and explain Sanskrit poetry in Hindi.

After a shaky start, I began to enjoy Sanskrit and had not only memorized all the gardaans, but also could translate Hindi passages into Sanskrit easily. While everyone was worried about my learning Sanskrit, I read Zane Gray's *Riders of Purple Sage* and other novels to improve my English.

The charade of working hard for my high school examination went to a feverish pitch by late February. The examination was scheduled in the middle of March, and I began to act like an important scholar preparing for it.

Once during this time, Sham was home for the weekend from Hoshiarpur. He was in his second year, and his examination was also scheduled in March. That Saturday night, we decided to study hard all night. The first problem was light. We felt that the hurricane lamp was not appropriate. There was a petromax lantern in our home, which we used at weddings only. Sham convinced Bhabhi that it was important to use the petromax in order to study better and save our eyes. She helped us set it up, dust it, and fill it with kerosene oil.

The lighting of the petromax became a major project. First, there was no lamp for it. Sham begged Bhabhi for the money for a lamp. He then gave the money to a boy to run to the bazaar for us to buy a lamp. Soon the word was out that we were going to light the petromax and about ten kids gathered there in our house for the festivity. Sham, being the elder brother, took over the responsibility of lighting the petromax. Since it was his first effort, it took more than a half hour to successfully light it. His audience, which had been frustrated, applauded; and after watching the bright light for about ten minutes, they got bored and left. We placed the petromax in a strategic place so we could both benefit from the bright light.

It was almost 9:00 p.m. by then, and we were getting sleepy. Sham suggested that we drink some coffee as he had heard that coffee helped people stay awake. We had coffee beans that Narain had brought a year earlier from Bangalore, where he served in the air force. The fact that the beans might be old did not enter our minds. We did not know how to make coffee and had never drunk even a drop before in our lives. We also did not know that coffee beans needed to be grounded.

The first step was to start a fire. Since dinner was over, our kitchen fire was cold. It took me a half hour to get the fire going and the water boiling. We added coffee beans to the boiling water, just like when we made tea, added milk and sugar and boiled some more. The coffee was bitter and tasted awful, but we drank it smacking our lips. Anything that required so much work to cook should taste good!

After drinking our coffee, we went to sleep.

10

The High School Examination

MID-MARCH CAME, AND I WAS READY FOR the examination. I have to admit that I did not prepare much for it; reading novels took priority over studying. I felt comfortable that I was going to pass the examination in first division (equivalent to getting straight A's). Narain had gotten first division and Sham second division, which is like getting a B average. Babuji encouraged me to make the merit list. I said, I could never make the merit list. Private students rarely earned that distinction, and no one from our village had made the merit list yet. How could I, who did not even attend school, make that?

High school examinations, known as matriculation, were, and still are, controlled by state universities. A centrally located high school was chosen as an examination center, and candidates from surrounding schools went there to take the test. Each day one subject was covered, and it took about a week to finish the whole examination. If a candidate failed in even one subject, he had to re-take the whole thing the following year.

More difficult than preparing for the examination was preparing myself to go to Ambota, the examination site, and face everyone. The memory of taking the sixth-grade examination was still fresh in my mind, and the mere thought of being there petrified me. I did not tell my fear to anyone and acted as if it was nothing. This was my personal fear and I was embarrassed. During the week before the examinations were to start, I spent more time agonizing about people ridiculing me than actually studying my textbooks.

"Are you planning to become the president of India?" I remembered this taunt from someone when he learned that I was planning to take the high school examination. I was sure a lot of smart aleck remarks awaited me from those who had not passed the examination or had dropped out of school in earlier grades.

The Big Day arrived. Sham wanted to help me with my appearance. While I was wishing to become invisible, he planned to make me stand out like a sore thumb. He brought out his best bush shirt (a half-sleeve shirt with open front and patch pockets, which was fashionable then), and pants, especially washed and ironed for the occasion. When I saw the clothes, I gave out a loud, "No!"

"I am not going to wear this fancy suit," I declared. "Everyone will laugh at me."

"Why should they laugh at you for being dressed nicely?" Sham was puzzled and rightly so.

Babuji had already gone to his medical store, so I could not get his help. Bhabhi liked the idea and supported Sham. I gave in to their combined front. I had to wear something nice anyway.

The bush shirt and pants were bleached white and, I had to admit, looked really good on me. The pure white suit was complemented by a pair of well-polished black shoes, also belonging to Sham. They were a size too big for me, and I walked a bit awkwardly, but not as awkwardly as I felt.

As Sham and I marched toward Ambota, boys began to join us. The word that the deaf guy was coming to take the examination had spread. They wanted to see me, but now they wanted to see my regal clothes also. By the time we arrived in Ambota, I was literally leading a procession with Sham holding my one hand and pulling me to hurry. He had a busy time because he had to field all kind of questions and yell at boys who dared to come too close to us.

There were about 300 boys from about forty villages who were taking the examination. Since we were an hour early, we had time on our hands, and everyone gathered around us. I kept looking at the ground or at buildings or trees. I did not look at other students, but rather I just looked at everything that could not stare back at me. I was by far the best dressed examinee in the whole center! I wanted to be invisible, but in my shiny white suit, I was as invisible as the full moon on a black night. Sham introduced me to the head examiner who kept looking at my regalia while listening to my brother talk about my deafness. The examiner was appropriately impressed and took me to my seat himself—long before anyone else. I sat there on the bench behind the desk in a large empty hall and looked at the barred windows full of curious faces.

It was not exactly an ideal setting for a statewide examination, but I survived. The examination was two hours long, but I finished it in less than one hour since I found it easy. However, I should have used time to review my answers and make revisions. I never checked my work in any subject during examinations. Not then, not ever.

I came out after handing the finished paper to the proctor. All the students were inside taking the examination, and I saw Sham sitting under the pipal tree on a brick platform talking to three men. On seeing me, he ran toward me very concerned and gestured if something was wrong. I yelled that I had finished the paper. He was relieved but not very happy about my finishing it in a hurry.

"You should have gone over your work at least twice," he admonished me.

"It was too easy and not worth going over a second time," I countered, and the case was closed.

Instead of talking about the next day's examination, which was geometry, Sham began to discuss the wardrobe that he had planned for me to wear for the encore. I stopped in my tracks and told him that if he dressed me up like a doll again, I was not going to take any more examinations. He was surprised and also hurt that I did not appreciate his efforts to make me look good. However, he agreed that I would be wearing my own clothes for the rest of the examinations.

I was back on the farm after the examinations were over. The result would be announced in all the newspapers two months later. My career as a student was over. I passed the high school examination in first division. Babuji was very proud of me, as was everyone in the family. I was the only one who was disappointed. I was secretly mad at myself for not following everyone's advice and reviewing my work. Making the merit list would have been nice. But at the same time, I told myself that being on the merit list would not have helped me in anyway. I could not "spread my diploma and sleep on it," as they said in Gagret about things that were not of much use.

11

Travels and Other Adventures

I MAY BE GIVING YOU THE IMPRESSION THAT I had no fun or adventures while living in Gagret. I did travel, and living in Gagret was an adventure unto itself. I traveled two or three times each year despite our limited means and the fact that no one in Gagret ever left the little village except as a member of a wedding party or on the way to the *Shivbari*, the open area outside the village where all the dead were cremated, for the last ride on four shoulders.

Seeing places—near and far, strange and awesome—was in my blood. I visited family in other cities also; however, I will spare you the details of those trips. Still, there were some fun-filled and funny travel experiences. For example, there was the time when I wanted to see snow.

Snow! No one in my village had ever seen snow. They did not even know what it looked like.

The Hindi and Urdu words for *snow* and *ice* are the same—*baraf.* Whenever I had learned about baraf falling in the mountains and other places where the weather conditions were sufficient to produce it, I always had mistakenly assumed that what fell from the sky was ice or a steady stream of hail stones, with which I was very familiar. The idea of getting my head pelted with falling ice was not very appealing. My mistaken impression changed when I saw some beautiful pictures of snow-covered scenes in photographs in airline calendars, which B. K. Sharma, our brother-in-law, brought from his office. He worked for Air India and received calendars from almost all the international airlines that flew to India.

The powdery, gleaming white stuff that covered homes, trees, and meadows in those photographs was beautiful. My improving English also helped me learn that ice and snow were two different forms of baraf.

Armed with this knowledge and tempted by the intoxicating beauty of snow in those photographs, I decided that I had to see it.

My eldest sister, Brahmi, she of the milk cure for deafness, lived part of the year in Theog where the uncles of her husband, Roshan Lal Joshi, had a hardware store and owned some land. Spending a few weeks or even a month in Theog had several benefits: I could see snow; spend time with my nephew Prag, who was more of a friend than a nephew, as well as my two younger nephews Sat Pal and Paisu; and also get away from the drudgery of farm work.

Now the problem was getting Babuji's permission.

I started with some innocent questions about baraf. Why did English have two separate words for baraf while Hindi had only one? When I asked this question, he was eating his dinner and talking to Bhabhi about something. He took a break from these two chores to answer me on his palm: "It could be because we do not have snow everywhere in India." I let it rest there.

A couple of days later, I brought up with him the issue of how there was much less work to be done on the farm during the winter. He agreed and told me I could join the servants in making ropes and doing other chores if I was bored. I was not looking for that answer and decided to approach him at a new angle. Since no other strategy presented itself, I decided to take the bull by the horns and wait for the right time to ask Babuji about going to Theog.

One evening when he appeared in a good mood while eating his dinner, I said out of the blue, "Babuji, I want to see the snow!"

He was puzzled at first, then treated this statement as yet another of my impossible dreams. He said, "I also want to see the snow," and continued to talk to Bhabhi. I was not very happy with this slight of my great plans, and decided to push my luck.

"You know they have snow in Theog," I ventured. The cat was out of the bag.

"No," he said flatly. "You are not going to Theog." To him, the matter was closed.

I knew he had reasons to deny my request. I was deaf, and he did not like the idea of my traveling alone. Sending me there uninvited for such a nebulous and outrageously silly reason as seeing snow was out of the question. Then, of course, there was the question of money. Traveling more than 500 miles both ways by train and bus would cost money. He did not have to tell me these reasons; I understood the importance of each. But I had to see the snow, nevertheless!

I broached the subject again a few days later using the carpe diem approach. In a jumble of several sentences, I tried to tell him that it would not cost much; I could travel alone as I had already done. I also promised to return within two weeks before the sugarcane harvest season began. He knew now that there would be no end of my asking, so he scribbled in haste, "OK, we shall think about it."

I remained adamant. "Will you please write a letter to Jijaji Roshan Lal that I am coming?" I asked in a voice that I hoped would melt steel, not just Babuji's heart, like melting snow.

"OK, I will do that tomorrow," he said. He wanted to get rid of me.

The next day, when I took Babuji's lunch to the pharmacy, I asked if he had sent the letter to Jijaji. He looked puzzled. Obviously, he had forgotten our conversation.

"You said last night that you were going to write a letter to Jijaji explaining that I was coming to Theog." I acted upset.

"OK, I will do that later," he promised. But I knew better. I took some money out of the cash box and ran to the post office, which was right next door in the building we owned, and returned with an inland letter, something akin to an aerogram. Babuji looked sadly at it and then at me and shook his head in desperation. I sat in the easy chair and watched while he, sitting at his desk, wrote the letter to Jijaji.

Of course, my visit was no problem for Jijaji and his family. He wrote back asking Babuji to let him know the exact date of my arrival so someone could meet me at the bus stop. He also asked that I bring heavy woolen clothes as it would get very cold when the snow fell. He did not have to tell me all that. I already decided to take Babuji's heavy railway coat, which came below my knees and was very heavy.

I took a bus to Hoshiarpur and then another to Jalandhar, arriving there around 7 p.m. Because the train to Kalka was set to arrive at 1:30 in the morning, I found myself with about six hours to kill.

Even though I was an irregular smoker, to pass the time, I bought a pack of cigarettes and chain-smoked them. Every hour, I bought piping hot tea to keep myself warm, even though I was sweating under the heavy overcoat. I had decided to wear it in order to look like one of the railway employees, as most of them wore similar overcoats. This allowed me access to the assistant station master's office, which had a comfortable bench, on which I stretched myself.

By the time the train arrived, my tongue was painfully swollen from smoking, and I had a very bitter taste in my mouth from all the tea. I had tried to act like a railways employee on night duty. Since I was not used to heavy use of nicotine and caffeine, I had to pay the price.

During my five or so hours in and out of the assistant station master's office, I made sure that no one learned of my deafness. In addition to facing all those questions (how did you become deaf?), I might have been thrown off the comfortable bench. If anyone talked to me, I smiled, blowing smoke into the talker's face or even offering him a smoke. I would make a vague statement like, "I am waiting for my elder brother who is a conductor," and then walk to the door, pretending to look for him.

The train came and I found a seat in a crowded third-class compartment. It was very uncomfortable. The windows were closed, but the wind blew hard from various holes. I wished I was in my own bed at home. But then I remembered how much I had fought to get in this uncomfortable position. My head ached, my swollen tongue bothered me, and my back hurt from several hours of standing, walking, and sitting while trying to look cool. Somehow, I dozed off and did not wake up until the train arrived in Kalka.

At Kalka, I took a bus to Shimla. The narrow winding road rose more than 5,000 feet in sixty miles, and the ride took more than five hours. The small bus bounced and jolted the passengers at each turn.

Shimla was the summer capital of India during the British rule. The whole government—from the viceroy and his staff to the humble *khalasis* (peon)—moved to Shimla from sweltering Delhi in April. After India achieved independence in 1947, the Indian government stopped the practice of moving the government back and forth every six months. Shimla had, over time, become a thriving summer resort of the rich. I was not one of those, though.

From Shimla, I took another, smaller bus bound for Theog. This 20-mile ride took another two hours and was even bumpier than the previous road. I was in Theog by about 4 p.m. The 200-mile trip had taken almost twenty-four hours. I was dead tired, but thrilled to see Prag, who was waiting for me at the bus stop. He asked me why I was late;

he had been waiting for me for two hours. We had not agreed on a specific time of my arrival, but I was late according to his calculation.

Prag took me to his granduncle's hardware store where Jijaji Roshan Lal, Kaka Ram, his younger brother, and their uncle Partap Chand were sitting wrapped in their pashmeena pattus (light blankets) and talking to their customers. Everyone except for Jijaji was smoking a hookah. I touched everyone's feet, as all young people did to show respect, and they looked very happy to see me. They told everyone, as I learned from Prag later, how smart I was. I had traveled alone despite my deafness. Their customers and their acquaintances shook their heads in wonderment.

From there, Prag took me to their home where I met my sister Brahmi and the other ladies. The wives of Kaka Ram and Partap Chand also lived there. Both of them stayed veiled in my presence. By custom, even in their in-law's house, the married women remained veiled from the men. I never really saw their faces or talked to them. They communicated to me through Sister Brahmi, but they said little except to check to see if I was hungry or wanted some hot tea.

The next morning, Jijaji, who knew well of my love for reading, took me to the town's brand-new library. He introduced me to the librarian, a Mr. Sood, who knew him well. Most of the books were still in boxes, but Mr. Sood assured me that I could borrow any book—even those that were not cataloged yet. I picked a few Tarzan novels by Edgar Rice Burroughs, much to the disappointment of Jijaji, who hoped I would pick books about philosophy and biographies of great men. Reading novels, according to him, was a waste of time and also unhealthy for the mind. Nevertheless, I stuck to my choice by smiling and shyly avoiding his suggestions.

I spent the better part of the day reading Edgar Rice Burroughs and several Hindi novelists. I learned that Mr. Sood was also a poet who had published a collection of Hindi poems. I was impressed as he was the first published author I had met in my life. I was not much interested in poetry, however. To please him, I borrowed his book of poems for a few days but could not make sense of his work.

Each day, we waited for the snow to fall. I was in no big hurry as I was enjoying my novels and wanted to spend as much time as I could there. Each day, all the members of my host family would express regret at the lateness of the snow and assure me that it would fall soon.

I spent the evenings with Prag after he returned from school. My two other nephews were too young to play with us. Prag and I would take long walks, and I would summarize my daily readings for his benefit. The rest of my time was spent reading, sleeping, and eating. Life was becoming enjoyable.

Finally, the snow fell! I was reading one of the Tarzan novels in my warm bed, when Prag rushed in and scribbled *baraf* on his palm. His granduncle had sent him running. I dressed hastily and came out to see the thick wads of wool winding their way to earth. It did not fall like rain or hail. It was really different.

We went to the family store where I watched the snow while everyone very happily watched me watch it. After a few minutes, I got bored with it and returned to Tarzan and the warm bed.

It snowed for three days and accumulated to more than one foot. I enjoyed the scenery, which looked like the photographs I had seen, and felt good and important for "being there."

Soon I was bored with the snow. It was beautiful, but it also trapped you inside the house. After two days of observing snowfall, I was ready to return home to Gagret. However, the road from Theog to Shimla was packed with snow, and there were no snow plows. I was told it would be a few weeks before the bus service resumed.

I read more novels and took walks with Prag, but was beginning to miss Gagret and even the sugarcane harvesting, which was pure hard work. After a week of being snowbound, getting back home became the main goal for me. I began to bug Jijaji about going to Gagret. He explained that there was no way to go to Shimla, which was twenty miles away; I had to wait until the snow melted. Dejectedly, I went to the library and borrowed more books.

Two weeks and about thirty books later, I was still there. I kept badgering Jijaji daily about finding a way for me to go to Shimla, and from there to Gagret. He must have gotten tired of my incessant badgering and looked for a way to send me back.

One morning, Jijaji told me that Mr. Sood, the poet-librarian, was going to Shimla on foot. He said I could go with him and another person, but I would have to walk all the way. I agreed and was excited about going back home. Jijaji explained that walking twenty miles on packed ice would be very hard, but I did not care.

The next day, we set out early in the morning. I had all my clothes in a bag, along with a few chapatis and pickled mango, and I wore the heavy overcoat for the trip. I did not have any walking shoes as we always walked on bare feet. Walking on packed ice without shoes was not possible, so for the first time in my life, I had to take a long hike wearing shoes. This proved to be the major problem with the trip.

Walking on bare earth with bare feet is easy. You walk nimbly and fast. Walking on snow and ice in dress shoes is very hard. The shoes tend to slip, so you have to walk gingerly, and they are not very comfortable either. However, I persevered until we made it back. Mr. Sood and his friend talked and laughed while walking. I thought of the English verse, "A merry heart goes all the way but a sad one tires in a mile." I was not sad, but bored, which is worse than being sad. I decided to join the conversation and hailed Mr. Sood.

"Mr. Sood," I said, "I really enjoyed your poems." This got his attention, but he looked puzzled.

There was no further response, so I pushed on. "I especially liked the part of the poem in which the dejected lover says, 'Thousands of times the spring returned to the garden/Had you returned for a few minutes/ It would not have cost you anything/But it would have saved someone's face!'" I sang Mr. Sood's poem to him hoping he would be glad to hear I had memorized part of his work.

There was no reaction. Both of them walked quietly and looked annoyed that I had broken up their interesting talk. After a few minutes of walking silently, they resumed their talks, and I was forgotten.

I felt embarrassed and insulted and did not have the nerve to talk again. Deaf people trying to make conversation with hearing people, who associate with them by chance, face this problem all the time. Unless they are fluent in sign language or are very interested in you, hearing people do not make much effort to communicate with the deaf.

We stopped once for half an hour at a tea stall in Kufri, which was halfway between Theog and Shimla. I ate my chapatis hurriedly and washed them down with a glass of piping hot tea, which Mr. Sood had ordered for us all.

We arrived in Shimla after seven hours. I bid goodbye to Mr. Sood and his friend and headed for the bus stop to get to Kalka. Gagret never looked so good!

Another memorable trip was to Delhi and then Kanpur. It was January of 1961, a year after the long march in the snow, and the work on the farm was slow as usual. Babuji, as a retired railway officer, was allowed three first-class train passes a year to anywhere in India, but he rarely used them. Through letters, I made plans with Ramesh and Prag to visit Delhi and later Kanpur during the Republic Day celebration.* Ramesh lived in Delhi, and Prag had two months of vacation from his school. I asked Babuji to get passes for Sham and me. Sham, of course, was not going. I had other plans for his pass. Babuji agreed without much fuss, knowing well that it was easier to get a pass than to put up with my constant bugging.

The plan was simple. From Hoshiarpur to Delhi, I was going to be Sham and Prag would be me. The ticket did not mention any names; just the ages of two boys. As first-class passengers, we could bring a servant who traveled in third class. We did not have a servant, so his pass was not used. I had other plans for the servant's pass.

Prag and I traveled in first class dressed in our best clothes, behaving like first-class passengers should—sitting quietly and reading magazines. There was still the problem of communication. Out of embarrassment, I did not want people to know I was deaf, and every time Prag tried to write something on his palm, I would wave him away and start talking about whatever came to my mind or showing him a page from my magazine and making comments on it.

In Delhi, we had a ball. We stayed mainly with Narain and his family, but visited various relatives daily, sometimes spending the night at their homes. Relatives would give us a rupee when we left, which helped with our travel expenses.

Ramesh, as planned, joined us for our trip to Kanpur. Now the question of who would ride in third class came up. Since I was the one with the pass and was also the eldest—I was six months older than Ramesh—one of the first-class seats was mine by default.

"I should ride first class," said Ramesh, "since I am older than Prag."

*The Republic Day, which falls on January 26, is the equivalent of the Fourth of July in the United States. It is India's day of independence.

"I have already ridden in the first class," Prag countered. "Therefore, it is my seat now."

"Since you have already ridden in the first class, it is my turn now," Ramesh argued.

We went back and forth. They asked me to decide whom I wanted to ride with me in first class. That was a hard decision and would have made whoever I condemned to ride in third class feel slighted. I took Prag aside and told him that he would ride first class on the return trip from Kanpur and then again from Delhi to Hoshiarpur. This way, I told him, he was riding in the first class three times more than Ramesh would. "So," I pleaded with him, "let Ramesh ride that portion of the trip." Prag was not happy, but understood my reasoning as well as my dilemma.

"You can have the first class," he told Ramesh. "Put it in your anus and give a shriek of joy at exactly 12:00 midnight." Prag could not help giving sage advice while relinquishing the privilege.

With Narain's help, Ramesh and I packed bedding in a holdall. Prag just had a blanket, but he would be sitting the entire trip. I had taken several fancy magazines—most of them in French and German, neither of which I knew—from Jijaji who had taken them from some airplane. We spread our bed on the fancy berths and pretended to read the foreign magazines. The magazines were illustrated, and I read about the marriage of Farah Diba to the Shah of Iran. Gosh, did they know how to live! I spent some time figuring out how much her jewelry cost. Her necklace alone, I calculated, was worth 300 years of our farmhand's salary! I passed this information to Ramesh who was "reading" a German magazine, but he cut me off in the middle of my sentence with his index finger on his lips—I was talking too loud. I looked at the other passengers, who obviously had paid for their first-class berths, and saw annoyance on their faces. After that, I remained silent.

We were met at Kanpur railway station by Mahesh and Ganesh, our cousins. Prag joined us wrapped in his blanket and acting like a servant. At first he refused to talk to us as he had to sit all night on a hard bench while we were asleep on our soft berths. He had told his traveling companions that he was an orphan and worked for "those people in the first class" as a dishwasher. He was disappointed that people did not feel sorry for him. According to them, he was lucky to get such wonderful bosses who took him with them on their travels.

"You had your fun," Prag told Ramesh. "On our return trip, you are going by third class and I am getting my seat in the first class back."

Ramesh was puzzled. "No," he said. "You can ride in the first class from Delhi to Hoshiarpur. The return trip from here to Delhi is mine."

"No, it is not." Prag looked at me for support. "Madan has already promised that I will ride first class on our way back."

I was on the spot again. I told both of them to enjoy our visit to Kanpur and wait for the class war later.

Our week in Kanpur was fun. We talked, played cards, had fabulous meals at our uncle Ram Prashad's restaurant, ran around in the dank and dark lanes of Kanpur, and watched movies whenever we could bum money from our uncle and aunt.

The question of who would sit in the first-class car on the return journey was brought up repeatedly by Prag. I tried my best to talk to both of them privately, but neither budged. Finally, Prag demanded that either all of us should ride in first class or all should ride in third class. Since everyone was adamant, I decided to take the plunge: We all rode in a dirty and crowded third-class compartment from Kanpur to Delhi.

12

Careers or the Lack of Them

FARMING WAS NEVER MY CAREER OF CHOICE.
But then, I had no other choice. It was there and was thrust upon me
like the sky is thrust upon us all. It was purely physical work. You did
it seven days a week, twelve months a year, in any weather. Farming just
was not for me, but it was all I had. The thing I disliked about it most
of all was that it lacked glamour.

Just like anyone else in Gagret, or for that matter, the world, I wanted
a glamorous job. A job for which I wore fancy clothes and shiny shoes,
slicked back my hair, and whistled while I worked. Needless to say, I
did none of those things while farming in Gagret.

Getting up early in the morning and trudging half a mile to the kudhi,
shoveling cow shit with a wooden spade, putting it in a large cast iron
bowl, carrying the bowl to a manure ditch, is, I am telling you, not
glamorous. The stench of the mixture of cattle shit and urine fermenting
overnight can hit your olfactory nerves with such force that you feel it
crawling up your nose to your brain, numbing it.

Milking a cow or a water buffalo looks cute in pictures, but the actual
experience is not so Currier and Ives. First, you have to squat in the shit-
and urine-soaked ground, wipe the soaked-with-you-know-what udder
with water while getting used to the powerful mixture of fumes. Then,
while you are milking, you have to fight off the flies that are trying to
get into the milk and your face. While you are busy milking with both
hands and using your elbows to ward off flies, the cow is also trying to
keep the flies off her torso. God gave cows long bushy tails for this
purpose. Suddenly, while you are milking and warding off flies, the urine-
soaked tail of the cow will hit you right in the face. Still, you have no
choice but to continue milking after wiping the slop from your face and
now-burning eyes.

Of course, these are the worst examples of the "glamour" of working on an Indian farm. There were nice things like fresh air, beautiful hills, the crystal-clear waters of the river Swan, the cold water of deep wells, the cool shade under the banyan tree on a hot day, the friendly and happy people, and the feeling of being home. But I longed for a job that allowed me to wear nice and flashy duds. According to everyone in the village, including my family, a deaf person could do only one kind of work— manual labor. I was fortunate, according to my village well-wishers, to be a landlord—a fancy British term—which sounds pretty glamorous!* Landlord or not, I still hated the work and kept thinking about other jobs.

I do not know how the idea of working as truck *cleander* entered my head. A truck driver's assistant is called a cleander, a mispronunciation of the English word *cleaner*. The cleander's main job was to help start the truck by turning the heavy motor with the help of the crank inserted in the front of the engine. As the truck was starting, the cleander had to put the crank under the driver's seat very quickly, stand at the ready as the truck passed him, and then jump into the back of the already speeding truck. The driver would accelerate without caring whether the cleander had gotten into the truck or not.

As the truck roared down the winding hill road, the cleander would perch on a sidewall of the open truck or sit on top of the cargo and smoke a cigarette with his hair flying in the wind. This was a glamorous pose and therefore got my attention. Then there was the charm of being on the road, spending each night in different towns or villages, meeting new people, and learning to drive the truck.

"Bhabhi," I told my mother one evening, "I think I will become a cleander."

"What?" Bhabhi was aghast. A cleander was one of the lowest jobs around.

---

*My family owned land, therefore we were landlords. More than half our land, however, had been "loaned out" to sharecroppers over a century ago. These sharecroppers stopped giving us our share sixty or seventy years earlier as a result of some kind of "deal" my grandfather had made with them.

"Your brain has taken a twist again." She used the Punjabi expression for being crazy. She did not say anything more, thinking I was just teasing her.

At night, when Babuji was eating dinner, I mentioned my career choice. He looked at me for a second and continued to eat. My great announcement about a future career did not even deserve a response, even an angry one, from him.

I ran my idea by Antru and Teerath, my grass-cutting buddies. They both thought it was a good idea. This helped strengthen my resolve, and I worked on the next step.

Tilak Raj or Tilku, as we called him, was one of my former classmates. He was the star athlete and captained both the soccer and volleyball teams of the high school. After graduation from high school, he decided to become a truck driver instead of following in his father's footsteps and running the family sweetmeat shop. Tilku was a wheeler-dealer and was able to purchase an old truck. I used to hitch rides on his truck to Hoshiarpur to watch movies. He was a good guy and introduced me to other truck drivers as "Babu Hakim Rai's son." His introduction had helped me hitch rides on several trucks as Babuji was well-known in the whole district. I would watch the cleanders closely to learn the tricks of the trade during these trips. Soon hitching rides on trucks became a goal in and of itself.

One day, I joined Tilku, who was drinking tea in a sweetmeat shop. "Tilku," I asked, "how would it be if I became your cleander?"

Tilku almost spat out his tea. He looked at me with eyes wide open but controlled himself. Being a good-hearted guy, he said, "Why not? Let me know when you are ready."

"But first," he added as an afterthought, "you have to ask Babuji."

I assured him I would and began to think about running away from home since getting Babuji's permission was akin to asking his permission to commit hara-kiri. I was excited about my new career and thought about ways I could convince Babuji to let me try it for a while. I did not know that Tilku had already shared our talk with Babuji, who had told Tilku to set me straight.

One day, while I was going to the bazaar, Tilku, who was coming from Hoshiarpur, stopped his truck and picked me up. I sat down, sharing the driver's seat with him, and put my hands on the steering wheel, pretending to drive. While slapping my back in greeting with his thick palm, he said, "Let us have some samosas and tea."

I agreed, and after parking his truck on the roadside, we walked to his favorite sweetmeat shop and sat down. I looked around proudly—as if I was already his cleander. His real cleander sat next to the truck smoking a cigarette and wiping the hood with a rag. He was not invited to tea and samosas. The difference in status hit me.

"So you still want to be a cleander?" Tilku asked while we waited for tea.

"Of course," I said, acting like a fellow professional. "Give me a few days to bring Babuji around."

Tilku became serious. "Do you know how hard and dirty this work is?"

"I know," I told him with a smile. "I have worked harder on the fields, and that work, as you know, is dirtier than this."

"No, you do not understand." Tilku was serious. I was surprised at this change of attitude. He went on to explain the difficulties faced by a cleander. They have to sit in the open truck bed in hot weather, in rain, and in the winter. At night, they have to sleep anywhere—in the truck bed or on the pavement using whatever they have to cover themselves. It was a seven-day-a-week job, and the salary was minimal.

"The salary a cleander makes is not enough even to buy food," added Tilku.

I sat there reading as he scribbled the bleak message on his calloused truck driver's palm, samosa and tea forgotten.

I attempted to cajole him into letting me try the job for a few weeks to see how I might like it. He shook his head in a vehement "no" and pointed to his cleander who was wiping the fenders now.

"Can you imagine being that person?" he asked.

I looked at his cleander. He was very thin, almost emaciated. He wore very old and extremely dirty clothes. He did not look happy. Actually, he looked quite forlorn.

That night, I told Babuji that I had decided not to become a cleander. He smiled. I knew he had given Tilku the task of firing me from the job before even hiring me.

13

My First Camera

I WOULD BE REMISS IF I DID NOT MENTION photography when talking of my imagined career choices. My interest in photography started with the great desire to be photographed. There were two people in our family who owned cameras—my cousin Bakshi Ram and my uncle Bhardwaj, Bhua Daropadi's husband. Uncle Bhardwaj was the richest person in our extended family, and he owned a Rolliecord, which cost fifteen times more than the Kodak box camera that Bhai Bakshi Ram owned. I figured this out because my interest in cameras started in my early teens.

Photographs in Gagret were taken only during weddings and only in our family. No other families in town owned a camera. Bhai Bakshi Ram took great pride in his camera. It was obvious that he could ill afford it, but he loved to take photographs. Since film and processing were expensive, he brought only one roll, which allowed eight exposures. The groom and the bride were the main subjects for these photographs, almost all of which were group shots; there was no room for photographs of individual people. When Bhai Bakshi Ram would photograph weddings, I would try to get into every group picture. He would chase me away as he had a theme for each group picture—the bride and all her friends, the groom and all his friends, and so forth. Almost all the groups, except for that of the groom, were composed of women. Men, for some reason I still cannot figure out, did not want to be photographed.

Still, I would manage to get myself into one or two group photographs at each wedding; however, I never could get a solo shot of myself. I longed to have my own photograph. Begging Bhai Bakshi for a solo photograph did not help since everyone bugged him for that privilege and it was not possible to satisfy more than eighty guests with a quota

of eight photographs. My desire to get a solo photograph led me to think
of getting my own camera someday and becoming a photographer.

Bhai Vishnu's wedding was in 1952. Vishnu is the younger brother
of Bhai Bakshi. I had become deaf only a month earlier and was very
self-conscious and always trying to make sure no one noticed me. If I
saw anyone talking and looking at me, I automatically concluded they
were talking about me and my deafness.

On the last day of the wedding, Bhai Bakshi was taking his eight
photographs. He had only one shot left, and the theme for this one was
jawaiis, or *sons-in-law*—meaning men who had joined our family by
marrying our daughters. He put two chairs on the ground for the two
eldest members of the group. Then, while Bhai Bakshi was busy composing them in the tiny viewfinder, I dashed in and jumped into Jija Roshan
Lal's lap. He had a soft spot for me and put both arms around me. Bhai
Bakshi saw his theme being broken. He pointed at me and told me to
get out. I was very embarrassed as thirty or so people were watching the
historic photograph being taken. Well, you have to remember, every
photograph that Bhai Bakshi Ram took was historic. I removed Jija
Roshan Lal's hands around me and slipped down from his lap. The trip
of four or so yards from his lap to the onlookers was one of the longest
trips in my life. I wished that the ground would part wide enough for
me to disappear into it. But when I reached the onlookers, they pushed
me back and told me to go back as the four in-laws were calling me to
join them. Bhai Bakshi could not overrule them. He indicated for me to
go back and be in the picture. I was feeling too humiliated and kept
walking. But several people forced me to go back, and soon I was astride
the lap from which I had slipped down in disgrace a minute earlier. I
could not look up, and they had to force me to look into the camera.

All this for getting into a photograph!

By the time I was thirteen, I decided to buy a camera and began to bug
Babuji every time I saw someone with one. He humored me with,
"We will see" or "When we have money." This went on for a couple
of years.

One night before going to bed, when Babuji was drinking warm milk
and talking to Bhabhi, I popped the question again. He must have been

in a bad mood, or perhaps our financial situation was getting worse. He got upset, put down the glass of milk with a thud, and wrote on his palm forcefully, "OK, if you must have a camera, let us sell the water buffalo and buy one for you."

I felt sick to my stomach. The water buffalo were very important for our family. Indian food depends heavily on milk and dairy products. We had butter, yogurt, and whey in addition to milk. Selling the water buffalo would have impacted our daily meals. Purchasing milk would have cost a lot more money, which was in short supply. I walked out of the room like a dog with its tails between its legs; I felt that Babuji did not have to threaten me with such dire action.

After that, I never asked for a camera. Still the desire to get a camera and shoot award-winning photographs haunted me. More than that, I wanted to be in control of who appeared in the group photographs I was going to take at weddings and family gatherings. I decided I should make a lot of money somehow and buy a camera so I would not be accused of jeopardizing our family's milk supply.

Buy a camera I did! I am not very proud of the way I got that camera, but all is fair in love, war, and getting a camera.

In December 1956, Babuji learned through his friend Kanshi Ram about an American doctor named Dr. Rosen who was coming to Bombay. It was said that this doctor had discovered a new method of making deaf people able to hear. I believed it because I knew America was very advanced in science, including medicine. I also believed there were no deaf people in America, since this wonderful doctor must have cured everyone.

Earlier in 1954, we made a long trip to Vellore, near Madras, in southern India. This trip was orchestrated by Babuji's friend Kanshi Ram. A very famous ear, nose, and throat (ENT) specialist named Jacob Chandy was located there. After spending three minutes with me, Dr. Chandy told Babuji that I was not going to become hearing again. After that, we did not visit any more doctors. However, Babuji still felt that we could not afford to miss this new opportunity. I was all for the trip—I had never visited Bombay. Actually, no one in our family, including Babuji, had visited Bombay. So, despite our economic woes, Babuji decided to make the trip to the American doctor. He borrowed money from someone. Those were the days when borrowing had become habit since Babuji had lost most of his retirement money in a couple of business ventures.

I enjoyed the trip immensely. We stopped in Delhi for a couple of days where I visited with Ramesh and Surinder, another cousin I was very close to. The train ride, 1,000 miles in first class, was a treat in and of itself.

We stayed with a Sikh friend of Kanshi Ram in Dadar, a suburb of Bombay, and commuted daily to the hospital, which was a mile long and always crowded with people. Dr. Rosen, the wonderful American doctor, was going to visit this hospital. I never knew what was going on as Babuji and Kanshi Ram talked to various people who would point them in one or the other direction. Babuji later explained that the hospital people were not sure when the famous doctor was coming. Some said he had already come and gone, and others said he was due any day. One thing was clear, having him examine you was like asking the moon to come down. With me following along, Kanshi Ram and Babuji trudged through the endless crowded corridors of the huge hospital daily. We would return to the Sikh friend's home at night, and while Babuji talked to Kanshi Ram and his friend, I read various magazines that were in ample supply in the house.

A week or so after these daily visits, we were finally ushered into the large office of the head of the ENT department. Kanshi Ram's friend had called a friend in a high office, who had, in turn, called another friend to grant us admission. This important doctor, who was going to host Dr. Rosen, talked a few minutes to Babuji and Kanshi Ram and asked questions. Babuji indicated that I should step forward so the doctor could take a look at me. I stood up with my legs shaking; he was going to decide whether the American Dr. Rosen was going to cure me or not. But the doctor waved me back and kept talking. Then he stood up, which was a signal for all of us to leave his office, and we walked out. It was not hard for me to guess that he had refused to allow us to see the famous American doctor.

In the corridor, Babuji and Kanshi Ram talked for a few minutes, and then we walked toward the exit. They both looked very tired. It was obvious that this long trip had come to naught. I knew Babuji's mood and decided not to ask him anything until we were alone.

Outside the hospital, we parted ways. Kanshi Ram took a taxi, and Babuji, apparently having nowhere to go, just stood there with me holding his index finger. I was afraid to look at him—he looked defeated. He had borrowed money for this trip to Bombay, and we had already spent two weeks there only to learn that we could not see the American doctor.

We walked aimlessly through the streets, looking at window displays with expensive items and at people rushing by us. Finally, I could hold it in no more.

"Babuji, what did the doctor say?" He did not hear me. Apparently the busy street was too noisy.

I tugged at his hand and repeated my question in a higher decibel. He stopped and looked at me sadly and then traced on his palm: "The doctor said it was not necessary for you to see the American doctor. Your deafness cannot be cured." He had dropped the bomb.

Even though we had been told two years earlier that my deafness was incurable, the glowing news stories about this American doctor had created new hopes. Now they were all dashed to the hard footpath under our feet. I was crestfallen.

We did not talk after that. He knew I was upset, and I knew he was very disappointed. We were wandering around an upscale shopping area. The shops had fancy stuff that we could not afford. We just kept walking aimlessly looking very interested in merchandise that we were never going to own.

While passing a photographic store, I saw a box camera for sale with the price tag of 29 rupees. I could not believe that camera could be bought for only 29 rupees. A water buffalo cost more than 300 rupees then. You could buy ten cameras with money to spare with that much. I tugged at Babuji's hand.

"I want that camera!" I said, adding to my voice all the sorrow of a young boy who was never going to hear again.

Babuji stood there frozen. I let go of his hand and climbed the four corrugated stairs to the door of the store and looked back at him. He sighed and walked toward me. I could not wait for him. I opened the door, went in, and gave a big smile to the salesman behind the counter.

"I want that Agfa Clack." That was the brand and model name of the camera.

The salesman ignored me and waited for Babuji to come in. Babuji shook his head in the affirmative in response to the salesman's questioning look.

I had a shiny black camera with a beautiful lens in my hand. I held it like a newborn baby and gave Babuji a big smile. He smiled back at me sadly and talked to the salesman for a minute.

We walked out of the store with me holding the camera in both my hands and all my grief about deafness forgotten. My euphoria must have been contagious. Babuji also smiled.

I wanted to show the camera to someone I knew. I wanted to buy film and take pictures. I wanted to arrange people in a group with authority and a serious look. However, I did not know anyone in Bombay and had to wait for several days before we returned to Delhi. There, after we had all chipped in money to buy film, I took photographs of Ramesh and Surinder.

That was my first camera. I have bought several cameras since then, some of them very expensive. None of the cameras, however, gave me the ecstatic pleasure that this 29-rupee camera did. Still, the memory of purchasing this camera is bittersweet. I had gotten something I wanted very badly, but I also had taken advantage of my father's depressed mood. I had, in fact, taken advantage of my deafness.

14

Becoming a Sadhu

I WAS STILL LOOKING FOR A CAREER. MY HIGH school education had not prepared me for any jobs, and I thought you have to be able to hear to work for other people. Higher education was out of the question since I knew none of the colleges in Hoshiarpur were going to admit a deaf person.

Then, I had an inspiration!

I had grown up in a religious family. Bhabhi worshipped Krishna and Rama, as well as other Hindu gods. Babuji meditated for almost an hour daily and read the *Bhagavad Gita*, a Hindu devotional work in poetic form. Both my widow aunts—Parvati and Savitri—lived for worshipping gods. You could not be anything but religious in such a family. I read the *Ramayana* and the *Mahabharata* as well as the *Bhagavad Gita* without even thinking why I read them. I enjoyed the two epic stories but did not really understand the message in the *Bhagavad Gita*. It was too deep for me.

I decided to test God.

Bhua Parvati's ongoing accusation that my deafness was the result of my refusal to believe in God strengthened my resolve. I had a short private conversation with God and prayed to him to make me hearing: "If you make me hearing, I will worship you all my life and live like a holy man." I gave my solemn promise to God and gave him three months to prove his existence by making me hearing.

For the next three months, I prayed daily after taking my bath. I read the *Bhagavad Gita*, chanted mantras, and sang various *bhajans*, or hymns. I had a very strong faith in various gods and was sure that I was going to become hearing within the timeline I had given them. I did not tell anyone about this holy ultimatum, fearing they would make fun of me. Additionally, I wanted this to be a surprise for the family.

The deadline passed and I did not regain my hearing. The next day, I stopped worshipping God and declared myself an atheist. I began to make disparaging remarks about sadhus and other holy men, including the Gurkha Baba and the Mahatma of Indora. Bhabhi and Bhua would be shocked at my remarks and would cover their ears in order not to hear my blasphemy. They even complained to Babuji, who, in his own stoic way, told them to ignore me and I would stop. Of course, I did not have the nerve to insult holy men in front of Babuji.

However, deep down I still had the faith; not in various gods, but in a God that was watching over me from somewhere. That God did not need a temple or church or mosque; God was there to talk with me whenever I needed him. Gandhi's belief about God being one helped me shape my belief that religions were just kind of middle parties between people and their gods. I made peace with my own god and left things there.

But I was talking about careers! I am coming to that.

India is a country of sadhus, or holy men. These sadhus come in all shapes and sizes with all kinds of beliefs and degrees. Educationally, they range from being totally illiterate to being scholars. Some of them roam around the country and others stay in one temple, or *ashram*—buildings attached to temples.

I decided to become a sadhu.

Knowing well this choice of "career" would also be ridiculed and rejected, I did not share my decision with anyone—not even with Antru and Tirath who had not minded my designs on becoming a cleander. I just let this idea lay there in the back of my mind and waited for the right opportunity, as I continued to milk the cows and water buffaloes, plow, cut grass, and do all kinds of farm jobs that I hated.

A *mahatma*, or a great soul, passed through Gagret and stayed a few weeks in our house. He was a learned man who lived in Rishikesh, a holy place not far from the origin of the Ganges. When he had arrived in Gagret and asked for someone religious, a villager had directed him to Babuji's shop. Babuji talked to him for a while and liked him, thinking this guy was not a common sadhu. He was a scholar and discussed the *Bhagavad Gita* in Sanskrit with Babuji, who invited him to stay at our home. Each evening, he would come home with Babuji, eat dinner with him, and sit with the village people who visited Babuji each night. In the morning, he would go with Babuji to his shop and sit there all day or walk around the village. He talked little, but I noticed that whenever he talked, he got everyone's attention. He had a very peaceful smile on his face and he radiated holiness. He became my role model.

One evening, when Babuji was worshipping and the mahatma was sitting alone, apparently meditating, I approached him. Point blank, I asked him if he would become my guru and if I could return to Rishikesh with him. He nodded with the peaceful and sage smile on his face. He pointed toward where Babuji was worshipping, moving his eyes upward with a questioning look. He had told me without speaking or writing that I had to have Babuji's permission first.

That was not what I had expected. I wished he would just tell Babuji that his deaf son needed to go to Rishikesh to find knowledge and peace. But it was apparent that he was a real sage; he did not want to offend his generous host. It was also quite possible that he did not want a deaf disciple.

Over the next few days, I developed a strategy; I knew that Babuji would call me silly for articulating such an idea, or just burst out laughing. Renouncing the world was not a career he was going to recommend for his son. As usual, I started dropping hints here and there. I told him I had been reading the *Bhagavad Gita* again and how the temporariness of the world was depressing me. Babuji smiled and agreed with me, but did not offer any solution to my problem. I knew that he knew I was cooking up something. Later, when he was smoking his hookah and the visiting sage was sitting beside him, I started talking about my own experiences that were so parallel with Buddha's. Babuji listened and exchanged glances with the sage. I did not know if he was expressing pride in his son's profound thoughts or simply telling him, "Look, he is up to something."

One evening, I saw Bhabhi thanking her gods with hands clasped while she was talking to Bhua Parvati. Ever curious, I asked what was up. They both, in gestures, explained that the sage was leaving the next day. They were tired of cooking special meals for this guest for almost a month and were happy he was leaving. They were both religious women and knew serving a sage was a great thing, but they were also practical. Enough is enough, so they were happy. But that got me worried. Time was running out, and I had to act fast.

That evening, as soon as Babuji came home, I waylaid him as he walked from his room to the worship room. I walked, holding his hand, and told him that I wanted to become a sadhu and to go with the sage to Rishikesh. He did not even break his stride. While sitting down on his mat in front of pictures and statues of gods and the family's meager religious library, he gave me an admonishing look with his index finger waving to and fro in a determined fashion. It was a firm **NO**, underlined, in capitals and in bold. I retreated—you did not argue with Babuji when he was this firm.

I was upset and ready to cry. I walked to the front of the house where Babuji's bedroom and meeting room were. There I found the sage sitting on a mat and meditating. I planted myself in front of him and implored him to speak to Babuji on my behalf. This was an insult to the sage and also an inexcusable effrontery—you did not interrupt someone who was meditating. However, I was too upset to remember such rules. With tears running down my face, I begged him to please do something. He opened his eyes and looked at me with a fixed glare. He was not smiling, nor did he look angry. It was an admonishing look. He had communicated a million messages to me without moving his lips or fingers, or batting his eyes. I fled.

I did not eat that night. Both Bhua Parvati and Bhabhi came to ask me to come to eat and later brought a *thali*, a large brass plate, of flat bread and vegetables to my bed. I refused to eat or talk to them. They finally gave up.

I was on a fast unto death like Gandhi. I was not going to eat unless I was allowed to become a sadhu.

Bhabhi, Bhua Parvati, and a host of other ladies took turns cajoling me to eat. Sham, who was home from college, also tried to force food on me. I stayed adamant and kept my eyes closed.

You could not argue with a deaf person with closed eyes!

Babuji did not come to ask me to eat. He was obviously angry at me for the silly notion I had and did not want to dignify it by even referring to it. So, I stayed in bed all day and night, only to go out to relieve myself. Bhabhi had spread the word, and women from our *behda* (cluster of houses) took turns telling me to eat and not be silly. They, of course, had to jostle me around as I would close my eyes whenever they came into my room.

On the evening of the third day of my fast, I was summoned by Babuji to come to his meeting room. I am sure Bhabhi, using her tears and ongoing nagging, had forced him to call me. Holding my arms, Sham escorted me to Babuji. He was, as usual, smoking his hookah. He looked at me and wrote on his palm: "Go eat! Stop being silly."

It was hard to read what he was writing as my eyes were blind with tears. But you did not ignore Babuji.

"I do not want to eat. I want to continue my *maran barat*." That is Hindi for fast unto death.

Babuji was upset. He waved his arm with his forefinger extended and told me to go. I interpreted it as "go die if you want" and walked away from him fast with Sham in my wake.

Instead of going to the bedroom, I began to walk toward the path that led to the well and the bazaar. Sham touched me on my shoulder to redirect me, but I ignored him. He stepped in front of me, but I pushed him and yelled, "I am going to die," and began to run.

I was weak from three days of hunger, but a manic strength had overcome me. The night was pitch dark, and the cobblestones and loose rocks in the narrow zigzagging path made walking dangerous. But my daily walks had acquainted me with each stone and rock, and I could run on the path in total darkness with bare feet.

Sham apparently called out to Vishwa and Antru. I could feel them running after me. Halfway to the well, Antru, who was the faster runner, tackled me to the ground and there I lay exhausted.

I began to wail loudly. The disappointment, the hunger, the tiredness, and the helplessness overcame me. For about five minutes, I just lay there in the dirt and pebbles with the three boys hovering over me. They tried to get me to my feet, but I ignored them and kept on crying. Then they had an idea, and the three of them picked me up by my arms and legs and started toward the house. I was too tired to fight and let them carry me. My arms and legs hurt, and at times, my back hit and dragged on the cobblestones.

My loud screams in the still night must have woken the whole village. As we passed each house, I saw women and children framed in the doors of their houses. I was ashamed and embarrassed and was glad that it was night and they could not see my face.

I was carried back to my bed. I pretended to sleep while fighting hiccups from crying. Soon Bhabhi and Bhua materialized with a thali full of food. I had no strength left to fight or even to say no, so I let them feed me. Needless to say, I ate a lot and then promptly went to sleep.

I woke up in the middle of night with an unbearable pain in my stomach. I tried to ignore it, but soon it was evident that it was not going away. If anything, it was getting worse. I felt like I had eaten razor blades that were cutting though my stomach. Finally, unable to bear it anymore, I yelled for Bhabhi. She lit the lamp, just as she had on the night I had become deaf, and asked me what was wrong. I told her about the awful pain in my stomach. Bhabhi went to the kitchen and prepared a poultice for my stomach. It did not help, so she started slowly rubbing alum on my stomach. However, each time she touched my stomach, I would scream in agony. This went on all night, and Bhabhi stayed awake trying to console me.

On learning about my new ailment, Babuji visited me on his way to the worship room. He wrote, "You should not have eaten too fast and too much." It was too late for that advice. I was thankful that he did not use this opportunity to tell me it was a punishment from the gods for being stubborn.

I suffered the whole day and rolled around in bed trying to fight the pain. Bhua Parvati, who was an expert at preparing all kind of remedies, made me drink some foul-tasting concoctions. I hated the smell and taste of whatever she prepared and even tried to convince her that my pain was gone so as to avoid having to take more. But Bhua Parvati could not be fooled, and she succeeded in feeding me a few spoonfuls of the poison. Whatever was in there, it worked. I spent a few hours throwing up the cause of my pain—all the food that I had wolfed down the night before.

This was the end of my plans to become a holy man! I told myself that God had loftier plans for me. I asked myself: What is loftier than being a full time ascetic?

Other careers such as becoming a doctor, a lawyer, a high government official, and so forth were beyond even my dreams, so I never really thought about them. Everything was tied to hearing, so I hoped that some day, I would become hearing and embark on a career that would, hopefully, be a little better than farming. But then, that was asking for a miracle.

15

Moving to Delhi

MY PROVERBIAL SHIP FINALLY CAME!
It arrived in 1961 in the form of a photography school for the deaf and a government law offering scholarships to the physically handicapped. At that time, the term *physically handicapped* for the Indian government meant "deaf, blind, and orthopedically handicapped." Bhai Narain sent Babuji a short letter explaining these developments and advised that I should come to Delhi to enroll in the school.

I was ready to go the very next day. By that time, I had become a full-fledged farmer. We had let one of our servants go. I plowed the fields and did everything that our farm servants did. My sudden departure meant we had to find a full-time servant to replace me. However, it was still summer, and plowing had not begun yet. Therefore, Babuji told me to pack and leave the next day.

As luck would have it, the monsoons set in that evening. It rained hard, and the next morning, we needed to start sowing corn. I felt responsible, and woke up early and ran about two miles to various *chamars'* (untouchables) homes to see if anyone was willing to plow for us. No one was available, and I ran into Babuji in the kudhi. He told me to pack and not to worry about plowing. I did not want to leave, but he was adamant. So I went home and stuffed all my clothes—three shirts and three pairs of pants, a pair of pajamas, and some underwear—into a satchel, touched the feet of everyone at home, and boarded a bus bound for Hoshiarpur. I took another bus to Jallandhar, and from there, the Flying Mail to Delhi.

The Flying Mail, as the name indicates, was the fastest train from Jallandhar to Delhi. I bought a second-class ticket for 7 rupees. The Indian government had eliminated the third class a few years earlier. This was a joke; third class had become second class and the second class had

87

become first class. The luxurious first-class *bogies*, as railcars are called in India, relics of the British era, were removed totally. The train only stopped for two minutes at Jallandhar Cantonment station, so you had to get on quickly or it would leave without you.

At the station, the platform was full of people with their baggage. I thanked my stars that I only had a small cloth bag, which swung on my shoulders easily. As the train approached, all the coolies loaded their assigned bags on their heads and shoulders and got ready, as did I.

The train hurtled in. The second-class bogies were not only full but literally bursting at the seams with people. There was no room to sit or stand. Even the corridors were full. I managed to jump onto the nearest door and hung to the door handle while standing on the first step. As the train moved, I managed to get my two feet on the main floor of the bogey. There I stood for seven hours as the train sped by fields where farmers were sowing corn. I smiled. I was done with farming! A new life was waiting for me in Delhi.

That night, feeling tired but very excited, I arrived at Subzi Mandi railway station, which was a Delhi suburb. Carrying my light satchel, I walked to the railway colony where Narain lived in a government apartment, about fifty yards from the station. They were not expecting me; there had not been enough time to send a letter about my plans. Back then, telephones were only for the well-heeled, and telegrams were sent only when there was bad news.

It was not hard to find Narain's apartment. I did not even have to knock because the doors on both sides—the "front room," which was really in the back, and the courtyard—were wide open. I walked in and, after touching the feet of Sister Kamala, Jijaji Balkishan, and Bharjai Krishna, I got into the very important and fun business of playing with my five nephews and nieces. I loved kids, and they, in turn, were always around me.

I lived at Narain's for the next four years. His block number was 52, and the quarter number was 5, hence we referred to the residence as 52/5.

Our quarter, one of sixteen quarters in a two-story building, had two rooms, one bathroom, one toilet, a verandah, and a huge brick courtyard. There was also a small storage room and a rather large kitchen. This two-room quarter was occupied by four adults and five children. I became one of the ten residents of 52/5. However, a steady flow of relatives and friends, who stayed there from a few hours to a few weeks, kept the number of people living there much higher.

Narain worked as a railway guard, the guy who waved a green flag to tell the engine driver to start the train. His hours were erratic. He was on duty when I arrived on the night of June 20, and would return sometime that evening.

Sister Kamala and her family—husband Balkishan and three sons—had moved in with Narain when he had been allotted this living quarter by the government. This was a mutually beneficial arrangement. Sister Kamala got a cheap place to live in Delhi, and Narain got a tenant who helped subsidize his meager salary with a rent of 20 rupees a month.

There were no designated areas such as a bedroom, living room, my room, or his room. Everything was shared and used in whatever way we needed it. The front room with the main entrance could be called the drawing or living room, as it had a sofa and two chairs, a ceiling fan, and a radio. A large bed was also part of the permanent fixture of this room. This bed was used for sitting during the day and for sleeping at night. Additional cots, depending on the number of men living in the house, were moved in at night. I recall as many as four of us sleeping in that small room.

The second room was for the women and children. It did not have any furniture except for another large bed. There were some large and small trunks used for storing clothes. At night, four or five cots were added to this room for Kamala, Bhabhi Krishna, and the five children.

Of course, this sleeping arrangement was during the colder months or when it rained. From early April to early October, we slept outside. Men slept in the outside fenced yard, and women and children slept in the enclosed courtyard.

Kamala had three sons—Surinder, Ashok, and Yash. In 1961, they were, respectively, ten, eight, and five years old. Narain had a daughter Sunita a bit over one year as well as a son Shashi, who was not yet four. As is the practice in India, children were called by their nicknames. Their real names were for school and outsiders only. Surinder was Mota, Ashok was Cuckoo, Yash was Bawa, Shashi was Puppoo, and Sunita was Kati. These nicknames stuck until they were adults.

Bhai Narain's children. Front row: Rajendar (Pinto), Sunita (Kati), Shashipal, Vinita (Manti), and Saini's son Babboo.

The morning after I first arrived, Bhai Narain woke up and had his first of many cups of tea, and we began discussing my training and career plans. The first step was to visit the office of the vocational rehabilitation department, which had announced the training scholarships. Meanwhile, I did some research and learned that a magazine vendor at the Subzi Mandi railway station rented books. I rented one and settled myself on the sofa in the living room under the fan and thought about those "poor people" plowing the fields in Gagret and other parts of the country. I felt smug and smiled.

Narain and I went to the central secretariat using a combination of transportation: a train, then a bus, and finally a scooter-rickshaw— commonly known as a *phut-phut* because of the noise it makes. We easily found the office of the vocational rehabilitation director. It was large with about thirty tables all covered with stacks of dusty and tattered files. Several ceiling fans tried to move the hot and humid air. The clerks lounged in their chairs, and khalasis dozed perched on their stools. No one appeared to be working, and our entrance was treated as an unwanted interruption.

Bhai Narain used his charm and talked to one of them. I stood there in my nicely pressed shirt and pants and my new shoes. The clerk Bhai Narain was talking to pointed to someone in the back, and we navigated our way through dusty tables and dustier files to the portly guy reading a paperback novel.

He was the head clerk and reluctantly put his novel aside while listening to Bhai Narain. After a few minutes, he gave a monosyllabic answer and picked up his book. We were dismissed.

Bhai Narain, who was always cheery, was getting a bit annoyed by now. Outside, he told me that no one there knew about this new scheme for offering scholarships and training programs for the physically handicapped. The head clerk had told him to go to the director's office for more information. The director's office was in the next building; we walked there briskly, holding our handkerchiefs on our heads to ward off the hot sun.

A khalasi and two clerks occupied the director's outer office. The three were talking and laughing, and they stopped their conversation when we entered. Bhai Narain smiled and began to talk, pointing his finger to the door with the "Director" plate on it. It took him a while to finally convince one of the clerks to see if the director would see us. After my three-plus hours pounding these corridors of power, I was sure the khalasi would emerge to tell us to go to yet another building. While Bhai Narain and I stood there, the clerks tried to look busy. The khalasi returned and motioned us into the office.

The director had a desert cooler in his window. This kind of "cooler" is simply a fan enclosed in a large square box made of grass stacked in a wooden frame. The grass is kept soaked to cool the air. Also, heavy curtains helped to keep his office cool and dark. The director looked scholarly with his horn-rimmed glasses and the pipe in his mouth. He pointed to the chairs in front of his huge desk and began to ask questions. Bhai Narain responded, and for the next half hour, they both talked. During their conversation, the director occasionally looked at me. At one point, Bhai Narain wrote on his palm and asked me to tell the director in English about what I wanted to do.

I stood up and said, "I want to be a photographer, sir!"

The director smiled and began to talk very animatedly with Bhai Narain. I wondered why he was so excited about my career choice. Later, I learned that it was my ability to speak and my knowledge of English that had him excited. He wrote a short note and gave it to Bhaiji.

This note requested that a Mr. Jolly, who was in another building, help "this deaf boy." A note from a higher official is like a golden key in the Indian bureaucracy. I do not know if it was Bhai Narain's charisma or my one-sentence declaration that got us that golden note.

Mr. Jolly and Bhai Narain became good friends within a few minutes. He not only offered us chairs to sit in, but also had a khalasi bring in cold water and hot tea. While they both talked, I sat there looking at my nails, the ceiling, and the office clerks who were reclining, talking to each other, or dozing off. None of them seemed to be working. I thought of the hundreds of thousands of clerks who pedaled bicycles or rode buses each morning. They brought their lunchboxes with them, disappearing into these buildings to sit, talk, drink tea, eat lunch, and relax. In the evening, they reversed their routes to their homes, looking very tired after their long hard day. None of these clerks knew about this new law that would change the lives of millions of handicapped children in India. It was part of their job to implement this law, but it seemed as if someone had forgotten to tell them about it or the law's announcement had been buried in the files piled in front of them.

Bhai Narain stood up and shook hands with Mr. Jolly. I clasped my hands and bowed my head like a good boy. We walked out and Narain summarized the good and bad results of our six hours in government offices.

Mr. Jolly had suggested that, instead of going to the photography school, I should learn the trade of printing. Since I could read and write well, printing made sense to me. He knew of a small print shop where he could get me an apprenticeship. I asked how much they would pay, and Bhai Narain laughed.

"We should be glad that they are going to provide you free training. Money will come later." He was tired, and his usual cheerful countenance was losing ground to the overwhelming depressing atmosphere of the government offices.

The next morning, we went to meet Mr. Jolly near the print shop, which was about three miles from our quarter. We took a shortcut through the train tracks and rode a bicycle rickshaw to the appointed place. Mr. Jolly was not there. We stood for almost an hour in the hot sun before he showed up and escorted us into the print shop. I walked behind them through the maze of bicycles, cows, rickshaws, motorcycles, and the occasional car. We entered a narrow lane paved in stone and bordered on both sides by an open sewer. The heat, humidity, and strong smell from the sewer made me wish I was back in Gagret, but I did not say a word.

The "print shop" was a 6-x-8-foot hole in the wall with one printing machine. Two brothers owned and worked in it. The walls were lined with wooden storage cabinets with very small drawers. These were for storing types in various sizes and fonts. The small floor was littered with ink-stained paper, composing handsets, discarded flyers, and rags.

At our approach, both brothers stopped working and stood with their ink-stained hands clasped. It was obvious that they had a high respect for Mr. Jolly, a government official. Mr. Jolly explained something to them, and Bhai Narain joined in the conversation. The four of them discussed various details of my life while I stood there sweating in the sultry heat, smelling printer's ink and sewage. At the end of their conversation, Bhai Narain put his hand on my shoulder and gestured that he was leaving.

"What?" I was aghast. "What will I do here?"

He pointed to the two brothers and told me that they would tell me what to do. As Bhaiji and Mr. Jolly disappeared around the corner, I looked at the two brothers. They were smiling.

I was going to be trained as a compositor. One of the brothers showed me a large box with cubby holes for various types. I learned that these cubbyholes were arranged just like a typewriter keyboard. The compositor had to memorize where to find each letter's cubbyhole. The brother demonstrated this by forming a sentence in the composing box. He was very fast. With his right hand, he picked letters without looking at the cubbyholes from whence they came and placed them in the compositors' box, and in the same motion, he fit the type in a line with his left hand. He formed the whole sentence in less than a minute. I was impressed.

I took off my nice shirt and shoes, rolled up my pants, and sat down on the floor. One of the brothers gave me a printing block, a steel block used to compose text, which was used to print a pamphlet. He told me to return the type to the correct cubbyholes. I thought it was easy and started on the project. It was not easy and took me almost an entire day to slowly find the correct cubbyhole and put the type in it. Once in a while, one of the brothers would stop whatever he was doing and show me how to do it fast. I was amazed at how fast they could put the types back—at least twenty times faster than I could. It was like a new typist doing the hunt-and-peck thing compared with a seasoned typist typing at 110 words per minute.

It was tedious and very boring work. The little shop was hot and could literally be called a sweatshop since I was sweating profusely. After about two hours, I began to miss Gagret and plowing. The hot sun was fine and so was milking a water buffalo while it moved a fly from my face with its tail!

I was too proud, however, to give in. I worked diligently and stopped only for drinking water or to take a leak, which I took standing in the alley and aiming at the wall. By 5:00 p.m., I had had enough and told the brothers I had to go. They tried to tell me that they closed at dark. I told them about my having some plans. They were nice, and I put on my shirt and shoes and walked back to 52/5. It was a very long walk and the sun was still hot. I had fancy clothes, shiny hair, and shiny shoes. These shoes and clothes were not ideal for walking under a hot sun. Gagret began to look more and more tempting.

Back home, Bhaiji had gone to work. Bharjai Krishna and Sister Kamla asked me how I liked my new job. "It is good," I lied. I was not ready to admit that I made a mistake by coming to Delhi. Returning to Gagret would have been very embarrassing. I spent the evening playing with the kids and reading a book. But my mind was on my new "career" and I wondered how long I would last putting types in cubby holes.

The next day, I went back to the print shop and worked all day. Gradually, I picked up speed in putting the types back into their pigeon holes. Once, one of the brothers gave me a proof print of the work he was assembling. It was in English, and I found several errors in it, which I pointed out to him. He was very happy and began to talk to the other brother animatedly. They clearly did not know much English and were happy to have a proofreader in the shop. I thought, "it would be fine to read proofs," but, as most of their work was either in Urdu or Hindi, they had so little to proofread and usually had the client do it for them.

All day long, I thought about how tedious the job was. By afternoon, I had made the decision: This was going to be my last day on this job! I did not have the heart to tell the two brothers, who were really nice and seemed to like the free labor I was providing.

Bhaiji was back when I arrived home. When he asked me how I liked the work, I told him I was ready to return to Gagret unless I got something better and more interesting. He smiled and told me that he had not been so happy about leaving me in that little print shop, but had wanted to see how I liked it. So, that was that. No more printing apprenticeship for me.

The next day, we went to Cannaught Place in New Delhi where the All India Photography Training Institute for the Deaf (PID) had been recently established. I got excited about becoming a professional photographer. Little did I know that the visit was going to open a whole new world for me.

16

Why Are They Flailing Their Hands?

THE NEXT MORNING, NARAIN WENT TO THE
Subzi Mandi railway station to make some phone calls. He knew the
station master, so he could make free calls. He returned looking happy;
the phone call was encouraging. After breakfast, we took a train to New
Delhi and walked a mile from the railway station to the office of the All
India Federation of the Deaf (AIFD), which was in the Theatre Communication Building in Cannaught Place. It was a brown, one-story structure,
built during World War II for American soldiers. We found the AIFD
office after being lost in dark corridors a couple of times.

Bhai Narain talked with B. G. Nigam, the general secretary of the
AIFD. This was the first time I had ever encountered another deaf person.
Nigam was a tall dark guy, dressed in a very expensive suit, who radiated
success and self-confidence. I sat there scared and, I am sure, radiated
my failure as a farmer and a printer.

Bhai Narain wrote notes explaining my situation and handed them
to Nigam, who could speak clearly enough for Bhai Narain to understand
him. I was impressed. This was one powerful deaf person. He had a fancy
office, four assistants, and a khalasi (or peon), sitting outside his office!

Bhai Narain filled out a form and gave 15 rupees to Nigam, who let
the money sit on the desktop in front of him as if it was something dirty
and called for one of his assistants, who picked up the form and the
money and went away.

I was registered as an AIFD student and was all agog with excitement
about starting to learn photography. But I was also apprehensive; I feared
this might turn out as bad as the printing press experience.

The All India Photography Training Institute for the Deaf (PID) turned
out to be an eight-by-eight-foot room behind the AIFD office. They had

As a student at the Photography Institute for the Deaf
in New Delhi in 1961.

converted the verandah behind the office into a small classroom, and
adjoining this small room was a darkroom, which could hold two people
maximum. Narain left me in the AIFD office, and I was escorted by one
of Nigam's assistants to the photography school whose signboard was
larger than the size of its total facilities.

There were only two students in the classroom, and the teacher was
to come later. They were both practicing retouching negatives with fancy
mechanical pencils. My escort looked at the two students, pointed at me,
and then pointed at one empty chair to indicate that I was a new student.
Both students looked at me cursorily, nodded their heads in understanding, and went back to working on the small dark patches on their notebooks with the retouching pencils.

Suddenly I saw the strangest thing in my life!

One of the students, I learned later his name was Khurana, suddenly began to gesture wildly to the other student, Goel. I looked in amazement and wondered what he was doing. People had often gestured to me and I had always successfully managed to misunderstand them. However, Goel seemed to be responding to Khurana with equal zeal, with his hands and fingers traveling in a curious but rhythmic movement that was not even close to gesturing. While they performed this ceremony with their hands, they gave me curious looks. I did not have to be a genius to know that they were discussing me. "But," I thought, "God, did they have to flail their upper extremities in a wild dance to talk about me?"

I kept looking at them as if hypnotized and followed their hand movements. They saw that I was looking hard and stopped. Khurana made a face at me and pointed to the chair. It was obvious that they did not like being stared at.

I stood there and the thought suddenly hit me: The two were actually "talking" with each other. The idea that people could communicate with their hands and, worse still, that people could understand this wild flailing of hands and fingers, was just inconceivable to me. However, their expressive faces and mannerisms demonstrated that they were communicating with each other just like two hearing people would communicate by speaking.

I remained transfixed by them and forgot about sitting in my chair. One of the guys tried to talk to me and, upon seeing the bewildered look on my face, must have concluded that I was ignorant and did not understand what he was saying. For all I knew, he might have told me to turn the chair upside down and sit on one of its legs.

The teacher, V. R. Goyle, came in an hour later. He was a good-looking young man of about thirty, dressed in an expensive bush shirt and pants. These deaf people, I thought, had money. There was hope for me!

Mr. Goyle looked happy to see me. Both Goel and Khurana began their finger dance while simultaneously pointing to me. Mr. Goyle smiled at me and signed something that I did not understand.

He then took the mechanical pencil from Khurana and showed it to me, pointed his left index finger at me, put the tip of his right index finger on the right side of his forehead, and then moved the finger in an arc in front of his face. I looked askance. He took Khurana's notebook and wrote *tomorrow* on it with the mechanical pencil and then made another arc with his forefinger in front of his face. Suddenly, I understood. He wanted me to buy and bring a mechanical pencil to class "tomorrow." I attempted to copy the sign, and the three of them broke into a merry laughter.

Mr. Goyle gave me a regular pencil with a needle-sharp lead. He tore a page from Goel's notebook and made four oval smudges with the pencil with the lead flat on its side. Then he demonstrated how to make those smudges evenly shaded by filling the lighter parts in with the pencil. The way he did this looked simple enough, and I shook my head and got the pencil and paper from him so I could start. He patted my shoulder and held both his palms together while facing me and making back-and-forth movements. I must have looked puzzled because he took the pencil and paper back and wrote "slowly." I nodded my head. Of course, I was not to work fast. However, I did not understand what making various shades of gray with a pencil had to do with photography. I kept quiet; I had neither the courage nor the means to communicate this question.

It took me less than five minutes to fill out the smudges. I had noted that both Goel and Khurana had worked at least half an hour on each oval smudge. I always did things fast and felt good that here was no exception. Proudly, I showed my work to Mr. Goyle, who looked at it and shook his head violently. He was not happy. He showed me Khurana's work and put my work next to it. I noticed the difference. Khurana had filled out the lighter areas so that they blended with the darker areas very subtly.

My next effort was not any better. It was hard for me to concentrate on those smudges and also spy on Mr. Goyle and the two students signing to each other. Observing these hand movements was more important to me than my assignment.

Mr. Goyle left after spending an hour with us. As soon as he was gone, Khurana and Goel put their pencils and notebooks away and started talking to each other again. I smiled at them, hoping they would include me in their conversation. They were not interested in me and continued to sign to each other.

During the lunch break, they both walked out of the classroom, and I followed them. As we exited the building, they both looked at me questioningly. I mimed drinking tea, telling them we could all go to a tea stall. They both shook their heads and pointed at me, telling me to go on my own.

They did not want me around them! It was not a very warm welcome. I assumed my lack of signing skills had turned them off. They were also both dressed in pretty nice clothes, and my shirt and pants screamed country bumpkin.

I had an idea and walked to the AIFD office and asked one of the assistants where and how I could learn to sign. He smiled and tried to talk to me, and when he learned I could not lipread, he wrote on a piece of paper, "Why do you want to learn signs? You speak very well. You do not need to sign like them." He was hearing, did not know signs, and thought signing was something inferior to speaking.

I insisted and he gave up. He looked around and found a small postcard and gave it to me. This was an alphabet card that pictured handshapes next to each letter. The assistant told me these were finger-spelling shapes, saying, "I think this will meet your need."

I carried the card back to the classroom and began to practice the two-handed manual alphabet. Khurana and Goel stopped talking and looked at me with amusement. I kept practicing and then decided to test myself.

I spelled, H-E-L-L-O.

They both smiled and spelled H-E-L-L-O back to me.

"Wow," I thought to myself, "I can talk without speaking."

At 1:00 p.m., the school closed. I learned that the summer hours were from 7:00 a.m. to 1:00 p.m., and the winter hours were from 9:00 a.m. to 3:00 p.m. Saturday was a half-day, and we had Sunday off. "I could get used to these hours!" I thought.

When I came home, I told everyone about the new skill I had learned. All showed a polite interest, but the kids were more interested than others. However, no one showed any interest in learning to fingerspell, and I did not think of it either. We were all so comfortable with tracing our fingers on our palms that changing our mode of communication did not enter anyone's mind.

I practiced fingerspelling all evening and was doing it fairly fast by next morning. I was thrilled about the possibility of communicating with this new mode.

The next morning, when I met Khurana and Goel outside the photography institute's door, I decided to demonstrate my skill.

G-O-O-D M-O-R-N-I-N-G. H-O-W A-R-E Y-O-U? I fingerspelled as fast as I could.

They looked puzzled, glanced at each other, and did not respond. The balloon of my excitement was punctured! I tried again and got the same reaction. Khurana decided to help me.

"We do not know much English," he wrote in Hindi on his notebook.

I felt dumb. I did not know that they did not know English. I needed to learn signs.

Goel could not even write Hindi, so I asked Khurana for help. I wrote, "Good morning. How are you?" in Hindi, and he translated the statement into signs. There was no sign for *good morning*, however. You just clasped your hands as in "namaste." He pointed at me, made the sign for "how," and pointed his finger at me. I was glad. That is how they signed "How are you?"

Mr. Goyle did not come to the PID that day as he was busy in his studio. Using gestures and writing, I learned a few new things about the school, Mr. Goyle, Khurana, and Goel. As we conversed, I began to pick up signs. By 1:00 p.m., I was able to communicate with them, albeit slowly.

We were using Indian Sign Language (ISL). Of course, no one called it that. It was just "signs." I became fascinated with this language. Each day, I picked up more signs, and by the end of the week, I was able to fully communicate with my two new friends and Mr. Goyle. I fell in love with sign language. It opened up a whole new world for me. Within a couple of weeks, I was also flailing my arms and fingers!

17

New Discoveries

I BEGAN TO LEARN PHOTOGRAPHY, BUT MORE than that I began to learn about an entirely new world of which I was becoming a bona fide member. Sign language was the key to this new world.

Soon I was leading a double life. One was the old life surrounded by my family and friends—all hearing—who communicated with me by tracing words on their palms with their index fingers. The second was the new one: the Deaf world with the PID at its center.

Mr. Goyle, the teacher, did not teach most of the time. He had a thriving photographic studio which required his full attention. He would show up erratically and give us an assignment and then return to his studio. I would confer with my fellow students. My sign language had improved and so had my knowledge about the Deaf world in Delhi.

Everyone had a sign name. Mr. Goyle was known as the "whistle." He used to bring a whistle to his school when he was very young, so he got that name sign. Khurana was "right-wrist-over-left-wrist separating and joining twice." This was a reference to his father being a police officer. Goel was "index finger raised up moving up and down on the left side of his forehead." He had a scar on his forehead. I got a similar sign except the finger moved back and forth across the lips. This referred to a scar on my upper lip.

The most famous sign was for B. G. Nigam, the general secretary of the All India Federation of the Deaf (AIFD). It was the tip of the index finger going from left to right on one's forehead. This was the sign for "black". Mr. Nigam was very dark—darker than most Indian people. Both Khurana and Goel talked endlessly about Mr. Nigam and how corrupt he was. They never said one positive word about him, the most

In front of Qutab Minar, a twelfth-century structure in Delhi. A fellow photography student shot this photo to show the effects of camera angles. The monument is almost 300 feet high.

powerful and successful deaf person in India. He was also the vice president of the World Federation of the Deaf.

Khurana and Goel complained that Mr. Nigam was angry and arrogant. I could not believe that the charming man with whom Bhai Narain had spoken with a few days earlier was so hated by other deaf people. According to Khurana and Goel, Nigam screamed at and even beat up people who did not agree with him. He was also corrupt, they said. He lived like a king and had no source of income except for being the general secretary of the AIFD. No one knew how much he was paid for that position. The way he lived, according to my new friends, cost thousands of rupees a month.

As I mentioned earlier, Mr. Goyle taught us only an hour or so daily. We used to talk and have fun while he was not there. Once in a while, Mr. Nigam would jump in from the window that separated his office from the classroom and talk with us for a few minutes. One day, he

Nephew Rajender, Bhabhi, our Babuji in 1965 in Gagret.

jumped in while the three of us were laughing about something and doing nothing. He got very angry and began to scold us. My sign language was not good enough and I understood almost nothing, but both Khurana and Goel looked visibly upset and embarrassed. They just kept quiet and stared at him. I was awed by his anger. His eyes were red and fiery. I was scared that he might hit us; however, he did not.

After he jumped back to his office area through the window, I asked the two what was wrong.

"He called us names for being lazy and dishonest and not working," they said.

They both became very eloquent in condemning Mr. Nigam for blaming us for not learning while no one was teaching us. They felt that he should get angry at Mr. Goyle and not at us. I asked why they did not complain about Mr. Goyle to Mr. Nigam. They responded that Mr. Goyle was Mr. Nigam's best friend; therefore, complaining about him would have only made Mr. Nigam madder.

I had an idea. I said, "Let us write a letter to Mr. Nigam and explain the situation." They said no.

"It will only make him mad. Let's leave it at that," said Khurana.

But I felt we needed to do something and decided to write the letter myself. I sat down and composed a letter in English addressed formally to Mr. B. G. Nigam. I added the formal salutation of "Sir" and ended with "your obedient servant." This was the format I had learned from English composition books.

Both Khurana and Goel were wide-eyed. They could not believe I could write English "like hearing people," as Goel put it. I showed the letter to them, and Khurana, who knew some English, tried to read it, but could not understand it. So, I translated the letter into signs for them. I asked Mr. Nigam to please make sure that this new photography school was successful. I said that the secret of a good school was a good teacher, and Mr. Goyle was a good teacher; however, his being good did not help if he was not there to teach us.

I asked Khurana and Goel to sign their names alongside mine. They refused. They were afraid of Mr. Nigam. "He will kick us out," said Goel. That worried me some, but I decided I was not going to come to school daily only to wait for Mr. Goyle to materialize whenever he wished. Of course, I was also learning signs and that was worth the daily trip, but I was really there to learn photography.

I folded the letter and parted the curtain in the window, looking for the office khalasi or one of the assistants. I thought it would be safer to have someone else deliver the letter. The assistant was sitting at his desk, typing on an old Underwood. He took the letter, unfolded it, and began to read. He beamed and looked at me repeatedly as he read it.

"Who wrote this letter?" he asked when he was done.

"I did," I replied. I was wondering why he had to ask this question.

"You know English!" He said wide-eyed.

"Yes," I said. Why was my knowledge of English such a big issue, I wondered.

The assistant told me to close the curtain and go back to my work.

"What work?" I asked him. "You read the letter. We have nothing to do here."

He put his finger to his lips to hush me and waved me away. I closed the curtains and sat down on my chair waiting for the sky to fall. Both Khurana and Goel sat there silently. They were scared and worried about what would happen. Their fear rubbed off on me and I began to regret writing that letter. I thought about the printing press and plowing chores at Gagret. But the arrow was out of the bow. All I could do was wait for it to hit its target.

We did not have to wait for long. A few minutes later, Mr. Nigam jumped out of the adjoining window. He had the letter in his hand. I was prepared for him to slap me and decided that if he hit me, I was going to hit back and then run for the door. However, Mr. Nigam was beaming. He waved my letter in the air and said, "This is a very good letter," and I began to breathe again.

He sat down in one chair and talked for a few minutes with us. He explained how Mr. Goyle could not come because he was very busy in his studio and how Mr. Goyle was making a great sacrifice by giving us even an hour daily. He went on and on and then said that he was looking for a new teacher so Mr. Goyle could focus on his business.

Then he looked at me—no stared at me—for a full minute. "You can write English," he said, smiling broadly. He showed the letter to Khurana and Goel and both pretended to read it.

Mr. Nigam patted my back and jumped back into his office through the window. Both Khurana and Goel came over and patted me on the back. I was not a dog anymore. Until that moment, they had been stand-offish toward me. I was the village bumpkin who did not know signs, dressed poorly, and asked them all kinds of dumb questions. Now, there I was, the writer of letters in English who had impressed the general secretary of the AIFD.

My status in that class of three people jumped from the bumpkin to the scholar. During the lunch break that day, they both asked me to join them. I moved up a notch in their eyes! We went to a nice teashop and they paid for my tea and snack. I felt good.

During lunch the next day, we walked together on Janpath, a road lined on one side with fancy shops in huge buildings built during the British era and on the other side with temporary structures established by refugees from Pakistan. The refugee shops were doing brisk business while the fancy shops in the gothic-style buildings were patronized only by the gentry.

We three walked on the refugee side, and as we got farther, Khurana signed WHISTLE and added the sign for "shop." They were going to show me Mr. Goyle's studio. It appeared that they went there daily, but until recently had not wanted me to join them. As we neared the studio, Goel and I stayed behind while Khurana went on to check something. He soon motioned us to join him. I learned later that Mr. Goyle did not approve of such visits and that they only visited when he was not there. At that time, Mr. Goyle was out to lunch with Mr. Nigam, so it was safe to visit the studio and chat with Mr. Goyle's two employees—Vasand Nagwani and M. Subramanium.

Both of them were at the counter. Subramanium was retouching a negative framed in a huge retouching box and Nagwani was sorting out films and negatives in envelopes for processing and printing. Goel introduced me to them.

"This is 'finger-on-lip,' new student," he said, pointing at me. To me, Goel said, "This is 'big-eye,'" pointing to Nagwani. "And this is 'M.'" That was Subramanium. He was from Madras, and the "M" was his sign name based on the state of his origin.

They shook hands with me while Khurana added, "He has a high school diploma." They looked impressed.

Goel embellished, "He can write English like a hearing man." Nagwani's eyes grew bigger, justifying his name sign.

Subramanium said, "I almost had a high school diploma but changed my mind." Nagwani laughed and said, "Subramanium is lying."

We all laughed. The north-south divide was evident among the deaf people also. Each state in India has its own culture and language. One can tell which state a person is from by just looking at him. The cultural and linguistic variances among the states are minor; however, the differences between the northern and southern states are huge. The rivalry between the North and South is very bitter.

Now I knew a total of six deaf people. I was the seventh. During our lunch breaks after that, Goel and Khurana began to introduce me around. There was another Nagwani and Duni Chand, Vasand's elder brother. He managed a bicycle and motorcycle stand, or parking place, contracted by the Deaf and Dumb Association of Delhi from the city government. He had an assistant who was also deaf, but had no name. His sign name was also "M" since he was from the south. Duni Chand's sign name was "bald" for obvious reasons.

What struck me as strange, however, was the fact that two brothers could both be deaf. I thought everyone who was deaf had become deaf due to one or another kind of sickness. Both Goel and Khurana said they became deaf when they were babies due to "high fever." But Vasand and Duni Chand were born deaf. Later I learned that they had a sister who was also deaf. I wondered if deafness was catching or some kind of family trait.

I was just learning the ABCs of deafness.

18

Visit to a Deaf Club

THE CYCLE STAND THAT DUNI CHAND NAGWANI managed had a sign which read "owned by the Deaf and Dumb Association, Delhi." I asked Khurana about it. He told me the association was "a bad group" and I should stay away from them. I learned slowly that there were four deaf groups in Delhi, who acted against each other's interests. I also learned that the Deaf and Dumb Association was the original deaf organization in India and was established by Mr. Nigam and his friends. Later, Mr. Nigam established the AIFD and let other people manage the Deaf and Dumb Association. However, his friends did not get along and the three of them defected, establishing their own organizations. Obviously, the deaf people were just like hearing people. Almost all of India's political parties had split over time with defectors establishing their own parties. For example, the National Congress Party of India, the party of such stalwarts as Gandhi and Nehru, split into several groups after Nehru's death. Personal agendas are always bigger than a party's agenda.

Khurana told me that his deaf club, known as the Deaf and Dumb Society, or DDS, had a function the following Sunday at 4:00 p.m. He gave me the address and invited me to attend the party. At the same time, he cautioned me against telling anyone about my attending or we both might be expelled from the PID. The enmity and competition among the deaf groups ran deep!

I was excited by the prospect of meeting many deaf people and practicing my signs all evening. On Sunday, I took a bus to Cannaught Place and walked all the way to the address Khurana had given me. It was the local YMCA. The YMCA had given permission to the DDS to use its premises for events. I did not want to be late, so I arrived a few minutes before 4:00 p.m. Khurana was not there. I looked around and saw no one signing. There were few hearing people walking around looking busy. I sat on a bench under a tree and waited. When no one showed up in an hour, I thought, "Maybe I am at the wrong place." I went in and asked the receptionist if the DDS was indeed meeting there.

The receptionist said, "Yes, they meet here every Sunday." So, I waited more.

I saw Khurana come with a couple of other deaf guys at 6:00 p.m. He acted as if he was on time. To him, "4:00 p.m." really meant "in the evening or afternoon." When I told him I had been waiting for two hours, he looked puzzled. Time, I learned, was relative among deaf people, as very few wore watches or could tell time.

Soon a group of about fifty deaf people, almost all men, had gathered. They were all signing to each other in small groups. Khurana introduced me to some people, but they all dismissed me as my clothes were not very fancy. Soon I noticed that the more popular deaf people were those who dressed in nice clothes. I was left alone as Khurana got busy with his own friends. I thought they were going to have some meeting, but that never occurred. All they did was talk to each other. At about 7:00 p.m., Khurana told me that samosas and Coke were available for us. I was not comfortable with accepting the free food and drink, but Khurana assured me it was alright. After the food was gone, they all gathered into groups again and talked while I watched them. I tried to butt into conversations, but was brushed aside. Finally, I gave up and started my trek back to the bus stop.

So much for the Deaf and Dumb Society!

Goel told me that the association met every Sunday at 4:00 p.m. and gave me the address of the meeting place. After my visit to Khurana's club, I was not so sure if I wanted to visit any more deaf clubs, but decided to check it out.

On that Sunday, I took a train to New Delhi railway station and walked to the address Goel had given me. It was in Paharganj, an old area of the city. The street was very narrow and reminded me of the lane that led to the famous print shop where I had worked for two days. I arrived at a huge old house with a large arched doorway. I went in and found myself in a dark hall. No one was there. On one side of the hall was a small library. No one was there either. I remembered how everyone arrived two hours late for the DDS meeting, so I went out and walked around looking at the wares in stores. Each time I passed the building, I went in only to find no one there.

Finally, at about 6:00 p.m., some deaf people began to filter in. The only people I knew were the Nagwani brothers. There were six or seven girls also. After being ignored by everyone, I decided to get a book and read it. I was disappointed to find that the bookcases were all locked. So, I read the titles through the glass doors and found several books that I wanted to check out. I asked one important-looking man if I could borrow a book. He gave me a flat "no." Books were not loaned out, I was told. I wondered, "What kind of library is this?"

Like with the DDS, this meeting consisted of people standing in small groups, talking non-stop, and eating samosas and tea at the end. At 8:00 p.m., the meeting ended, so I walked out and made my way to the railway station for the ride home.

I decided that deaf associations and societies were not for me. They did not accept me. Everyone talked with each other and I was just some unwanted person. This was not very good for my ego. I was the center of attention at home, and in Gagret, everyone knew me and paid attention to me. Here the deaf who could not read or write well did not even want to talk to me! I stopped going to clubs.

19

Making Deaf Friends

MEANWHILE, THERE WERE OTHER DEVELOP-
ments. Our class of three grew to five and then six. One of the new
students was Kesh Kumar. His name sign was "cheek." When he was
young, his cheeks were always red, hence the name. Kesh was a very
good-looking guy and very funny. He could communicate with me and
was an excellent mime. Soon we became good friends. Another new
student was Raj Kishore. He was also very good-looking with curly hair
and very light skin. His name sign was "lifting-the-hat," which means
"British." He could have passed for a European, especially in winter
because he was so pale.

With the arrival of Kesh Kumar, my time at the PID became more
interesting. He was a ball-and-a-half of fun and very creative. He was
impressed to learn that I was a high school graduate and could write in
English, in addition to Hindi, Urdu, Punjabi, and Sanskrit. He proudly
called himself "illiterate" by putting his right thumb first on his lips and
then pressing it on his open left palm, indicating the way illiterate people
signed their names on legal papers—by making a thumb impression. He
could tell the difference between Urdu and Hindi because Urdu was
written from right to left, but could not discern written Punjabi from
Hindi or Sanskrit. "That writing stuff is for hearing people," he said.

Illiterate or not, Kesh was bright. He could make up a joke in no
time. Everything was a joke to him, and I loved to match wits with him.
Soon we became inseparable and the others began to leave us alone or
rather Kesh would shoo them away.

It was from Kesh that I learned to communicate in signs effectively.
Kesh could communicate with anyone—deaf or hearing. One incident
that really impressed me occurred when we were talking to an American
artist in a coffeehouse.

Kesh had a number of hearing friends, and one of them was a painter. One day, this painter brought a visiting American painter to the coffeehouse with him. Kesh and I frequented the coffeehouse as the food was cheap and the atmosphere bohemian. Of course, Kesh and I did not know what a bohemian atmosphere was; we just liked it.

That day, Kesh's painter friend was sitting with the visiting American painter and several other artists who were more interested in the American than painting. Kesh and I joined them, and someone ordered coffee for us. One benefit of being deaf is that someone always orders coffee for you. Darshan, Kesh's painter friend, introduced us to everyone. He pointed toward us and told them who we were, or so it seemed, and then pointed to each of the people sitting around the table and said their names with exaggerated lip movements. We did not understand any of the names as we could not lipread, but we smiled and shook our heads at each introduction.

"He," Darshan pointed at the American painter and said, "America."

We understood. Darshan told the American painter about Kesh. Both Kesh and I could tell from his hand and body movements that he was explaining how Kesh was a professional classical dancer and how he was a funny guy. The American painter beamed. Kesh asked me to talk for him, and I voiced, "He wants to tell you a story."

The American painter kept smiling. Kesh started miming slowly about his being a painter (pointing at him and miming painting) and painting a woman (moving hands indicating a woman with an hourglass figure). Then he pointed at various parts of his face—eyes, nose, chin—and made painting movements. At the end, he pointed to his lips and vigorously shook his index finger indicating a firm "no." Then he mimed taking out lipstick, painting his lips, and then kissing an imaginary easel firmly. Everybody burst out laughing.

That is how Kesh communicated and associated with people. He was full of confidence and walked with an air of owning the world. He did not have any money, but had a wealth of talent that gave him the confidence few people—hearing or deaf—have. Opposite him, I felt like a village idiot and was afraid to talk to anyone. Being with him, though, gave me a lot of courage. It seemed strange that I, as one of the highest educated deaf people in Delhi, was learning a lot about life from a self-proclaimed illiterate deaf guy.

Kesh was born deaf and, like many deaf children of hearing parents, had no communication at home. He spent his early years wandering around the house and never learned to communicate with anyone until he was enrolled at the Lady Noyce School for the Deaf, a government-run school, in Delhi. He was already about ten years old, and all he had learned at the school up to that point was sign language. He did not even learn the alphabet. If he did, he had forgotten. He could write his name in English, but a friend had taught him. He could also fingerspell his name and count to 100.

I understood after speaking to Kesh several times that he was highly intelligent. How a smart person like him could not read and write after several years of schooling was hard for me to understand. But then, I had also met many other bright deaf men and women who were in the same boat as Kesh. Congenital deafness, I assumed, made learning to read and write very difficult. Among the many friends I made, only a few could read and write well, and most of them had become deaf later in life, like me.

Another friend I made was Raj Kishore (the "hat"). He had, just like Kesh, worked all his life as a tailor, the most popular occupation of the deaf during the early twentieth century. Tailoring did not require much education and involved minimal communication. I asked Raj Kishore why he was quitting tailoring to become a photographer.

"It is not a steady job," he explained. "Sometimes there is a lot of work, and sometimes there is nothing. The worst part is getting people to pay for the work you do." After learning photography, Raj and Kesh hoped to get jobs as darkroom technicians.

I was surprised to learn that Raj Kishore rode a bicycle to and from work. Riding trains was fine, but their timetable required my leaving home and school at specific times. Each day after school, Kesh would ask me to stop for a cup of tea and talk, but I was always in a hurry to catch the train. Kesh apparently also enjoyed my company and would walk to the railway station with me—even though I walked fast. I thought if I rode a bike, it would give me more time to hang out with my friends.

I asked Raj Kishore, "Your parents allow you to ride a bike?"

He was surprised at my question. "Of course. I have been riding it since I was a little boy."

"But riding a bike in side streets is easy; riding it in the overcrowded Delhi streets is very dangerous. You will never hear what hit you." I expressed the fears that were conveyed to me at home when I had brought up the idea of riding a bike to school.

Raj Kishore laughed. "Well, look at me. I am still alive and never had an accident. Hearing people have accidents all the time."

"Do you know," he went on, "deaf people in America and England drive cars. They have driving licenses."

It was my turn to laugh. I knew he was pulling the village boy's leg. "Sure," I replied, and just to keep up with his joke, I added, "they also fly airplanes."

But Raj Kishore was serious. "It is true. Please believe me. I am not making this up."

It must be true, I said to myself. But the idea of deaf people driving had floored me. Riding a bicycle in an almost-empty road from Gagret to Hoshiarpur was challenging enough. Coping with the traffic in Delhi must be very hard, I thought. And driving! I was aghast.

That night after dinner, my suggestion that I start riding a bike to school was opposed by everyone. Jijaji was totally against it, and Sister Kamla was ready to cry once she envisioned me sprawled in a street after being hit by a car. My explanation that I had already ridden my bike from Gagret to Hoshiarpur was mocked.

"That is different. It is Delhi, and it is hard enough for a hearing person to ride a bike here," they said. Jijaji mentioned that he had relinquished his bicycle to commute to work by train because the street traffic was murder.

"In Europe and America," I began to brag about my knowledge, "deaf people drive cars. They get driving licenses."

They all laughed. I was making up stories to strengthen my case, they said. Bhai Narain, however, had begun to waver and suggested that I ride my bike to visit my cousin Surinder a couple of miles from our home to test the waters. I volunteered to go there right then.

"It is after nine; not a good time for a visit," Narain said, stopping me. Jijaji, Sister Kamla, and Bharjai Krishna were totally opposed to the idea. They argued that if some deaf people were risking their lives on two wheels, this did not mean that I had to join them.

Nevertheless, a week later, I was riding my bike to school and hanging out with Kesh and Raj Kishore.

20

Me, a Teacher!

ONE OF THE REASONS I MOVED TO DELHI WAS
the availability of government scholarships. I had applied for one when
starting at the PID and was waiting for approval. We needed it badly;
Bhai Narain's salary barely supported his family. My tuition, food, and
other expenses were an additional burden on his already overextended
finances. Bhai Narain made calls to the office that granted scholarships,
but to no avail. Most of those clerks did not even know what he was
talking about. Finally, he went to the office and, after several hours of
asking around, learned that I had not received the scholarship as they
had "never received" my application. This, in bureaucratic language,
means they had either lost it or it was still sitting in some tall pile of files
in front of one of those sleeping clerks.

I was disappointed and hurt. Bhai Narain, with his characteristic
optimism, said, "It is no big deal," but it bothered me to be a burden
on him. I began to think of finding some job; however, unemployment
at the time in Delhi was over 20 percent for hearing people and much
higher for disabled people. Finally, I decided to bring the subject to Mr.
Nigam's attention.

The next time Mr. Nigam jumped into the little classroom, I told him
about the scholarship problem and added that I was thinking of dropping
out of school. I had no intention of doing that and had not even planned
to mention it to him. I just blurted it out, trying to make my case strong.
It did.

"No, you are not leaving this school," he said in an admonishing
manner. Then he had an idea: "We will find another scholarship for you."

The next day, I was told I now had two part-time jobs. First, I was
going to work in Mr. Goyle's studio after school and second, I was going

to teach an adult literacy class at night. Mr. Goyle was going to pay me 25 rupees a month, and the night class would pay me another 25 rupees. Thus, I was going to earn 50 rupees a month. I was overjoyed and did not even pay attention to the long hours this plan was going to require.

Thus started my sixteen-plus-hours-a-day routine. I left home at 6:30 in the morning to arrive at the school at 7:00 after a hard six-mile bike ride. At 1:00 p.m., I went to the V. R. Goyle Photo Studio and worked there until 9:00 p.m. when the shop closed. I was allowed to leave a few minutes early so I could return to the PID to teach an adult education class, which was started just so I could earn a little more money.

I was overjoyed! I was making 50 rupees a month, which then was about U.S.$11 at the exchange rate; it would be less than $2 at today's exchange rate. The idea that I was being exploited never entered my head. Mr. Goyle paid me less than 1 rupee a day or about $5 a month; this was as much as Mr. Nigam made in one day. The idea that I was making some money satisfied me, and the opportunities to do professional photography at the studio and be a teacher were much more valuable than any amount of money.

Teaching was something I really began to enjoy. About fifteen people signed up for my literacy class. They all had full-time jobs and their education varied from thumb-on-lips-moving-to-palm to the ability to spell some words. They all wanted to learn English because of its prestige. My suggestion that we learn Hindi was laughed out of the window. "What will we do with Hindi?" they asked in a chorus. I wanted to tell them that they would be able to read the great Hindi writers and poets, and that it was our national language; however, I knew it would have been useless. So, I taught English and some basic arithmetic.

The students attended erratically due to their jobs. If a boss wanted someone to stay at work longer, he had no choice but to stay and miss the class. There was no such thing as earning overtime pay, but working late reduced the chance of being fired. Knowing how important their jobs were, I did not make their frequent absences an issue.

They all made up for their irregularity with their dedication to learning. Each of my students was eager to beat the others out. Some of them made rapid progress while others plodded along. Soon, they were all spelling words on the two-handed manual alphabet that we used. One of the students, Jawaharlal Lal, who did not even know the alphabet when we started the class, began to spell with great gusto. He also began to use his limited English vocabulary in a very effective manner.

He liked a girl because of her red lips. Once, when I asked him in class to explain why he liked the girl by fingerspelling in English rather than signing, he thought for a while and then spelled "lip-red-kiss." I was impressed. Another time, he was having a hot argument with a deaf guy who knew English fairly well and could also talk. The guy called Jawaharlal Lal a "dog" because of his habit of moving lips without forming any words. Jawaharlal Lal retorted, "Me dog, you dogs." The guy made an ugly face.

"That is wrong English," the guy told Jawaharlal Lal, who looked at me for support. I was too busy trying not to laugh to do my duty as a teacher and correct Jawaharlal Lal. By pluralizing the word *dog*, he meant *bigger dog* or *worse dog*. The signs for "big" and "more" are the same in Indian Sign Language, and he was following ISL grammar.

The biggest challenge in teaching English to young men in their late twenties or early thirties, who had never even learned either the Hindi or English alphabets, was to help them understand that an English word can and does have more than one meaning, or that rules for making words plural did not always apply the same way. The plural of *boy* is *boys* and that of *girl* is *girls*. Therefore, they argued *man* should be *mans* and *woman* should be *womans*. They all agreed that either I was breaking rules or I did not know enough English despite my having passed my high school examination.

Jawaharlal, who was very creative, suggested that we forego English plurals since there were too many irregularities. His idea was to simply add "many" after the noun to indicate plurality. He wrote, "Man many eat big" instead of "Men eat a lot." My argument that each language has its own rules fell flat on his literally deaf ears. He was bright and had a following. Finally, I had to ask Mr. Nigam to come to the class one night and explain that I was not making up the rules. Mr. Nigam, who never missed an opportunity to ham it up, first told them that I was correct and then went on to lecture them on their impertinence to question a teacher's knowledge. He went on and on and took up the whole class time. Everyone was scared of his vile temper, so they kept quiet and listened to his tirade. They begged me never to invite him to the class again and told Jawaharlal to keep his ideas to himself.

After class, we would all walk together in a group with arms around one another to a nearby teashop. If there were ten of us, we would order five glasses of tea with five empty glasses to share in order to save money. The teashop owner did not like this practice, and this invasion of ten or more deaf people scared away his other customers. However, at 10:00 p.m., there were not many customers, so he accommodated us, but treated us very rudely.

For about twenty to forty-five minutes, we talked and laughed while sipping hot tea. This was the first time since I had become deaf that I had a good number of friends with which to share jokes and ideas; however, there were limitations.

None of them read the newspapers or magazines. Their ideas about the world in general were hazy. All their knowledge was based on personal observations supplemented by some explanations by deaf people who could read some or by hearing people who signed some. Either way, the limited reading skills of deaf people and the erratic signing of hearing people communicated more misinformation than facts.

However, I was amazed at the common sense they all had and the general information for survival they had accumulated. Those who could not read and write knew where to get on and off buses and how to pay the exact amount even when they could not count. Some of them, especially Jawaharlal and Kesh, were extremely intelligent. I taught Jawaharlal how to play chess, and after three or four practice sessions, he began to beat me regularly—and I was a fairly good chess player.

I used to arrive home at about 11:00 p.m. Everyone at home would be asleep. Bharjai Krishna used to leave my dinner on a plate with vegetables and dal in a saucer on the side. I would eat my dinner standing up in the dark kitchen. I usually fell asleep before my head hit the pillow.

The long day included six hours of learning, eight hours of work in Goyle Studio, one hour of teaching English, one hour of tea and talk, and one hour of brisk cycling for a total of twelve miles. I followed this routine six days a week and welcomed the Sunday which I spent with my family or visiting relatives.

All of it was pure fun, and I never tired or thought about jumping into a well.

21

Working in the Photo Studio

GOYLE STUDIO WAS ONE OF THE NINETY OR so shops on Janpath that were allotted to refugee businessmen from Pakistan. These refugee shops lined one side of Janpath, and stately shops in huge columned buildings, which catered to the wealthy, lined the opposite side of the street. These "temporary" structures were still there fourteen years after India and Pakistan were divided into separate countries. These businessmen had built up so much economic and political clout that the New Delhi Municipal Corporation was afraid to take the structures down. Each shop site was worth hundreds of thousands of rupees and was allotted to "deserving refugees," a euphemism for people who could pay heavy bribes or were related to the mayor or corporation commissioners.

The location of these shops was one of the best, if not the best, in all of New Delhi. Cannaught Place was the most modern shopping center in New Delhi, and two of the best hotels, the Imperial and the Janpath, were within walking distance. All the tourists visited this row, and the storekeepers had a roaring business in clothes, jewelry, artwork, and other baubles that tourists liked. The prices in these shops were "fixed," as the sign in front of each store declared. An American tourist would pay $20 for a trinket that a knowledgeable local could pick up for $2. However, locals never shopped in those stores.

I used to enjoy walking with my friends on this strip and looking at all the clothes and other wares that I could not afford. The idea that I was going to work in one of those stores behind a counter, where I would be talking to people from all over the world, was very exciting.

But, as always, what you expect and what actually happens are two different things. Instead of being behind the counter and dealing with fancy people, I found myself working in the darkroom, washing and drying prints, trimming and retouching them, and then putting them in envelopes with marked order numbers. All this work was done in a three-by-six-foot room with a small window. The front counter was taken up by "M," since he was an expert at retouching negatives, and the retouching cabinet was right behind the counter. Of the four people working there, I was the only one who could talk. I thought that fact might make me the logical choice for the cushy job. However, being new and only part-time, I had not yet earned the right to sit up front.

The limited opportunities I did have to work at the counter helped me develop some self-confidence. Since Goyle, Vasand, and Subramanium could not talk and their writing was rudimentary at best, they communicated via gestures. At times, they would call me from inside to explain something to the customer. I liked and looked forward to these opportunities.

Talking with strangers, especially men dressed in expensive suits and beautiful perfumed women, was not easy for me. I had left the little village of Gagret only a year earlier, and these fancy people made me nervous. I would begin to sweat and grow a lump in my throat the size of the tie knot of the man I was talking to. It was even harder to respond to women who appeared to belong to another planet. My voice, which was the reason for my coming out to the counter, would be lost. It took several months before I learned that these rich people were just regular people with money.

It was a perfect arrangement. I learned photography as a student at the PID and honed my skills as a darkroom technician at my studio job. I also had the opportunity to take photographs at weddings, news events, and various ceremonies. Photographing a wedding was nothing but fun. Only well-off people could afford to hire a professional photographer. At these weddings, they had huge buffet dinners spread out. The wedding ceremony, with the priest chanting mantras and the couple getting married throwing rice, flowers, sugar, and vermillion into the fire went on all night. There was little for a photographer to do but wait for another photo opportunity, which came when the bride was to leave for the groom's home. In between, I enjoyed the buffet, an endless supply of coffee, and sweetmeats. I had never eaten such good food before.

I used a large Rollieflex camera, which had an electronic flash gun and came with a larger flash battery, giving me the look of a professional photographer. I walked with a swagger and an air of importance. Finally! A glamorous job!

The glamour did not pay much, however. If I worked all night covering a wedding, I was still expected to work all the next day at the studio. I received no overtime pay. However, if I was sick or didn't go to work for whatever reason, Goyle deducted one day's wage. Still, he expected me to be thankful for the privilege of working in his studio, and I was.

Once, Goyle asked me to cover a wedding at the last minute. I had to leave the studio for the event at about 4:00 p.m. The wedding lasted until 1 a.m., and I arrived at Narain's residence at 52/5 at around 2 a.m. Bhai Narain and other occupants of the quarter were aware of my hours and did not worry. But at that time, Bhabhi, my ever-worrying mother, was visiting us. I had not called about arriving home so late because the residence had no telephone. When I arrived, after bicycling for more than twenty-five miles and working eighteen hours, Bhabhi opened the door. She came forward and put her hands on my face the way only mothers do. I pushed her aside; I was in a foul mood. She brought food and asked if I wanted her to warm it. I told her gruffly that I had already eaten. When she asked where I had eaten, I got mad and told her I was very sleepy.

At that time, Ramesh, B. K. Sharma's younger brother, who had also joined the ever-growing population at 52/5, arrived home on his bicycle. He looked at me and said, "Oh, you are back." That is when I learned that Bhabhi had sent him to Janpath to check the photo studio for me. I got madder and yelled at her for making the poor man ride the bike twelve miles in the middle of the night. She just looked at me and was obviously hurt. I was embarrassed, but did not say anything more and went to sleep.

Whenever I remember this incident, I think about Bhabhi—how loving she was and how much she cared for us. I did not understand her concern and care until I became a parent myself.

Working at the Goyle Studio gave me a lot of experience, and soon I could process and print films at the required speed and of professional quality, take portraits in the studio, and, in a cinch, retouch negatives. However, my negative retouching ability never was up to par. The more I tried, the worse I retouched. When I retouched negatives, I made the people uglier instead of more beautiful. Retouching negatives, just like lipreading, is an art—either you have it or you do not.

Within a few months at the Goyle Studio, I had developed several skills. I could produce professional quality photographs, shoot portraits and action photographs, and deal comfortably with clients. All these new skills gave me a lot of courage and self-confidence.

22

Learning about Leadership

MY TWO VISITS TO THE DEAF CLUBS THAT I recounted earlier did not encourage me to return to such places. However, due to pressure from Raj Kishore, who was a regular Delhi Deaf Association member, I did attend some special club events like the Independence Day picnic at the Lodi Gardens. I did not like going there; nobody paid any attention to me, and even Raj Kishore would be too busy to talk to me. So, I would just hang around with Kesh.

One thing bothered me about these gatherings. There was a distinct class system in the DDA. I am not talking about the caste system* —most of the members did not know what caste the others belonged too. Even when they knew, they did not care. The class system they had was related to money. The members coming from wealthy families had their own clique. My clothes clearly indicated that I was not wealthy, therefore, I did not belong to their group. I tried to associate with the poorer members, but they also gave me the cold shoulder. Despite my wearing pants and coats, I looked like a country bumpkin.

The attitude changed a little bit after I began to teach the night class. Many of my students, especially Jawaharlal, were popular, and they introduced me to people as their teacher. The news that I could read and write English and "speak like hearing people" helped move me up in the circle. But it took several months before I was invited to join the group of richer members who associated with Mr. Nigam.

*Indian society was divided into four groups in the second century B.C.: Brahmins (priests), Kshatriyas (warriors), Vaishyas (businessmen/farmers), and Sudras (service class). The caste system was banned by the government in 1948.

The Delhi Deaf Association, once a vibrant organization, was now dormant. The young deaf people in Delhi, under the leadership of Mr. Nigam, had established it in 1950. They had contacted some powerful politicians and with their help gotten an office in Kamla Market, a shopping center about a mile from Cannaught Place, and two bicycle parking stands. These ventures provided a steady income. In addition, the DDA started a wood shop in the office where a deaf carpenter made simple furniture. The DDA hosted annual picnics and held several general membership meetings.

Mr Nigam was very ambitious. He was not satisfied with the local DDA and managed to start a national organization—the All India Federation of the Deaf. After Mr. Nigam established the AIFD and took some of the group's more active members, like R. L. Aggarwal, with him, the DDA lost its clout. Mr. Nigam was more interested in the AIFD and appointed Mr. O. N. Sharma as the general secretary of the DDA. However, Mr. Nigam liked to hog power and required Sharma to work at the AIFD every evening. Since Sharma had a full-time job during the day, there was no time for him to work for the DDA. DDA slowly stagnated. Whenever people asked what was wrong with the DDA, Mr. Nigam simply pointed to Mr. Sharma.

Everyone knew that Mr. Nigam did not want the DDA to become active and take attention away from the AIFD; they discussed this issue openly in small groups. But no one had the nerve to tell that to Mr. Nigam. His legendary anger scared everyone.

Another young man arrived in Delhi at this time. Suraj Kanchanbras was living with his parents in Dehradun, about sixty miles from Delhi. Suraj just showed up one morning in the AIFD office, and we were told he was working there full-time. I asked Kesh and Raj Kishore about Suraj. Kesh did not know him well, but Raj Kishore did, and he told me that Suraj was very smart, could write pretty well, and was a good leader.

Suraj was only twenty-five, but he was serious like an old man. I never saw him smile. We saw him in the corridors walking very fast, head bowed deep in thought. I was awed by his demeanor and never tried to talk to him. He was upper class and only associated with Mr. Nigam, Goyle, and two successful tailors, Harish Chugh and Dayal Rameshwar, as well as other leaders who rode taxis and ate in swanky restaurants.

One evening while I was teaching night school, Suraj walked into my classroom. Since he was considered a leader and an important AIFD staff member, all the students stood up and clasped their hands to say "Namaste." Suraj, in his usual serious manner, told them to sit down and spelled to me: "After class, you come to AIFD office." This was his way of making sure no one understood what he said. I said, "Fine," and he went away without a smile or another word.

I was puzzled as to why they wanted me in the inner sanctum, and the class was even more puzzled. Jawaharlal said, "Maybe they plan to close the school? Mr. Nigam might be trying to save 25 rupees so he could spend it in a restaurant in one evening."

I got worried and could not focus on teaching for the rest of the class time.

After class, I entered the AIFD office with my heart thumping. I saw Mr. Nigam sitting in his chair with Suraj, Sharma, Harish Chugh, Ram Parkash Mehra, Rattan Lal Aggarwal, Rameshwar, and some other members of Mr. Nigam's entourage at the other end of the huge desk. They were all laughing about something and stopped when I came in. I thought it might be time to start thinking about working somewhere else.

After inviting me to sit down, Mr. Nigam explained the purpose of our meeting: "You know the DDA is not functioning since Sharma became its general secretary. We need to find ways to make DDA an active organization again." Mr. Nigam was a very skilled actor. He looked as if someone had died and he was reading a eulogy. I felt relieved; my teaching job was not at stake; instead I was part of a group discussing the future of a major Delhi deaf organization.

Sharma stood up and tried to object, but shut up when Mr. Nigam pointed his index finger in warning. Sharma sat down as if a gun had been pointed at him. Mr. Nigam continued to lecture. He was a ham and enjoyed the audience.

"The deaf people in Delhi area are suffering because of Sharma's neglect. The DDA did wonderful things for the deaf when I was its general secretary and Aggarwal was the treasurer. We had saved over 10,000 rupees when I moved to the AIFD." He paused dramatically and asked Sharma, "How much money is there now?"

Sharma said, "Nothing, but ..."

Mr. Nigam cut him off: "What happened to the money we collected and saved by hard work?"

Sharma started to explain, "You took . . ."

He was cut off again by Mr. Nigam, whose legendary anger was building by the second. I felt scared and sorry for Sharma as all eyes were on him, and everyone in the room apparently blamed him for the demise of the DDA. I had heard all of them say that it was Mr. Nigam who never let Sharma work in the DDA, that he forced him to work at the AIFD. However, here, no one had the nerve to say anything. These men who spoke so eloquently and bravely about Mr. Nigam being a crook were sitting there looking accusingly at Sharma. No doubt they were as scared as I was.

Suddenly, Suraj faced Sharma and told him in no uncertain terms that he, Sharma, was the cause of the stagnation in the DDA, and out of the blue, the quiet and reserved Suraj punched Sharma right on his glasses.

We were taken aback. Mr. Nigam had created a clone. We could not believe that Suraj could get angry, so angry that he would hit Sharma, who was older than him and deserved respect, not a fist.

No one moved, and it was Mr. Nigam who intervened. He pointed his threatening finger again—this time at Suraj, telling him to stop. But Mr. Nigam was smiling. He apparently was feeling good; someone else had done his dirty work for him!

Suraj sat down. He looked spent. The emotional outburst had taken its toll. Sharma sat there with his broken glasses in his hand. His eyes were very bad, and I doubted he could see the glasses clearly enough to discern how much damage had been done to them.

Mr. Nigam motioned to Vassand, the resident handyman, who went forward and took the glasses from Sharma's hands. After a short examination, he shook his head like a surgeon who has just found terminal cancer in a patient. The glasses could not be fixed.

The change in Mr. Nigam's personality was dramatic. He was no longer an aggressive scary figure, but a benevolent big brother now. I could not tell whether he was a good actor or genuinely concerned about Sharma, who looked pitiful without his glasses.

Mr. Nigam sized up the whole situation and took over. He asked if anyone knew of an optometrist that was open after 10:00 p.m. That was a rhetorical question. We all shook our heads in unison. None of us wore glasses, and we did not know an optometrist from a taxidermist. He shook his head in great disappointment and told Sharma that he had to wait until the next morning to get his glasses fixed. Sharma did not understand him. His eyesight was so bad that he could not tell a man from a horse without his glasses; understanding signs was out of the question.

Mr. Nigam ordered three of us, including me, to walk Sharma to the bus stand and put him on a bus going to his home. He came close to Sharma and tried to sign at a specific angle. Apparently this was the not the first time the man had lost his glasses during a heated discussion, and Mr. Nigam knew how to communicate to a glasses-less Sharma.

We walked with Sharma, who appeared to have night-blindness also. He was walking like a drunk, and when I tried to hold his arm to steady him, he pushed me aside and began to call me names. Understandably, he was very angry; he had been humiliated in front of ordinary DDA members. He began taking his anger out on us and kept signing, not his strong suit, blaming Mr. Nigam for getting Suraj angry and having him, a much younger man, hit him in front of everyone.

I felt empathy for Sharma. We had a lot in common. He had become deaf at the age of twelve and had managed to get a bachelor's degree. I had seen his father communicate with him by writing on his palm. He was working as a clerk with the New Delhi Municipal Corporation, a very good job for a deaf person. He had moved up and belonged to Mr. Nigam's inner circle. I decided that if being a part of his inner circle meant getting beaten up, I did not want to be there.

After getting Sharma on his bus, I started for home. While riding my bicycle, I thought about the whole situation. Mr. Nigam had clearly set the whole situation up and prompted Suraj to violence. He had also gathered an audience for the purpose of humiliating Sharma. As I pedaled, I wondered why I had been invited to this drama. As much as I disliked the incident, I felt elated that I was becoming more important in Mr. Nigam's eyes.

A week later, a general meeting of the DDA was called. Rameshwar and several other of Mr. Nigam's toadies went around telling everyone that they must attend the meeting because the DDA election was to be held. I had never seen an election of an organization; therefore, I went out of curiosity. I wondered if they would use ballot boxes and give speeches. Who would replace Sharma as scapegoat? Or would Sharma run again?

The meeting was scheduled for 4:00 p.m. I arrived at Cannaught Place a little before that despite knowing that no one would be there. The meeting was to be held on the lawn just outside the PID room, and sure enough, no one was there. So, I walked outside of the building and stood looking for someone who was using hands to communicate. Soon, deaf people began to emerge in twos and threes. No one was in a hurry. When Kesh and Jawaharlal showed up, I joined them and began to listen to their chatting.

They believed that whoever became the general secretary of the DDA would be a failure as Mr. Nigam did not want the association to flourish. The general secretary of the DDA would become a challenge to him. I wondered why, then, did Mr. Nigam want to hold these elections? That question was too deep for me.

At about 5:00 p.m., we saw Mr. Nigam get out of a taxi accompanied by Rameshwar and Suraj. He walked quickly, like a very important leader, with his entourage in tow. We all followed them at a distance. Instead of going to his office, Mr. Nigam headed straight to the lawn and suddenly stopped, looking around. His face contorted with anger.

"Where is everyone and where are the arrangements for the meeting?" he asked. He looked at Suraj and Rameshwar. He also glanced fleetingly at us, apparently to gauge our reaction to his anger.

Rameshwar, who was a genius at grasping situations, jumped to attention and looked at us.

"Why did you not bring out chairs and the dhurrie?" he addressed no one in particular. The trio looked at us as if we were responsible for setting up the meeting space. We looked at each other. Since we had no one to yell at, we kept quiet and fidgeted.

Mr. Nigam took out his office key and tossed it at Rameshwar who, being a good cricket player, caught it deftly. Rameshwar gestured to Jawaharlal and two other guys to follow him. They left and Mr. Nigam began to examine the walls and trees, while Suraj checked the length of the grass, which was almost gone as it was summer.

Within five minutes, five folding chairs were set up in a line and a dhurrie was spread out. Mr. Nigam sat down in the middle chair with Suraj next to him. Sharma, the present general secretary; Aggarwal, the treasurer, and one other founder of the DDA occupied the other chairs. We, as common deaf people, stood around waiting for an order. Finally, Mr. Nigam signed in a huff, "What are you all waiting for? Sit down." We all sat down cross-legged, quietly looking at the dignitaries adorning the folding chairs. The small number of women sat on the front part of the dhurrie.

Mr. Nigam sat there, slowly taking in the riffraff, including myself. He looked very pensive and inspired. I thought again that this guy was either very concerned about the deaf people in India or was a great actor. As Mr. Nigam's eyes lingered on the women in front, especially the beautiful ones, I smiled to myself and thought, "He is human after all."

Finally, after what seemed like an eternity, Nigam stood up and, with the seriousness of a person delivering an eulogy, began to sign. "Brothers and sisters," he said. "We have a very depressing situation here. The DDA, which Aggarwal and I established with the help of some other people, is dying. I was very busy with the AIFD and the World Federation of the Deaf, therefore, I could not pay attention to the DDA. I thought all was well, but when I checked recently, I found that all my life's work was thrown out the window. I have been crying ever since. I feel like crying now, but I think crying will not help. Therefore, I am here to make sure that DDA is resurrected."

He went on, and I listened with a pounding heart. This guy, by simply talking about the stagnant organization, could instill fear in his audience, especially me, a villager and a new member of the group. I looked at the other four people in folding chairs. For a deaf person, sitting in the same row as someone who is signing is the worst. To see the signing, the four of them had to twist their necks and hold their palms in front of their eyes to ward off the sunlight. I do not think they understood him, but they did not want to leave their chairs of status and stand or sit where they could see him better. Being in the chair of position was more important to them than being in a practical and rational position.

Mr. Nigam went on to say that he wanted new blood and new leadership. He wanted a new general secretary to be elected. He wanted a volunteer to stand up and accept the challenging position to save the DDA. I looked around. No one stood up. People either kept staring at Mr. Nigam or looking at others' heads to see if anyone was going to stand up.

Suddenly, out of the blue, I decided to stand up. "Someone has to do the job," I thought to myself. "Why not me?" However, I could not stand up. My body refused to obey my mind. I sat their frozen because the idea of standing up in front of fifty people petrified me. Earlier, I was sweating slightly from the heat and humidity. Now I was sweating profusely from fear and nervousness.

Someone poked me in the back, and I looked around slowly. It was Jawaharlal. He was nudging me to stand up. I looked at Mr. Nigam, who was getting angry now. "Is not there anyone who has sucked his mother's milk?" he asked. That was an insult. It propelled me up. I stood there with sweat flowing from my forehead and armpits. My legs were trembling, and I could not raise my head to look at him. Instead I looked at the upturned faces of the guys sitting in front of me. They were all smiling.

Jawaharlal poked the back of my leg, and I looked back at him. He pointed at Mr. Nigam and signed for me to look there. Mr. Nigam had been talking to me but I had been too busy looking at the ground and people's faces to see him.

Mr. Nigam asked me to approach him. I moved, tracing my path through the sitting people, and after what felt like a few years, was standing in front of everyone. Mr. Nigam patted my back. I felt a little better, but my legs still trembled.

"Here is your new general secretary," he told the audience. Then he had a thought. He looked at the four chair straddlers. "But he is new and does not know the system. We need help." He looked at them and then I saw his eyes sparkle.

He pointed at Suraj. "You know how DDA operates, but you cannot write very well. Let us make you the general secretary and Madan the joint secretary. You two will make an excellent team."

The election à la Nigam was over. Later, I learned that the DDA bylaws required a vote by all the members present. However, Mr. Nigam, who had developed the bylaws, decided to ignore them. He was the bylaws! The members present either did not know the bylaws, did not care or were afraid to challenge the Big Man. Most of them wanted to get the so-called election over with so they could go to a tea shop and chat.

Mr. Nigam shook hands with me. This was the first time he had shaken my hand. In India, one did not shake hands with people of lower status. I had climbed a rung up in the Delhi Deaf community's hierarchy. He had me shake Suraj's hand and then asked everyone to quiet down. I wanted to go back and sit down in the anonymity of the people sitting on the dhurrie, but he held onto me.

"With Suraj and Madan, we will be able to raise the DDA to its old glory. But they need your help. Will you all cooperate with them?" It was not a question, but an order. Everyone raised their hands and we were "elected" unanimously.

As I look back, my standing up on that hot and sultry evening was not just a physical act; it was a venture into a new life. This helped me stand up on my own feet and later help others. The walk from the anonymity of the dhurrie to the folding chair of importance only took a few steps, but sometimes, such steps lead to another world.

23

Life Becomes Busier

THAT WAS MY INITIATION INTO THE WORLD of leadership. Suraj and I met the next day. He was serious as usual. He discussed his plans for rejuvenating the DDA. He wanted to establish regular weekly membership meetings, open the defunct library, have cinema nights, start a cricket club, and so forth. After he had shared his plans for the DDA, he told me he wanted me to start writing letters to various government and private organizations asking for money and permission to start some of the programs. He did not ask me for ideas for expanding the DDA, and I was glad since I did not have any. Anyhow, it was clear that my main role would be to write letters and be his sidekick. That was fine with me.

My life changed again. I already was working from 7:00 a.m. to 11:00 p.m. six days a week. Now Sunday was also gone. On Sunday morning, I would ride my bike about eight miles to the Ferozshah Kotla playgrounds, which were just outside the national cricket stadium.

I had never played cricket, but I needed to show support for the new DDA cricket team of which I was now a member by default. We practiced every Sunday from 9 a.m. to noon. Then I would ride my bicycle back to Subzi Mandi. The main thing I remember about these practices was the headache I used to develop because of hunger. I used to leave home in the morning after drinking one cup of tea. There was no food or drink available at the playground. My headache would go away after returning to 52/5 and devouring a huge lunch. After lunch, I would rest for a few hours. Resting meant playing with my nephews and nieces and talking with adults and guests. Bhai Narain was a popular guy and had a big heart. All his friends and our relatives dropped by to chat. Bharjai Krishna and sister Kamla spent most of their Sunday afternoon making tea and snacks. Some of these guests lingered for dinner also.

At about 4:00 p.m., I would take the bike again and ride six miles to Kamla Market, where I would meet Suraj at the tiny DDA office in the back of the DDA wood shop. The office had a small desk with two chairs for us. A very old Remington typewriter sat prominently on the desk. After discussing a few ideas, I would write letters while Suraj did accounts. I looked wistfully at the typewriter, which was older than me, but was afraid to touch it. Typewriters were a mystery, and I was afraid I'd break them.

Around 6:00 p.m., various DDA members would start to drop in. There was no room to sit, so they would hang around in the corridor between the rows of closed shops. We conducted short meetings in the corridor to agree on activities for the DDA. After that, we drank tea and broke into smaller groups to chat. Suraj would go back to Cannaught Place to spend the evening with Nigam and his court, while I stayed there to hobnob with my friends.

Slowly, we made changes. The wood shop was not getting much business. We decided to close it and use the area for a small library and game room. The letters I sent resulted in enough donations for us to purchase some furniture, several board games, books, and subscriptions to some magazines. Soon the old wood shop was transformed into a nice meeting and club room.

I enjoyed this role as an important member of the Deaf community. It gave me a sense of accomplishment, and I liked the attention that I got as an office holder. The deaf people who used to avoid me were now hovering around me.

This had a downside as well. I began to learn that the main goal of the AIFD was to raise enough money to run the office and pay for Nigam's annual trip abroad. Each year, Nigam went to another country for the World Federation of the Deaf's annual conference or some other meeting, and the AIFD paid all the expenses. The rupee was fine in India, but it did not buy much abroad. A roundtrip ticket to Europe and hotel costs easily added up to about 10,000 rupees, which was more than the combined annual salaries of the four AIFD staff members and more than thirty years of my salary as a teacher in the adult literacy class!

Everyone in the organization understood that Nigam was dipping into the till and using the federation money for his lavish lifestyle and expensive trips, yet no one had the nerve to discuss this with the members

At a picnic with deaf friends: Harish Chugh, his wife, Rajkishore's wife, Rajkishore.

of his entourage, including Suraj. No one wanted to be the sacrificial goat and be subjected to Nigam's wrath for speaking up.

Where did this money come from? Nigam never missed a chance to tell us how he had earned a lot of money while working in Germany for two years and had saved every mark. He would claim that he never touched one *paisa* (penny) from the AIFD. No one believed him, but everyone, including me, nodded their head in agreement.

One source of income was the annual Flag Week. During November of every year, National Flag Week for the Deaf was observed. The AIFD put a lot of effort into planning this event each year. The PID was closed for one week and about 100 deaf people were let loose all over the city in groups of three or four to collect donations by selling miniature Indian flags.

I did not like this work, but there was no choice. We had to "volunteer" for this "begging work," as Kesh called it. We were told that the PID operated with the money raised during Flag Week. Nigam and his close friends also worked as volunteers, but only for a few hours and only to pin flags on VIPs, such as the president and the prime minister. Their photographs were published in newspapers. We, the lowly ones, did the dirty work of pinning flags on office clerks who could ill afford to give us money.

Later, I learned that the AIFD earned about 5,000 rupees each year from this campaign. I figured it covered half of Nigam's annual trip to Europe or America. It bothered me that we all had to go out and beg for paisas so Nigam could make his trip.

During my long bicycle rides and while working in the darkroom, I would plan ways to expose Nigam. I would discuss my thoughts with Kesh and my other friends. They told me it was not worth my time and effort, and Nigam would crush me like a mosquito. Thus my grandiose plans were never implemented. I was very brave when alone or with my trusted friends, but I was the proverbial chicken when it came to actually confronting Mr. Nigam.

However, I continued to enjoy my busy schedule. Each day was a new challenge. Once again, I was settled for life!

24

Goyle's Death

I HAD ALREADY BEEN IN DELHI FOR A YEAR and was feeling good about myself and what was happening in my life. Then an incident changed things.

On July 13, I arrived at the PID a little before 7 a.m. and found the door still locked. Soon other students, including Kesh, Raj Kishore, Khurana, and Goel, showed up. We waited in the narrow and dark corridor for Goyle or one of his assistants to come and open the door. It was not uncommon for them to be late. We enjoyed this free time by talking to each other and wiping the sweat from our brows with handkerchiefs.

One hour passed and no one had arrived yet. This was fine with us; we could talk and tell jokes. "Let him be late," we said. The atmosphere was relaxed because we knew Nigam was out of town. Were he around, he would have berated us for standing around and doing nothing, even though it was not our fault.

Kesh began to tell, or rather invent, all kinds of jokes right on the spot. He decided that Nigam had gone somewhere with a woman on a false honeymoon.

"That is not very nice," Raj Kishore said. He was very proper and did not like Kesh ridiculing the number one leader of the deaf in India. "He is too interested in improving the lot of deaf people to be chasing women like you."

Kesh was waiting for such an opening and began to taunt Raj Kishore by asking him if Nigam was a eunuch. Then Kesh, a master mime and actor, began to copy Nigam's walk as if he were a *hijra*, a common Indian eunuch or transvestite. We laughed at Kesh's acting. Even Raj Kishore had a hard time not smiling.

Then we saw Suraj at the end of the corridor walking toward us. We quieted down and stood there at attention. Suraj looked puzzled.

"What are you doing here?" he asked. Kesh pointed at the locked door and shrugged his shoulders, mimicking American tourists. We would have burst out laughing but for Suraj's stoic presence. Raj Kishore became uncomfortable again, but did not say anything. He knew that we would shun him if he ratted on Kesh and his Nigam imitation.

Suraj told us to wait and opened the AIFD office. We stood there quietly. He returned in a minute with a key and opened the PID. We went in, opened all the windows to let some air in, turned the fan on, and began to clean the worktables with rags. This was our duty as students. Suraj stood in the middle of the room under the fan and asked if anyone had seen Vassand or Subramanium. We replied that we had not. It was almost 9:00 a.m., and Goyle had never been that late before. Suraj sent Raj Kishore to the Goyle Studio to find him. Raj Kishore left and Suraj asked us to start working on our projects. Kesh, Goel, and I headed into the darkroom. Khurana decided to stay out and work on coloring a portrait. We did not have color film then, so we colored the black and white prints for people who wanted color pictures.

We had not even finished putting the chemicals in the trays, when Suraj poked his head through the darkroom door and asked us to come out. We were puzzled. He asked us to sit down and told us that Raj Kishore had learned from Vassand that Goyle had a motor scooter accident the night before and had died. We sat there feeling shell-shocked. I had just seen him the evening before. He was so alive. Now he was dead!

This was not my first experience with death. People died in Gagret all the time, and it was customary to cremate the bodies. I had the dubious honor of carrying a couple of *seedhis*, the ladder-like bamboo structures used for carrying the dead, to Shiv Bari where we cremated our dead. All deaths hurt, but Goyle's death had an impact on me.

Besides being my teacher, he was my role model. He could not read or write, but he was an excellent photographer. He, a deaf man, had run a successful business in a hearing world. He had just bought himself a Vespa, the very popular Italian motor scooter. Owning a Vespa was a status symbol, and no other deaf person in Delhi owned one. This status symbol that he loved so much had killed him.

We sat there in silence as Raj Kishore told us the details. Goyle had gone for dinner at his friend's house the night before. After dinner, he had ridden his Vespa home. His parents, with whom he still lived, were used to his coming home late. However, when he had not arrived home by morning, they began to make inquires. His friend said that he had left around 10 p.m. after dinner. Where could he have gone?

They called the police and hospitals, and after a few hours of probing, they traced him to a hospital where his body lay. He had fallen from his scooter at a turn on an isolated road and his head struck a rock. He died from the impact.

Hindus, unlike Muslims and Christians, cremate their dead. We were told to go to the Pusa Road cremation grounds where his body was to be cremated that afternoon. We rode the bus or our bikes to the crematory and waited with more than 200 others who had come to join the ritual and "throw in wood."

We stood there in groups in the shade of the few trees. The sun was fiercely hot. The body was brought from the hospital and put on the wood pyre while the priest chanted mantras. Goyle's father followed the priest's instructions and threw flowers, water, rice, and vermillion into the pyre before setting it ablaze. We all picked up twigs and threw them into the burning pyre.

Seeing a man with whom I had been talking only fourteen hours earlier being put on a pile of logs and then burned was a great lesson on the brevity of life. As I watched, I thought of meeting Goyle for the first time, and then being hired by him. I thought of his generosity.

A few months earlier, I had borrowed a close-up lens from him for taking some photographs at home. I carried the expensive lens in my lunchbox, which I tied, as usual, to the carrier on my bicycle. When I arrived home one evening, I found the lunchbox missing. I had been carrying my lunchbox that way for almost a year and had never lost it. Trying to find it on the six-mile bicycle route in heavy traffic was like searching for a needle in a haystack.

The close-up lens cost about 100 rupees, four months of my salary at the Goyle Studio. I did not have the nerve right away to tell him that I had lost the expensive piece; I decided that I would pay him. So after three days of trying to collect courage, I approached him.

"How much did the close-up lens cost?" I asked.

He smiled and waved me away. He already knew that I had lost it. My classmates with whom I had shared my plight had already told him what happened. He was just waiting for me to admit it.

"Forget it," he said. "But promise to be more careful in the future."

I breathed a sigh of relief and thanked him. He waved me away as if it was nothing. My classmates who were waiting eagerly for a good tongue-, or rather hand-lashing, were disappointed.

Now, I looked at the burning pyre and thought of him, and hoped that I would be equally generous to someone in my life.

As the fire began to die, people started to leave. His students and employees got together and cried. We had all grown close during the year of working together.

Mr. Goyle's father called to Vassand, Raj Kishore, Subramanium, and me, telling us in gesture to come to the studio the next day at the usual time. He asked Vassand to print a few large copies of his son's portrait and frame two of them. Then we left. The school and the studio were closed for the day.

The next morning, I arrived a bit before the shop was to open. Vassand was already there and had hung an 8-x-10 enlargement of V. R. Goyle in a golden frame. He had also purchased a flower garland and a box of incense. Mr. Goyle's father arrived by taxi. He walked slowly, like any father in his late sixties who had lost his young son would walk—looking tired and beaten.

The senior Mr. Goyle led us in installing his son's image. The photograph was hung so people could see it as they entered the studio. The marigold garland was draped over it. Mr. Goyle shook hands with us and told us, partly in gestures and partly in signs, to go home as the shop was going to be closed that day and to return the next day to work as usual.

However, a lot of things were not usual after that.

25

Changes in School and Work

MR. GOYLE'S DEATH AFFECTED OUR LIVES way beyond what we had imagined. Suraj told us to continue practicing various skills—negative retouching, taking portraits, developing and printing film, retouching prints, and whatever else we had done before. He asked me to decide on who would do what and then left.

Everyone wanted to work in the darkroom, which created some controversy. It took me awhile to restore order, and I had to use the memory of our respected departed teacher to make them follow my directions. We worked very seriously for half the day and then began to slack off. The death of our teacher weighed heavy on us. We wondered who our next teacher would be. After a couple of hours, Kesh suggested we sit down and discuss our plans for the future. I agreed.

"Who will teach us new skills and who will criticize and provide input on our work to improve it?" Kesh asked. "We cannot learn photography by ourselves."

All of us agreed that it was a cause for concern. We knew how the AIFD operated. They would ignore us unless we made them understand that a new teacher was a must. We decided to discuss the issue with Suraj. Raj Kishore went to the AIFD office next door and brought Suraj with him. Suraj was not happy at being called by lowly students and asked us why we were making problems.

"We need to know when a new teacher will come in," declared Kesh.

"Soon as Mr. Nigam returns," Suraj said with his usual serious demeanor.

"Where is he?" Kesh asked, "Has he gone to England or some other country?"

Suraj raised a warning finger at Kesh and told him not to be disrespectful to Mr. Nigam. He was, according to Suraj, out conducing important business. He would return soon.

"His best friend has just died," Kesh continued, "and he is conducting important business?"

It was obvious Suraj did not know where Mr. Nigam was. He looked a bit worried about it. I felt sorry for him. He was trying to shield someone whom he respected but also had begun to doubt. I was also impressed with his authority and wished I had even half of it.

For the next two weeks, we kept practicing what we already knew. In between, we wasted time talking to each other and sneaking out for long tea breaks while covering for each other. Suraj would come in once in a while to check on us, but all he could do was preach to us. Kesh tried to give him a hard time, but Suraj would cut him off with "Do not talk silly."

We had to wait for Mr. Nigam to return so he could hire a teacher to replace Goyle. But where was he? When was he returning? We were told to shut up and wait.

One morning, when we were all working on various projects, Mr. Nigam came rushing into the room. He was fully dressed in a dark suit and tie. He stepped quickly to the table where Goyle's garlanded photograph was sitting and bowed his head in front of it; he appeared to be crying. We saw his body shake as he sobbed. Suraj came in and patted his shoulder, but Mr. Nigam pushed him away without even looking. He kept his head on his forearm and kept sobbing. Puzzled by his behavior, we looked at each other. To me Kesh signed, "He is fooling us," when the others were not looking. I did not think of it before, but Kesh was right. The guy was acting.

After about a half an hour, Mr. Nigam's sobs decreased and he let Suraj guide him to a chair. He wiped his tears and refused to look at us. He would look at Goyle's photograph and start to cry again. This drama went on for more than hour. Finally, his crying subsided and he started to talk to us.

"We have been friends for thirteen years. We were like brothers. I do not know how I will be able to live without him."

After that, he began to talk about the future. He was going to get the best teacher for us and soon. Then he was gone.

We began to talk to each other about Mr. Nigam and his sorrow. Kesh laughed, "I saw him last night with Suraj and Rameshwar as the three walked out of that fancy restaurant. He was not crying then. He was just trying to impress us with his great love!"

I believed Kesh. A grown man does not cry like that, especially in front of young students. He wanted to show us how much he cared; but, in fact, he had demonstrated that he did not care for anyone except himself.

Of course, a new teacher was not hired anytime soon. Suraj would tell us that a teacher was coming soon, but this "soon" changed from weeks to months, and we still had no teacher.

Finally after three months, they hired a hearing man named Yadav. We did not know where or how Mr. Nigam had found him. He just showed up in the PID room with Mr. Nigam in the middle of the day and interrupted our deep discussion. We moved to our work areas and stood at attention like good students.

Mr. Nigam introduced Mr. Yadav as having a lot of experience in the film industry as a photographer. He was, according to Mr. Nigam, also a writer and a director. We were impressed and glad to know that Mr. Nigam had not just picked up anybody off the street.

Mr. Yadav did not know sign language. That was expected; he was hearing. However, soon we also learned that he did not know photography, at least the kind we were learning. He claimed to be learning sign language, but was never really able to communicate effectively with the hardcore deaf people.

He did work as a photographer, but all he did was take some still photographs. His darkroom expertise was abysmal. He spent almost half an hour adjusting lights when he took photographs of a little girl. We were used to the efficiency of Mr. Goyle. He had established everything in concrete. Mr. Yadav was an artist who believed in and encouraged creativity. Mr. Goyle treated us as journeymen apprentices and taught the trade of photography. Mr. Yadav believed the PID was a school and considered photography an art. Mr. Goyle's approach fitted us better, as we were planning to work as darkroom assistants or negative retouchers in some commercial photographer's shop.

Through his stooges, word got to Mr. Nigam about our dissatisfaction with Mr. Yadav. He came into the PID one morning and explained how wonderful Mr. Yadav was. "He is a writer and an artist," he told us.

"He cannot even retouch a negative," Kesh said. Mr. Nigam was a master in the arts of debate and fact distortion. He explained why he had picked Mr. Yadav. We already knew how to retouch negatives and how to process and print film. Mr. Yadav, continued Mr. Nigam, was going to teach us the artistic aspects of photography.

"He cannot sign at all," Kesh complained.

"He will learn," said Mr. Nigam. "Look at Madan. He did not know signs at all. Now he signs better than you." We laughed, but we also knew that Mr. Yadav lacked the motivation or desire to learn signs.

However, we agreed with him, as we knew Mr. Nigam would never give up and would keep inventing rationales to justify his selection. We also knew the main reason he had selected Mr. Yadav: He had excellent writing skills and so was made to draft all kinds of letters begging for government grants. He was also, we later learned, ghostwriting a book about deafness for Mr. Nigam. This Hindi book was published later as *A World Without Silence*. Mr. Yadav, who knew nothing about deafness, spent most of his time in the American Library doing research. That work paid off; *A World Without Silence* was a very well-written book. I doubt Mr. Nigam, the declared author, could read it as it was written in very fancy Hindi. Mr. Nigam's Hindi was rudimentary, and his English was limited to a lot of vocabulary to impress other deaf people.

One change was made after this meeting: Mr. Nigam decided that Mr. Yadav would teach by writing and I would interpret his written messages into signs. We all agreed as we knew disagreement with Mr. Nigam would only get us into hot water. Even Kesh, who enjoyed needling him, shut up.

The first class using Mr. Yadav's writing and my signing was a bust thanks to Kesh. I enjoyed reading Mr. Yadav's writing. He had beautiful handwriting and wrote very fast. Kesh, however, insisted on distorting everything that I signed.

Mr. Yadav wrote, "I will show you a negative." I signed this statement. The sign for negative is same as the sign for black—the index finger running downward on the temple. Kesh responded, "He means he is pea brained." The sign for pea brain is similar, except the index finger goes lower and closes with the thumb—to show the size of the brain.

I had a hard time not laughing. The others began to giggle as well. Kesh's fertile mind distorted everything that Mr. Yadav wrote and I signed into a hilarious situation. Soon Mr. Yadav knew he was not getting anywhere and left the classroom.

We laughed like crazy at his hasty departure, but also got worried. We thought he might complain to Mr. Nigam, and then we would be subjected to his wrath. However, Mr. Yadav never told Mr. Nigam, and we decided not to complain about his signs. We had started to like him as a person.

As previously stated, Mr. Yadav spent most of his time out of the classroom, apparently doing research for Mr. Nigam. That was fine with us. We continued our daily routine of retouching negatives, taking photographs, developing films, and making prints. Kesh and I began to cut classes for a little fun. Once such a trip almost got us arrested, but that is another story.

26

Have Tongue, Will Speak!

SEEING THAT THERE WAS NO TEACHER IN THE school, Kesh and I decided one morning to skip class and go for an adventure. Little did we know that we were going to have the adventure of a lifetime!

The president of India lives in the *Rashtarpati Bhawan* (President's House). Each March, the house's garden and grounds, known as the Mogul Gardens, were opened to the public. This particular year, Kesh and I decided to go see them. We did not own a camera and could not borrow one from the PID.

It was spring and we were in our early twenties. The excitement of being in the fresh air instead of cooped up in the darkroom had us in good spirits. Kesh kept on talking about his professional dancing program and I kept nodding my head.

The garden was really beautiful! It had a million varieties of roses and other flowers. We walked around looking at them, admiring their beauty. After about an hour, however, we had had enough and were ready to leave, when we saw the president, Dr. Rajendra Prasad, who had been sick for a few weeks, being wheeled around in the secure part of the garden. We stopped in our tracks and watched him; we even moved a bit closer to get a better view of India's number one man.

Once he was out of sight, we decided to call it a day and started to walk toward one of the exits. As we arrived at the gate, a uniformed policeman blocked our way and told us something. I asked if this was the exit. He just said something and pointed to the path. I did not understand him but assumed he was telling us that the gate was closed for some reason. Kesh and I continued talking and laughing and found the other exit. However, just as we reached it, two policemen blocked us and pointed to a path that ran between the rose bushes. We were both puzzled, and I asked if there was another gate. One of the policemen just kept talking and pointing toward the path. We saw that he was allowing other people to exit the grounds. I told him we were deaf and to please write down the reason for not allowing us to leave so we could understand it.

No answer, just a stern hand pointing to the path between the rose bushes!

I told Kesh that we would try the other gate again. As we walked, Kesh, who had the sharp and observant eyes of a person who had been born deaf, signed to me that we were being followed by six or seven policemen. I did not believe him and looked behind us. Sure enough, several policemen and one inspector were following us.

Something was wrong.

We kept walking and looking back. Sure enough, they were about ten feet behind us. I told Kesh, "Let us try the other exit and see what happens."

We were stopped again!

I asked the policeman why he was sending us back and forth. He pointed to the police inspector who stood there with his baton under his armpit and hands clasped in front of him. He was looking at us with great interest. I walked to the police inspector with Kesh in tow and complained to him: "Look, this policeman is giving us the runaround and is not allowing us to leave."

The police inspector began to talk to me in a calm and officious manner. I told him we were both deaf and requested that he write on a piece of paper explaining what the problem was. He remained still so I fished out a piece of paper and a pen from my pocket and extended them toward him. He ignored the items and started talking to me again. I stood there with a pen in one hand and the paper in the other, wondering what to do. Kesh tried his mime skills on him, which did not result in any positive results either.

Before we knew it, there were more than 100 people gathered around us in a circle. They all kept a respectable distance due to the police. They were more interested in this strange spectacle than the famous and rare roses. I kept talking to the police inspector, explaining about the roses and how beautiful they were, while simultaneously signing to Kesh my opinion of the police inspector's intellectual level. Kesh smiled, and we both looked at our captive audience. We were providing excellent entertainment.

While trying to look calm, I was also getting scared and wondering what was wrong. I told the inspector a third time that we could not lipread and that he must write and explain to us why we were not being allowed to go. It did not work, so I appealed to the crowd. Raising my voice to full volume, I told them in an appealing tone, "We are two deaf people and were looking at the flowers just like you, and this police inspector is holding us and not allowing us to leave. He is not even explaining the reason for keeping us here!"

The police inspector kept his marathon silence, and the people around us began to talk with each other. Finally, one guy broke ranks and came toward me. Two alert policemen jumped to stop him, but the inspector told them to stay away and talked to the brave person who showed him a paper with something scribbled on it. The inspector, after inspecting the paper, gave it to me.

The guy had written, "They do not believe you are deaf, and they think you were trying to kill the president."

I read it twice and could not believe it. I signed to Kesh, who mimed his amazement. I laughed and signed to him how dumb the policemen were. We both laughed, but I am sure the laugh must have looked like I was crying.

Very nicely, I told the policeman that we were deaf and had no reason to fake our deafness. We would never even think about harming our beloved president who supported deaf people a great deal. The police inspector stood there like a statue and kept talking. Our friend from the crowd transcribed what he was saying for me.

"If you are deaf, how can you talk like a hearing person?"

I explained how I had been deaf for only ten years, therefore, still had what he called "normal" speech. I volunteered that Kesh was born deaf and never learned to speak.

The inspector came forward and asked Kesh in gestures to open his mouth. Kesh opened his mouth. This made me really angry. It was derogatory. I told Kesh to close his mouth and confronted the policeman. This was a mistake; it only made the police inspector more suspicious.

Kesh had more sense than me and, pushing me aside, opened his mouth and went as close as possible to the police inspector who looked at his tongue closely and pushed Kesh back with his baton.

"He has a good tongue. He should be able to speak. They are faking." The police inspector expressed his erudite observation, which our friend transcribed for my benefit.

I could not believe this ignorance. The anger and frustration were building up in me, and I felt like hitting the policeman. However, knowing how violent Indian police are, I checked myself and calmly began to talk to him.

"I know you are doing your duty, but believe me, we are both deaf. We wandered into the wrong area by mistake. You can call Mrs. Nigam — she is the president of the All India Federation of the Deaf—and ask her if we are deaf or not."

Dropping names always helps. This got the inspector's attention. Some of the men in the crowd had also started to talk to him, apparently in our support. Finally, after what seemed like ages, he stepped back and pointed us both toward the exit.

By that time, my patience had run out. The crowd around us had made me brave. I stepped six inches from the police inspector's face and began to yell at him. "You and your staff have nothing to do! There are people being murdered in the street, and all you are doing is following two innocent deaf people!" I noticed the look on the police inspector's face and knew this was a mistake. Kesh acted fast and pulled me away. I let him pull me, but also made a big show of trying to stay there.

We were let go. We had our adventure. We not only saw the president up close, but were also accused of trying to assassinate him. I spoke of my wonderful experience at home and everyone laughed. But we never told our friends in school; we were supposed to be sick at home that day.

27

New Teachers

MR. YADAV BECAME MORE AND MORE IMPORTANT to Mr. Nigam as a writer, and his presence in the classroom became rarer and rarer. We knew there was no alternative but to stay quiet and wait to get our diplomas so we could get jobs.

Mr. Nigam, however, surprised us again. One day, he brought in a very well-dressed mustached man with military bearing. This was Mr. Lal, another teacher.

"You will have two teachers now," declared Mr. Nigam. "Mr. Lal is an expert in darkroom and other technology. He worked for the Indian Navy as a photographer." We were impressed again.

We were also disappointed again. Mr. Lal did not know much about darkroom work and almost nothing about lighting and retouching. He *had* worked as an aerial photographer in the Navy, but his job had been to click the shutter while lying on the belly of a small plane. He had picked up some darkroom skills from his Navy buddies. That was all, but we liked Mr. Lal.

Mr. Lal soon grasped the situation. He began to talk to us. He picked up some signs and could reasonably communicate with all the students. With me, he wrote and I spoke. Soon, I became his official interpreter. This plan had failed with Mr. Yadav due to Kesh's own efforts at interpreting my interpreted messages. With Mr. Lal, it worked as we all became his friends. He even went out for tea with us—which was a no-no for a teacher. A teacher was not supposed to socialize with his students; however, Mr. Lal had lived in England and other countries and had different ideas. I socialized with my students as we were all deaf and friends.

I enjoyed Mr. Lal because he was patient. He treated us as regular people and not as deaf people. Despite the fact that he had never met a deaf person before, he adapted to us as if he had known us all his life.

He talked about his family and asked about ours and joked with us. The most important thing about him was that he was in class on time every day and worked with us until the school closed in the afternoon.

A couple of new students were admitted, and I learned about something that was stranger than signing—lipreading. Govind Uppal and Rupam Goswami were both profoundly deaf; they did not sign. But not only could they talk, they also understood people just by looking at their lips.

Mr. Lal, on the first day of Govind's and Rupam's arrival, talked to them as if they were hearing. I could not believe it, and, seeing my role as the unofficial interpreter diminished, I asked Mr. Lal what this charade was about.

"They can lipread me," he said. His lips were barely visible under his heavy military moustache.

I still could not believe it and decided to test them. I looked at them and asked in Hindi, "What is your name?" Govind spoke his name and Mr. Lal beamed. Rupam got confused.

"He does not know much Hindi," Mr. Lal wrote. "He is from Assam and knows some Bengali, but is fluent in English."

It took me awhile to accept the fact that other people could lipread, but I couldn't. Kesh told me he knew of deaf people who could lipread and that he could also lipread when hearing people yelled obscenities at him. That was his limit. I laughed and let the matter of lipreading go.

Meanwhile, things changed at the Goyle Studio. Vasand was the head honcho there because of his seniority. The first thing he did was to fire Subramanium. Raj Kishore and I witnessed that "firing." Without any warning, Vasand told Subramanium just before closing shop, "Do not come tomorrow."

Subramanium smiled. He thought Vasand was joking. "And day after tomorrow, right?" he tried to joke. But Vasand was not joking. "Right," he said very seriously. "You are finished here."

"But why?" Subramanium was not smiling anymore. "Who will do negative retouching?" He was the best one.

"Raj Kishore," Vasand told him. "Now go!"

Subramanium looked at us helplessly. Raj Kishore seemed to know already. He and Vasand were close. I looked at Vasand in order to support

Subramanium, but seeing his expression, I decided to stay quiet. He might tell me not to come tomorrow, I thought.

Subramanium's firing did not change our workload much. Raj Kishore picked up Subramanium's retouching, and I began to do more darkroom work. But we knew that Vasand did not fire Subramanium due to a lack of work. He fired him because he disliked him. They were never good friends. Vasand tolerated him because Goyle liked Subramanium's retouching skills. Now no one was there to stop Vasand from getting rid of his rival.

Soon Raj Kishore and I began to notice that Vasand was fixing the daily accounts. Each night after the studio was closed and shuttered, after counting the day's income, he picked up 5 or 10 rupees. His "take" began to increase on a weekly basis. Stealing and drinking are habits that feed themselves; Vasand did not make them a secret. To win our support, he began to order tea and snacks just before closing with, "I am buying that for you."

Since Vasand and Raj Kishore were close friends, I decided to stay mum about this. It was not my money, I told myself. Goyle's father could do with a few rupees less. Vasand's lifestyle changed. He began to visit fancy restaurants and pay for his friends' snacks. He became more popular. Money makes one popular very fast.

I finished my two years at the PID in July of 1963. The senior Goyle offered me full-time work in the studio with a salary of 125 rupees. This, with my 25 rupees from the night school, brought my total income to 150 rupees a month. This was not bad for a deaf boy. I was making more money than most other deaf people in the city.

Then things changed again!

About eight months later, one night when I was teaching the class, Mr. Nigam sent Suraj to get me. I followed him but was filled with trepidation. Mr. Nigam looked like he was in a good mood. He asked me to sit down, which was an honor. Mostly, he left people standing while he talked with them.

"You are going to start teaching in the PID tomorrow." He told me. I sat there in a shock. "Mr. Lal . . ." I started to say.

"We got rid of Mr. Lal today. Tomorrow you start teaching." He was smiling.

"What about my work at the Goyle Studio?" I asked.

"Vasand will find someone else," he told me, and the case was closed. I wanted to ask about the salary. I knew Mr. Lal was paid 300 rupees a month. I hoped I would be paid the same money.

"You will be paid 150 rupees a month," he said as if he was doing a great favor for me. I did not have the nerve to discuss it further. I calculated that with the night school salary, this would still be a 25-rupee raise for me. In addition, I would have free time after school was closed.

I said, "Fine," and clasped my hands in "Thank you." I was dizzy with this rapid change in my career.

The next day, I rode my bicycle straight to the PID and learned that Mr. Nigam had also hired Kesh to teach. I was the head teacher and responsible for teaching theory and keeping accounts. Kesh was to teach darkroom skills and would be paid 125 rupees a month. We were both happy as we were close friends, and working together all day was something we enjoyed.

Vasand learned about my change of jobs through the grapevine. When I saw him the following evening—he was in my night class—I told him why I was not at the Goyle Studio all day. He said sadly that he knew. He needed another hand, but he was also afraid of Mr. Nigam and did not say anything. I felt better.

We had six students at the PID. Of these, Uppal, Bhushan, and Goswami had joined the PID when Kesh and I were still students. It was a little awkward for the two of us to change our roles from that of fellow student to teachers; however, gradually we adjusted to it. We all got along very well. The classes were fun. Kesh kept everyone on their toes with his quick wit and humor.

At the end of the month, I got my first check from the AIFD. It was for only 150 rupees. I asked for my night class teaching money as well and was told that the 150 rupees was for both of my jobs. I did not like it, but there was nothing to do about it. One could not negotiate with Mr. Nigam. I was also too proud to talk money. But it hurt.

This was not all. About a month after we had started teaching, Kesh and I were told by Suraj that Mr. Nigam wanted us to stay in school and work after the students were gone.

"What work?" Kesh asked.

"I will give it to you tomorrow," Suraj said with his usual seriousness.

Kesh and I were not happy. Kesh, in his anger, even declared that he was going to quit. But we both knew we had no choice but to accept this additional workload without additional salary.

The next day, we were told to take photographs of new houses being built in Hauz Khas, a posh suburb in New Delhi. Mr. Nigam's elder brother was an architect. These photographs were for him.

It was May and the sun was really hot at 1:00 p.m. We took two cameras and a few rolls of film and rode the bus to Hauz Khas. We were told that we would be reimbursed for our bus fare. When we exited the bus at Hauz Khas, I saw some people throwing away their tickets when getting off.

I had an idea! I told Kesh to pick up all the bus tickets that he could find on the pavement and started to do that myself. Kesh was puzzled, but he also knew from my expression that these tickets would be valuable. We made our way to the nearest tea stall and ordered piping hot tea. Kesh kept asking me what we were going to do with the bus tickets we had picked up.

I explained that since we were being forced to work without any salary, and since this work was really for Mr. Nigam's brother and not for deaf people, we had to get even.

"How? By recycling these used tickets?" Kesh signed. "You are crazy."

I told him of my plan. "We will shoot photographs like crazy today and finish up all the film. We will tell Suraj that we have finished one roll and will return to Hauz Khas tomorrow to shoot more photographs."

"OK, then?" Kesh was still puzzled.

"Tomorrow we will go see a movie from 3 to 6 p.m." I smiled.

Kesh understood after thinking for a few seconds. He slapped his thigh hard and began to laugh. He was thrilled with the idea. The idea of pulling a fast one on Mr. Nigam was more tempting than watching the movie.

The next day and the day after that, we made a big show of leaving the PID with our cameras on our shoulders for the big shoot. After passing the bus stop, we walked to an air-conditioned restaurant and had coffee to while away the time. At 3:00 p.m., we snuck into a movie house and enjoyed still more air conditioning. This was much better than pounding pavements in three-digit heat doing something that we thought was improper. The fact that our cheating was also improper did not occur to us. After all, we were getting even.

We submitted the bus tickets for reimbursement. This paid for our cinema tickets. We laughed at the mere idea of cheating on the Great Cheat.

28

Adventures in Signing

MY FLUENCY IN SIGNING INCREASED AS I
made more friends and used it on a regular basis. However, I was still
shy about signing in public. The main reason was that signing was not
a common sight in India in the early 1960s. Every time my friends and
I signed in public, we drew a crowd of curious onlookers who behaved
in a variety of ways.

There are four kinds of "sign observers." There are glancers,
watchers, starers, and gawkers. The glancers just look at signers for
a few seconds while passing and never look back. We seldom took notice
of glancers as they were serious people who minded their own business,
and sights like two or more persons flailing their arms do not distract
them.

The watchers, on the other hand, stop suddenly in their tracks. They
look at you signing for a full minute, as if they are seeing a horse talking
and then, with their eyes wide, they start walking away from you while
still watching. They do that until they run headlong into a telephone pole
or another person.

Starers are, well, those who just stare. They stop whatever they are
doing when they see someone signing. They come as close to you as they
can and follow your hands and fingers like a boy watching a butterfly
that he wants to catch. Starers make deaf people, especially shy ones like
me, nervous. We can ignore those who watch us from a distance, but
someone staring at you with intensity can disorient you to the point of
losing interest in what you are talking about. One has to either stop
signing or stare back at the starer, who suddenly looks puzzled, wondering
what stopped the action. Then, seeing that we are staring back at him,
he makes a hasty retreat.

The worst kinds of sign watchers are gawkers. They stop and gawk at you, follow your signs, and then try to copy them. They usually end up putting their finger up their nostrils or in their eyes in trying. Some of them become bolder and incorporate some common ribald gestures into their mimicry. One common gesture is making an "O" with the left hand and inserting one's index finger in it with a piston-like movement.

Deaf people deal with the starers and gawkers in our individual ways. Some of us ignore them totally, and others tell them nicely or rudely to get moving. Some will even start a fight if the gawkers refuse to stop gawking and become obnoxious. I found myself involved in many situations with interested onlookers of every stripe. One incident, however, stands out in my memory very clearly.

After a day's work, Kesh and I were on a bus having a nice time chatting. The bus was crowded, and we had to stand in the aisle, holding onto straps attached to the ceiling railing. This meant we had to sign with one hand; however, we kept signing, or rather Kesh kept signing with me nodding or smiling as the situation demanded. He was telling me a funny story that he had invented just then. He was using his talent as a mime to make the story even more interesting.

Kesh was too engrossed in his storytelling to notice, but I saw that everyone sitting on the bus was staring at us. At first I ignored it, but then I began to feel uncomfortable with more than fifty pairs of eyes gazing at us. Kesh noticed my expression and, being very observant, figured out the cause. He told me to ignore them. Then, seeing that I was not paying full attention to his story, he decided to do something to eliminate the competition.

"I know you do not like people staring at us. Do you want me to stop them?" he asked.

"How?" I asked. "Are you going to throw them out of the bus or order them to stop looking at us?"

"Watch me." His fertile mind had thought up some plan and I began to worry.

Without any warning, Kesh pointed out the window with the expression of having seen a ghost. He kept looking there for a few seconds as the bus passed the area he was pointing to. I got concerned and looked outside, following the direction of his pointed finger. There was nothing

Kesh (front) hamming it up at a deaf association picnic.

unusual to be seen, and looked back at Kesh, who winked at me and
continued with his story.

I noticed that our audience had followed Kesh's cue, just like me, and
all of them were looking outside the bus. Of course, there was nothing
to see, and they guessed that they had missed seeing the scary thing and
went back to watching the show the two deaf guys were staging in
the aisle.

A few minutes later, Kesh again pointed out the window with great
fear on his face; but this time, he pointed toward the other side of the
bus. The whole bus looked in that direction and Kesh continued his story.
I began to smile at his antics. Some members of our audience muttered
something to their neighbors and went back to staring at us.

At that point, Kesh suddenly jumped and pointed at the floor of the
bus with his eyes bulging in fear, as if he had seen a snake there. People
quickly looked at the floor in fear. Some even stood up to get a better
view. Kesh had already resumed his story as if nothing had happened.

It must have dawned on most of the passengers that Kesh was pulling
a trick on them. They began to talk to each other. Some smiled in amusement and some looked offended; however, all of them stopped looking

at us. They were either looking outside or examining their hands or staring at the back of the passenger sitting ahead of them.

During the rest of the journey, everyone on the bus ignored us. When Kesh's stop came, he walked proudly down the aisle, smiling at the people who refused to look at him, and jumped out of the still-moving bus. I found an empty seat and waved to him.

29

The Interview of a Lifetime

I WAS COMFORTABLY SETTLED IN MY NEW routine as a teacher at the Photography Institute for the Deaf (PID) and was feeling good about myself. As the joint secretary of the Delhi Deaf Association and a teacher in the night school operated by the All India Federation of the Deaf (AIFD), I held a prestigious position in the Deaf community in Delhi. My workdays were busy but brought numerous joys. Teaching at the PID was fun, and doing volunteer work for the DDA gave me a sense of accomplishment. I spent time with my deaf friends in the evening, drinking tea and laughing at the world. I had begun to think that the course of my life was set, just like three years earlier when I thought I was going to be a farmer for life. All this changed when I saw a three-line advertisement in the *Indian Express*.

It was a Sunday in May. My family and I had slept in the open courtyard and had just woken up to the enjoyable early morning cool of eighty-plus degrees. Bhai Narain, Jijaji Sharma, and I were sitting on cots reading the paper and drinking tea. Karishna, Narain's wife, and Sister Kamla were cutting vegetables for lunch. The six nephews and nieces were still asleep.

The advertisement jumped off the newspaper page at me. The National Physical Laboratory in Delhi needed an assistant photographer. The salary ranged from 150 to 250 rupees. I showed the advertisement to Narain, who read it twice and then pressed his lips together—his habit when he was thinking hard.

"You should apply for it," he said. It was not a suggestion; it was an order.

I said I didn't think I could get that job. Also, I found the salary lacking. Narain, who knew the government salary structure, explained that 150 rupees was the "basic salary," and that with all the other benefits, the total would be about 250 rupees. I was wide-eyed. The fact that the salary would be equal to what Narain was making—he was nine years older than me, had a college education, and was hearing—was unbelievable to me.

"No, I do not think I have any chance," I said decisively. "Everyone who can click the shutter release button will apply for it. This is a government job, and someone whose uncle has a high position will get it anyway. Why bother?"

Narain was irritated. "Maybe you will get this job and maybe not," he admonished. "It will not hurt if you apply. They won't kill you for applying." Jijaji Sharma, who had always thought that I was being exploited by the AIFD, agreed.

That settled it. I was going to apply for the job. The deadline was still two weeks away, but I decided to get it over with. I went into our living-sleeping-family-guest room and found ruled paper and a pen.

The next day, I dropped the letter into the mailbox outside the PID. I did not tell anyone about it, lest they laugh at my audacity. I was also afraid of Nigam and his temper. He would have called me a traitor for even thinking about leaving the teaching job.

Then I got busy with my daily routine and forgot all about it. However, three weeks later, I got a form letter from the National Physical Laboratory (NPL). I was invited for a "practical examination in photography" and an interview. I read the letter repeatedly until I had memorized every word in it. Even in my wildest dreams I hadn't thought that I would be called for an interview. I had not mentioned my deafness in my letter and was sure that as soon as they discovered it, I would be kicked out before the interview.

Narain was all smiles when he saw the letter. "I told you it would not hurt," he said.

"I have not gotten the job yet," I responded. "Maybe, they will laugh at me when they learn I am deaf and tell me to get out fast."

"We shall see," said Narain, ever the optimist. "Who knows? You might get the job." He laughed and patted my back. Jijaji Sharma agreed. He frequently got angry when I put myself down.

The night before the practical test, we had a planning conference. Narain, Sharma, and Ramesh told me how to behave and how to answer the questions. They suggested that Narain go with me so he could explain to the interview committee that I was deaf and also help me by writing out their questions.

I did not like the idea. I said, "If you go with me, we will be giving them the impression that I am a little kid and require your help even at work."

They all laughed at that and it was decided that I would go alone.

I was a nervous wreck as I left to go take the practical test. Bhai Narain called the PID folks and told them I was sick and would be out that day. I did not want anyone to know that I was looking for another job. In the morning, I took a bus to the National Physical Laboratory, which was a huge government building surrounded by six-foot-high walls and tall trees. I told the guard at the gate that I had an interview and showed him the letter. I kept looking at him to make sure he was not asking me a question, as I did not want him or anyone to know that I was deaf. The guard did not say anything; he just put my name on an admission slip, and I walked toward the huge and scary building, following the shrub-lined red gravel road.

Upon entering the main door of the NPL, I saw a small crowd gathered in the large lobby. I showed my letter to a guy sitting behind a small desk. He checked my name with the list in front of him and said something, pointing to the group of young men. I assumed he wanted me to join that group. They were my competition.

My heart sank! I stood in one corner and looked at all these men who were competing for this one job. Slowly, I counted and came up with the number—seventy-three, including myself. I silently cursed Bhai Narain for putting me in this situation. I thought about walking out of the lobby, taking a bus, and going home. However, after considering the taunting I would receive at home ("You chickened out!"), I decided to stay there, telling myself, "Now that I have my head in the tandoor (oven), why worry about getting burned?" I walked around and smiled at people. One group especially got my attention. Six people seemed to know each other very well, and people passing through the lobby stopped to shake their hands, exchange a few words, and laugh, slapping each other's backs. It seemed these guys worked here and were being interviewed for the same position. This sent a clear message to me: You have NO chance here, boy!

One thin guy came over to me and started talking. I told him I was deaf and asked him to please write. He took out a pen and we began to converse, him writing and me talking. I learned that actually there were two open positions, the other being junior technical assistant. That position paid more than the assistant photographer. I figured this improved my chances.

At 11 a.m., after an hour waiting in the lobby, a bespectacled man in his thirties came in with a clipboard. He talked for a few minutes and then walked away with one of the applicants in tow. Apparently, this guy was going to take the test first.

Time passed as applicants went to take the test and then returned. I told my new friend to please tell me when my name was called. He agreed; however, he was called before me and left the building after his test. He was a nice guy. On his way out, he told a few people about me and they all shook their heads in unison while looking at me. I smiled at them.

Finally, my name was called. About thirty people were still waiting, and all of them pointed their fingers at me in unison. The guy with the clipboard looked at me with a puzzled expression. He must have wondered at this drama. At that point, a few of my competitors told him that I was deaf. I could not lipread, but could clearly understand their gestures.

Mr. Mehta, the man with the clipboard, was the senior technical assistant. He walked with a swagger and made the "O" sign with his thumb and forefinger to tell me that all was fine. This gesture really warmed me up, and my nervousness lessened a bit. We walked down a long corridor lined with solid wooden doors on both sides. "These must be laboratories where national-level research was being conducted," I thought. I felt important by being in proximity to these important rooms.

I was impressed with the huge air-conditioned darkroom where I took the test. This darkroom was ten times bigger than any darkroom I had ever worked in. Mr. Mehta gave me a typed sheet with instructions. I was given a negative and a scientific magazine. My job was to print and develop an 8-x-10 enlargement from the negative and then copy the magazine on a photostat machine. These were simple enough tasks. After

I developed both prints, Mr. Mehta turned the light on. He viewed both and made another "O" sign. He looked pleased. That gave me some hope.

I walked back to the lobby where the remaining interviewees were still waiting. I made an "O" sign to all of them as I exited triumphantly. At home that evening, I told the story of my great test to everyone in the family. The older nephews wanted to hear it again and again. The younger ones sat there, understanding little, but enjoying the atmosphere of a story being told. I enjoyed their innocent interest in the advancement of my career.

I was to be interviewed the next day. I felt surer of myself. I was told to be there at 10 a.m. All seventy-plus of us waited for our turn. Again, I asked that someone tell me when my name was called. Each time an interviewee would come out, we would stand up, all of us hoping to be called. I had to wait all day long. My turn came at about 3 p.m. Only five or six of us remained, and all of my fellow interviewees pointed their fingers dutifully at me when my name was called.

I went into a very large room. At the end of the room, five fancy people in suits and ties were sitting behind desks and talking to each other. In front of them were the photographs that the candidates had printed the day earlier. I walked in with my heart pounding. As there was no chair, I stood in front of the five desks littered with photographs, crossed my hands behind my back, and waited.

The man sitting in the center opened a manila envelope. I could see my name written on it. He looked at the prints and began to talk to me.

I said, "I am deaf, sir!" I spoke in English to impress them.

They all looked puzzled and began to talk to each other. One of them asked me something. I said, in a soldierly fashion, "I am deaf, sir. Will you please write on a paper?"

That brought more puzzled looks. They all began to talk at the same time and passed the contents of my envelope back and forth. More discussions followed, with all of them bearing expressions like a cow had just walked into the room. I stood at attention and tried to smile. The four or five minutes I stood there seemed like an eternity to me. My heart was still thumping and I was sweating in rivulets. However, I continued smiling as if being interviewed was a daily routine for me.

Finally, the man in the center, he was the director, wrote on a piece of paper in large letters: "You are deaf, how will you be able to work?"

I read the sentence from ten feet away and spoke standing at full attention: "The same way I did this work, sir!"

I pointed at the photographic prints in his hands. This led to another round of back-and-forth discussions. I stood there waiting and smiling like an idiot. The director then waved at me, which told me that I was dismissed. I bowed my head and left the room.

As I came out, the remaining guys looked at me. I did not make the "O" sign this time and left the building with a sinking heart.

The bus ride home was depressing, and I consoled myself by thinking that it was a good experience and that I had had fun. I replayed my five minutes in that room in my head again and again. Something about the facial expressions of two of those important people assured me that all was not lost. They might not pick me, but they must have been impressed with my work. Even from that distance, I could tell that the prints lying in front of them were not as good as mine.

After the interview, I busied myself with work and almost forgot the dreadful experience of the interview. I told myself that I was happy with my job as a teacher and I did not need that government job even with its much higher salary.

In less than a month, I received a letter. I had gotten the job!

I could not believe that I had beaten out a large number of hearing people for that position. Narain had a big "I told you so" smile on his face. I was going to start working at the NPL as an assistant photographer for a nice salary of 250 rupees on July 1.

That position did much more for me. Slowly I began to realize that deafness was not going to stop me from succeeding in life. All I had to do was to venture out, and I might get a better job than the one I had just gotten.

30

Getting Engaged

LIKE ALL YOUNG MEN, I DECIDED THAT I WAS not going to marry. Marriage, I thought, was for the birds; not for avant-garde people like me who had higher causes such as improving the lives of deaf people.

Working with deaf people had given me a lofty goal—making things better for us all. My friends told me horror stories about the deaf schools they had attended. The teachers did not care about them and did not even know how to sign. My dealings with Mr. Nigam had also shown me that deaf adults needed to be united against tyranny and manipulation. We needed better schools, better organization, and, perhaps, a college for the deaf. The idea of getting married just did not fit into this equation.

While still in photography school, I told Bhaiji that I was not going to marry. Period. Sister Kamla and Bharjai Krishna tried to convince me again and again to consent to getting married. "Bhabhi," they said, "is old, and there is a dire need for someone to look after Babuji and Bhabhi." Both Bhai Narain and Sham were working in different cities. Their wives lived with them and spent only one or two months at Gagret. My future wife was supposed to also follow this rotation.

"They are fine," I responded. I was firm. Bhaiji and Jijaji did not pursue the issue. They were men and had gone through this kind of fear of marriage—they knew I would come around sooner or later. My deaf friends did not care one way or the other. They were all unmarried, and some of them were ten or more years older than me.

Then Bhabhi came to Delhi to talk me into getting married. I would get mad when she even mentioned the word *marriage*. She stayed at 52/5 for a month and, because of my busy schedule, only saw me a few minutes at night and in the morning. I told her she had two daughters-in-law, therefore, she should be happy; she did not need a third one!

I really did not want to marry. I had big plans. I was going to dethrone Nigam and become the general secretary of the AIFD. I was going to work with the government and affect changes in the lives of deaf people in India. They were going to have government jobs and excellent schools. I was going to fight the government to get rights for the deaf.

Marriage did not fit into these plans.

For three years, I stayed adamant, and people stopped bothering me about it. Strangely, once they stopped asking me about getting married, I became interested. I thought to myself, "I will need someone to cook my meals and be with me." I needed a wife.

Who was I going to marry?

While I was studying for my high school examination, Bhua Parvati, after one of her trips to her in-laws' house in Lohra, brought back a small girl with her for a visit. The girl was seven, short, and extremely cute. I was sixteen years old at the time, and a kid her age was too old to play with and too young to hold any other kind of interest for me. She, however, soon became a part of the family because, despite her young age and tiny size, she could work. She washed dishes, made chapatis, cleaned the house, and even brought water from the well. Bhabhi, who hated work, had a great respect for hard-working people like Nikki, as the young girl was called. Her full name was Nirmala Devi.

Why am I talking about this seven-year-old girl? She was to be my future wife!

Marriages in India, especially in villages, are arranged. In Indian society, it is taken for granted by every young child—male or female—that their wise parents and the older members of their family will select a suitable boy or a girl for them to marry. Young people have no say in who their life mate will be.

When I was about thirteen years old, I read in a magazine how boys and girls in Europe and America could decide whom to marry. I was shocked. "How shameless!" I thought. "How dare they pick their own life mates?" I found it inconceivable that boys and girls would go out together on what they called a "date"—and that they did this with the full knowledge of their parents!

Nirmala with cousin Ganesh (Uncle Ramhrasad's son)
in Kanpur after we were married, April 1967.

The idea that one should have a voice in picking one's spouse just
never entered our minds. Our parents had married the person their parents
had picked for them, as had our grandparents. They knew what they
were doing, and they also used horoscopes to help make the decision.

The first step in arranging a marriage is to compare the horoscopes
of the prospective bride and groom to make sure all the stars agree. If
the stars do not clash, the boy and the girl are "made for each other."
After that, the matchmaker, who could be anyone who knows both sets
of parents, passes the word that all is well. At this point, the girl's parents
will send a gift—usually a piece of cloth and a coconut—to the boy
through the village barber to "seal the deal." Barbers played an important
role in all sorts of ceremonies.

A boy never marries a girl from the same village or even from an
adjoining village. The question of a boy seeing a girl before marriage

never arose. It was like a lottery; you won or you did not. This system worked. All the married people I knew were happy. They fought, of course, and there was little or no romance. The husband worked; the wife cooked and kept the house. They took care of their old parents and their children.

During one of my visits to Gagret, I was betrothed formally to Nikki of Lohara. At the time, I was twenty-two years old and working at the NPL. Without my knowledge, Bhua Parvati arranged the ceremony when she learned I was coming home for a visit. One evening, Babuji came home early. I wondered what was going on as he followed his schedule very strictly. He told me to go downstairs. I went and found in the courtyard a group of about ten women from our family as well as the neighborhood. They smiled at me, and I could see they were singing. I was made to sit on a settee, and the barber from Lohara came forward with a small bundle in his hand. He applied some sandalwood paste on my forehead and gave me a piece of cloth, a coconut, and one 5-rupee note. I was engaged to be married to a girl!

Bhabhi was crying with joy. She asked me to touch all the older women's feet as a sign of respect. I then went up and touched Babuji's feet. He acted as if nothing had happened.

That was in 1964. Nikki at that time would have been fourteen. I had not seen her since she was seven. We were not going to see each other until after we were married.

After this short engagement ceremony, I returned to Delhi and resumed my busy life. No one discussed marriage arrangements with me, but I picked up pieces here and there. It was decided that the marriage would take place "within a couple of years." That was just fine with me. Bhai Narain was twenty-three years old when he married, as was Sham. I was already twenty-five, but I felt I was too young to marry. I could wait!

31

The Air-Conditioned Darkroom

ON JULY 1, 1964, I STARTED WORKING AS AN
assistant photographer for the Indian National Scientific Documentation
Centre (INSDOC), a new department of the National Physical Laboratory
(NPL). The agency made copies of scientific journals and books for scientists all over India. This was before photocopying machines were common.

My first day on the job did not start well. For some reason, I did not
have my bicycle that day and tried to ride the bus. With my luck, the
buses going in my direction were full to the point of bursting at their
seams. People were hanging out of both doors, and the buses did not
even slow down at my stop. Then I tried to flag down some scooter
rickshaws, but they were full too. It seemed like everyone had a new job
that day and was rushing to report on time. Finally, I took a bus in the
opposite direction and then caught a ride with a scooter rickshaw. I
arrived fifteen minutes late at the NPL gate and found that I had only a
10-rupee note with which to pay the driver. The fare was 1 rupee, and
the driver had no change, so he claimed. I had no choice but to pay ten
times more than the usual fare and run inside to minimize my tardiness.

On entering the office, I found that only three other people had arrived
so far. So much for all the hassle of the morning and trying to be on
time. I was happy to be there. This was a nice big office adorned with
very expensive technical cameras and other equipment. More than that,
it was air-conditioned. The sweat I had worked up by running around
all morning froze in a few minutes. Most Indian government offices
were not air-conditioned back then; however, the reprographic section I
worked in was air-conditioned to protect the chemicals, film, and equipment from extreme heat.

Fourteen people, including myself, worked in our department, which
was headed by Mr. Krishnamurthy. The second in command was Mehta,

the senior technical assistant, or STA. Gopal and Bajaj were the photographers. Gaur and Raju were my fellow assistant photographers. Sunny, Sinha, and Prasad were our darkroom assistants. Finally, there were Kesar, Om, Sharma, and Sat Parkash—the *khalasis*, or peons.

I am introducing my coworkers in order of their positions because these positions played a very important role. Mr. Krishnamurthy, the boss, supervised us all. He was a well-known photographer with several international awards and publications in magazines to his credit. Mr. Mehta's work had also been published and exhibited. He also had commercial experience. Of the other staff, only Bajaj, Parkash, and Sunny had some training in other places as journeymen apprentices. The rest were hired as khalasis and had risen through the ranks.

My job supposedly was to use a reprographic camera to photograph scientific literature as requested by clients. However, since we only had two reprographic cameras, and they were used by Parkash and Bajaj, I was assigned to make photo prints in the darkroom instead.

That day, I shook hands with Mehta, Bajaj, and Gopal. Mr. Krishnamurthy, who was the boss, did not shake hands with me. Mr. Mehta was happy to see me. I learned that he had known Mr. Goyle in Lahore when they were kids. They worked in the same photo studio as apprentices. All my other coworkers gave me furtive looks and left me alone.

Mr. Mehta took me into the darkroom where Sinha, Sunny, Kesar, Om, Ramji, and Sat Parkash were either sitting on counters or standing. They were all in a deep discussion. When I entered, they all stood up to show respect for the STA position. Mr. Mehta introduced me to them. He must have been telling me their names and positions, but I could not lipread at all. I just nodded, smiled, and shook hands. Their reaction ranged from polite acceptance to open hostility. Om was especially openly belligerent. He was a very dark man dressed in a white shirt and pants.

Then Mr. Mehta took me to an enlarger and jabbed his index finger in my chest. I was to work on that enlarger. I had used the same machine during my test, so I was glad to have it. He pointed to the sink and then to Ramji and Sinha. These two were going to work on developing and fixing prints. Sunny was to work on the other enlarger. Kesar and Sat Prakash were to wash, dry, and trim the prints and put them together.

It was almost 11 a.m. now, and I wanted to start working. At the Goyle Studio, we were not allowed to waste even one minute. However, no one appeared to be in a hurry here. After Mr. Mehta left, they all started to talk with each other again. I could tell that they were discussing me; each time I looked at them, I caught them staring, and then they would look away.

After cleaning the lens and condenser, I checked the sheaf of negative wallets to prepare for printing. I shook a box of printing paper to see if it had enough paper; it was full. While I was going through the motions of getting ready for work, I hoped that someone would tell me that all was set and we should turn the lights off. However, they continued talking and looking at me. Sinha lit up a bidi and Om a cigarette. I remembered the sign outside the darkroom door proclaiming "No Smoking" and wondered if they were trying to tell me something by acting macho.

Sunny seemed to read my body language. He walked to me and wrote on paper, "Do you want to start now?" I nodded, and he walked toward the main light switch. I could see other people talking to him in unison, but he ignored them.

When the lights were off, I got the negatives out and opened the box of photographic paper. Slowly, after making a test print, I went to the large sink where Ramji was sitting on a stool and put the paper in the developing fluid. I dipped the sheet with my index finger, and in the murky darkness, I could see some shiny teeth; they were laughing at me. I was puzzled. Ramji pushed me aside and began to stroke the print with his gloved hand. I understood. It was Ramji's full-time job to attend to the developing tray. He put the print in the stop bath, and then Sinha retrieved it and put it in the fixing solution.

I got the hint and began to focus on printing. When I had five or six prints, I took them to Ramji. I glanced at Sunny. His enlarger was right next to Ramji to whom he would directly hand his prints. I was impressed by Sunny's speed. From past experience, I was used to burning or shading each print to make it perfect. Here, you made prints of printed material and just exposed it and threw it in the developing solution. I copied Sunny's system and began to pick up speed.

After about an hour, I understood the system and was working fairly fast. At about 12:15, I noticed that Om was standing next to me and telling me to stop printing. I told him that I would stop at 1:00 p.m. for lunch. He turned the enlarger off and put the paper inside the box. I was puzzled. He was just a khalasi! How could he be ordering me, an assistant photographer, who was two notches above him? I was learning the government system.

Someone turned the light on. I was furious at Om. "Why did you stop me from working?" I asked him.

Om had an amused look on his face. He put his index finger on his wristwatch and gestured that we were "finished."

"What do you mean? We still have forty-five minutes to lunch." I must have been loud; all of them were looking a bit nervous. Om told me in gestures to calm down. They were all looking toward the darkroom door. Obviously, they did not want the boss to hear me.

They all gathered around me. Om, who appeared to be their ringleader, began to write on a piece of paper in Urdu: "We have some rules here. We work from 11 to 12:30 and then from 1:45 to 3:00 p.m. You are not supposed to make more than 200 prints a day."

I was puzzled. They wanted me to work less while I was trying to work hard to impress the boss.

"But if I work less, I will be fired," I said and looked at others for support. They were all stone-faced and looked away. There was no support.

"If you work more, we all will be fired," Om wrote. Everyone nodded in agreement. It took me a while to understand that they wanted to keep production low and create an impression, a false one though, that there was not enough staff. I had a choice to join them or become a pariah.

I sat down on the counter and sulked. They were all sitting or standing in different parts of the darkroom while Om, with a cigarette dangling from the side of his mouth, was talking to them. He looked like a villain in an Indian movie.

At 12:45, Sunny came to me and signed "eat." He had his lunchbox in his hands. I had nothing with me. He opened his lunchbox and put it on the counter. Kesar, Sharma, and Sat Parkash added their lunchboxes. They smiled and asked me to join them. This was the first friendly gesture I had received from them. Om was also smiling as he joined the community lunch. Sinha and Ramji left; they usually ate together with some other friends. They were both from the state of Bihar, and all Biharis hung out together.

Om did not bring lunch; he was mooching like me. He was trying to be friendly now. As I complimented different lunch items, I asked Om if he also forgot his lunch like me. He found a paper and wrote, "I have five kids to support and have no money to eat." I did not feel sorry for him. He had a big stomach and obviously ate well. He kept writing: "The only thing I can bring is my roasted penis. Anyone is welcome to eat it."

I laughed. That was funny. The others did not laugh. They had heard this joke before and, I learned later, were tired of his mooching their food. However, no one had the courage to say so.

After lunch, we all walked to the cafeteria, where we found a table for six people. They ordered tea and talked. I looked at them and surveyed the large hall where about 300 people were eating lunch or drinking tea. Om walked from table to table. People offered him food, and he took a bite here and a bite there. He was a well-known character. He pointed at me while talking to others. His putting his index finger in his ear did not need any explanation. A deaf man was working in the NPL!

Later, while we were drinking the scalding tea, Om brought a very fat man to our table and introduced me to him as the manager of the cafeteria. While I was shaking the manager's hand, Om wrote down a lewd remark, insulting the manager's mother, and showed it to me. I did not know how to react. The manager snatched the paper from me to read what Om had written and guffawed. Then he wrote something about Om's mother and pointed at him. We all laughed, and soon people at the adjoining tables were also laughing.

Om was on a roll. He again wrote on the paper and yelled at everyone, "The manager eats roasted penis." This got more laughs.

I wondered how I was going to survive this lewd group. I did not know they were being polite and actually were being restrained in their behavior! More was to come. Making photocopies of scientific articles from journals and books was the secondary job in our office; the raison d'être for this group was to be as ribald as possible.

32

Working with Hearing People

SLOWLY, I BEGAN TO LEARN THE ROUTINE AT the INSDOC. We started to work in the darkroom at 11 or 11:15 and then continued until 12:30. The official lunch hour was from 1 to 2 p.m., but our unofficial lunch hour stretched close to two hours. We worked again after lunch for a little over an hour and then stopped for the day. During the seven-hour workday—from 10:00 a.m. to 5:00 p.m., we worked a total of three hours or less. During a six-day week, I put in eighteen hours, and I was one of the harder working people there.

Some people, like Om, never worked. He was a peon, but he believed he knew more about photography and darkroom techniques than all of us put together. He said he did not work because he was a khalasi and grossly underemployed. Then there was Raju. He lived about fifty miles from the office and each day arrived about two hours late. After arriving, he would sit and bother Gopal by telling dirty jokes. Gopal clearly liked to work; however, I could tell that he did not want to offend the majority who considered work against their religion. He would try his best to work while laughing at their jokes.

Mr. Krishnamurthy, we called him Sahib, knew who worked and who did not. He pushed those who worked and ignored the others. He clearly did not like the stragglers, but was afraid to challenge them, especially Om.

Not long after I started, they accepted me as part of the group. Sunny and Kesar learned to fingerspell, and the others started to write on their palms to talk to me. Sahib always wrote or asked Sunny to fingerspell for me. Communication, however, was always an issue. In the darkroom, it was difficult enough to see each other; reading lips was next to impossible. In addition, my lipreading ability was "a few points below that of a brick," as a friend had once pointed out to me.

We experienced numerous misunderstandings because, even if I did not understand something, I pretended that I did. Most of the time, things went smoothly; however, sometimes my bad habit caused problems.

Once Sahib wanted to reduce the density of an overexposed film. He asked me if I knew how to use the reducing agent. I did not understand him, but nodded my head anyway. Sunny was nearby, helping Sahib print some photographs, but his gloved hands were in the sink so he could not spell anything for me. He did, however, raise his eyes in warning. I knew I had misunderstood Sahib but was too afraid, too proud, or too dumb to admit my mistake. So, I just picked up the film and walked into our other darkroom.

Needless to say, I made a mess of the project. Sunny later told me that Sahib was livid at my mistake. "That deaf guy should let me know if he does not understand me," he had yelled. But he never came to tell me that I had messed up. Neither did he ask me to do another project for him. Thus, this misunderstanding cut me off from being able to show off my skills.

Another time, my inability to understand him got me in real hot water! Bajaj once brought some pornographic photographs to work and made negatives of them on his reprographic camera. Then he came into the darkroom and made some prints of the hardcore photographs. We all looked wide-eyed at the Americans in the pictures. Sex is a taboo subject in Indian society, and our knowledge about sex was limited to its use for making babies. The erotic sculpture in Khajuraho was, of course, thousands of years old. While we had all previously seen photographs of those statues, seeing American men and women engaged in unimaginable sexual acts left us breathless. Needless to say, many of us wanted our own personal copies of these photographs. Sinha and Ramji refused to even look at them and touched their ears to show they would never look at such sinful scenes.

Bajaj gave me the negatives and asked me to make several copies for other staff members. I made the prints, Kesar developed them, and Sat Parkash was to dry them. We told Sat Parkash to make sure Sahib was not around when he dried the prints. He wanted his own set of prints and assured us that he would be careful.

As luck would have it, Sahib walked in while Sat Parkash was drying the prints. Those prints were lying face down, but they were only 2-x-3 inches in size. All the prints made in our darkroom were generally 7-x-5 inches or larger. So naturally, Sahib was puzzled and, wondering why the prints were so small, picked up a photograph. At that moment, I was in the darkroom, reading a book. I later learned from different people what happened.

Sahib looked at one photograph and got so mad that he started shaking. He yelled at Sat Parkash and told him that he was fired. Sat Parkash looked around helplessly at the others sitting there. They were all equally guilty, but no one wanted to take the blame. Sat Parkash thought fast and said, "These belong to Vasishta, sir!"

"Where is he?" Sahib yelled.

"In the darkroom, sir!" Sat Parkash pointed his shaking finger at the door.

Sahib picked up all the prints and stomped into the darkroom where I was blissfully reading my book. I looked up when his shadow blocked the light and then stood up. He cut a scary figure. His eyes were red, and he was shaking his right index finger at me while holding the dirty photographs in his left hand. It took me but one second to know I was in a pickle. You do not need signs or lipreading skills to understand the message in a situation like this.

I did not understand what he said. All I could do was shake my head. After two seconds, he stomped to the trash can and threw the photographs in it. He went out, and I sat back down, now feeling very scared. I wondered why he seemed to be so mad at me and not at the others.

Soon as he left, Sunny and Kesar walked in. They had seen the drama outside and had heard Sahib yelling at me. Sahib had asked me if I had brought the negatives for these photographs to work. I had said, "yes" without understanding him. Sunny told me that I was being made the scapegoat. I was now terrified. I could lose my job here. My deafness had gotten me into this situation. All of us were equally guilty of this crime—it was a crime, after all. We had used government property for producing pornographic material. I thought if Sahib went out and re-ported me, I would go to jail. I thought of my family learning about what I had done and the embarrassment that would follow.

Kesar told me not to worry. Sahib was just sitting outside in his chair and had stopped yelling. I felt a little better; but at the same time, I felt awful. What would Sahib think of me—that I was a dirty-minded little deaf boy—that I was the only one involved in printing the pornographic photographs? I thought of going out and telling him that I was not the guilty party, but my pride would not let me do that.

After a few minutes of thinking, I made a decision. I got a sheet of paper and a pen and wrote my resignation letter on it. I wrote that I was very sorry about what had happened, and I did not want him to have an awful person like me working for him. "Therefore," I ended my letter, "I am submitting my resignation effective immediately."

I did not tell anyone about what I had written. Sunny and Kesar tried to look, but I told them firmly that it was personal. I walked outside where Sahib was talking to other members of the staff. Without a word, I handed him my letter and walked back into the darkroom. Sunny and Kesar looked scared. They asked me what I had written. They were scared that I was fingering everyone. I told them in a choking voice that I had quit and began to clean out the drawer where I kept a few personal items.

My eyes were full of tears by that time. The embarrassment, worry about looking for another job, and everyone knowing what I had done had driven me to tears. Sunny and Kesar left me alone and talked to each other.

Just as I was finishing putting my stuff in a small bag, Sahib walked in. He had my resignation letter in his left hand and was pointing at it with his right index finger, just like he had done with the dirty pictures only a few minutes earlier. He shook his index finger to and fro in a strong "no" motion. I was wondering what he meant when he walked to the trashcan again and threw my letter into it.

He walked back to me, patted me on my shoulder, and then left the darkroom.

I felt drained emotionally and sat down in my chair. Sunny and Kesar now understood that I had submitted my resignation, but Sahib had torn it up. They looked at me in a strange way. I could not understand whether it was awe or ridicule or wonder. I was too tired to think.

Gradually, things got back to normal. No one ever mentioned the incident again; however, I noticed that my coworkers began treating me with a lot more respect after that.

33

What Is Gallaudet?

SURAJ, WHO HAD BECOME A GOOD FRIEND
while we worked together in the DDA office, told me one evening, "You
need to take two days off from work."

"Why?" I asked. Taking a couple of days off work required submitting
a written application to Sahib and then waiting a couple of days for
approval.

Suraj showed me a letter from an American deaf woman. She was
traveling around the world and was going to stop for a couple of days
in New Delhi. The date of her arrival was going to be the very next day!

Mr. Nigam asked Suraj to assign me the task of escorting the deaf
American woman around Delhi. The reason for my selection was my
knowledge of English. Onkar Sharma could have done it, but either he
was busy or Nigam did not want to bestow this honor on him. Serving
as an escort for the American visitor was indeed an honor.

I had never met a deaf person from America before. Actually, I had
never met a deaf person from another country before either. Therefore,
I was excited. Learning about deaf people in America would be wonderful,
I thought. Perhaps this woman would have some good ideas that could
be implemented at the DDA.

So, I had Bhai Narain call my job the next morning, telling whoever
answered the phone that I was sick. I dressed and bicycled to the AIFD
office. Kesh decided to join us; he wanted to get to know the American
woman also. The AIFD hired a taxi for the whole day so we could show
her all the landmarks in old and New Delhi. We planned an itinerary to
make sure we could show the lady the Qutab Minar, the Red Fort, the
Gandhi Memorial, and other places that most tourists visit.

We waited for the American woman to arrive and wondered if she
was old or young, beautiful or ugly, friendly or standoffish. Kesh, as

usual, found an opportunity to make this event sound hilarious. He told me that this woman was going to look like Audrey Hepburn, his favorite actress; *My Fair Lady* was still playing in Delhi at the time. He also said that she had flown all the way from America just to meet this "deaf and dumb" Indian boy who could write English. It was all in fun, and we had a good laugh.

The American lady arrived, and she was exactly the opposite of what we had expected. She had grey hair, cut very short, wore glasses, and was dressed in simple clothes. She looked very earnest and businesslike, but was thin like Audrey Hepburn. Her name was Hester Bennet.

Kesh and I took her to the waiting taxi, and the three of us sat down in the backseat. We took her to all the important and historic sites in Delhi. As we rode, I wrote on a notebook, explaining the history and background of each monument we showed her. Kesh could not read, but he could communicate with her better than I. We three got along very well. I was very impressed with her. A deaf woman in her forties was traveling around the world all by herself! I wanted to do that too, but wondered where I could get that kind of money. Just traveling to Bombay was difficult enough for me.

Hester, whose nickname was Polly, had a twin sister who was also deaf. Her sister's nickname was Peggy. Hester told us how having twins ran in her family; she also had twin daughters who were in their late teens. She had worked all her life and saved enough money to travel around the world.

"Are not you afraid traveling alone?" I wrote the question that Kesh had asked.

She was puzzled. "Why should I be afraid?" I looked at Kesh admonishingly. Hester continued, "I always meet friendly and helpful people like you."

Despite the communication gap, the three of us became good friends by the end of the second day of her visit. Hester learned a few Indian signs, and Kesh and I picked up some American signs. I would write a word and show her the Indian sign, and she would give me the American sign; however, most of our conversation was carried out with writing and gestures.

On the second day, we took her to the coffee house where the local deaf people congregated. A hearing man whom Kesh knew joined us. He bought us all coffee and began to ask Hester about America. What did she do? What was she doing in India? Then he came to the real reason for joining us.

"I want to go to America," he wrote. "Can you help me?"

Hester told him she would be happy to help him, but did not know how to do that. She expressed her regret for not being able to help. Kesh became angry at the man for making that request and told him, in not-so-subtle gestures, to get lost.

I apologized to Hester, but she told me she did not mind being asked to help people to go to America. She had gotten used to it.

"In every country, I was asked by people to help them move to America," she said with a laugh.

"I am glad that I am an American. Everyone wants to move there. I was born there!" She continued smiling.

Eventually, it became time for us to say goodbye. I told her how much I enjoyed talking to her and learning about America. She thanked us for our time and patience. Then, she had a thought.

"You have such good English," she wrote. "Why don't you go to Gallaudet?"

"What is Gallaudet?" I asked.

34

Working at the NPL

SUNNY, KESAR, AND I BECAME GOOD FRIENDS. Sat Parkash also joined our little group. We were all in our early twenties and the youngest people in our office, so it was logical for us to hang out together.

Working at INSDOC was fun. We had little to do, and the companionship was just wonderful. We joked a lot and found different ways to enjoy life. Life at twenty-three could not have been better. Sunny and I began to go to the cinema during the workday. Leaving the office undetected was easy. One of us would ask Mr. Krishnamurthy for permission to leave early "for some urgent work." He liked us both due to our production abilities and never said "no." If I had permission to leave at 3:00 p.m., I would slip out at 2:00 p.m., and Sunny, who had no permission, would also leave a few minutes later. He would be going to the bathroom and then end up meeting me at the bus stop, where we would then go to the cinema house.

Meanwhile, I started teaching night school again after a short lapse. On the day I started working at INSDOC, I had decided to quit my job at the AIFD. It was, after all, six miles from my new workplace. At the end of my third day at INSDOC, I saw Suraj standing outside the NPL gate, waiting for me. He smiled and asked me why I had not come to the AIFD for three days.

"Too much work here," I lied. "But soon I will start to come."

"Why not today?" asked Suraj. "Let us go together. Your students miss you."

I thought about my students. I thought about their traveling to the class after working all day and riding several miles in crowded buses to Cannaught Place. I thought about them waiting for me and then going to the tea shop when I did not arrive. I felt awful and followed Suraj onto a bus going to Cannaught Place.

Soon, I was leading two lives—one in the hearing world, at work and with my family, and one in the Deaf world. I was very comfortable in both situations. Life was good!

Even Nigam began to give me more attention. I was the only other deaf person, other than Onkar Sharma, who had a government job. However, my job was better-paying, and I was just twenty-three years old, ten years younger than Sharma. When the AIFD decided to send the DDA cricket team to play a friendly match with the Calcutta Association of the Deaf, Nigam chose me to be the manager. That was a big honor. My boss at work, who was a big cricket fan, was very impressed that I was managing a cricket team that was going all the way to Calcutta to play. I perhaps gave the impression that I was a great cricket player when, in fact, I was the worst player on the team; however, I chose not to set him straight.

Our residence at 52/5 saw some changes as well. Sister Kamla and her family moved out to their own apartment, leaving seven of us living in the two-room dwelling. This did not last long. Bhai Narain got a better quarter, and we all moved about a mile to Kishan Ganj. The new quarter also had two rooms; but these were bigger. It was located on the second floor, and we also had an open third floor with an additional latrine. The new quarter was known as 21/6.

Housing in Delhi was very expensive and hard to find. Bhai Narain, who could not say "no," ended up renting the second room to a friend's friend. This was Saini. After moving in, Saini and his wife Santosh became very close friends of ours. They had a little son, Babbu, who was the same age as Narain's son Pintu. Soon we were living like one family.

Bhai Narain was a big spender. He always managed to spend his salary before he received it. Now that I had a better-paying job, he decided he needed to splurge a little more. When I received my first paycheck, he bought a box of Corn Flakes breakfast cereal and Ritz crackers. This was the first time he had ever purchased these luxury items. We opened the cereal box on a Sunday morning, when all seven of us were there, and ate our first Corn Flakes breakfast. Each of us had a few teaspoons of flakes dissolved in boiled milk. It tasted good. Later, we had one cracker each, except for Pintu, the youngest boy, who was still being breast-fed.

As I said before, a steady stream of friends visited Bhai Narain. They were, of course, served Ritz crackers with tea. One of these friends spread the word that we were rich, as we were now eating "the British way." This resulted in more people visiting us, much to Bharjai Krishna's ire. The box of Ritz crackers did not last more than two days, and then we were back to Indian snacks. Our prosperity was short-lived.

Bhai Narain decided that, since I had acquired a better job, I must look the part. So, he went out and bought material for a woolen suit and several shirts. I took this to my deaf tailor friend, who was also a student in my night class, and had my clothes fitted nicely. He was an excellent tailor and, being my student, sewed the cloths for a nominal charge. The new wardrobe made me look successful, and I began to walk with my head up and chest out. If you consider yourself successful, you feel good. It does not matter what other people think.

I continued to work as joint secretary of the DDA in the evening, teaching the night class, playing cricket on Sunday morning, and supervising the DDA club activities in the evening. There were some differences now. I was given deferential treatment. Tea was brought to me without my asking, and members of the DDA hovered around me. My status in the Deaf community had risen! I had not understood before then how having a good government job could change their opinion of me. Girls who had not even looked at me before began to pay attention. I was wary and ignored them—more out of shyness than anything else.

"It is time to get married and start a family," I thought.

35

Looking for a New Career

AFTER GETTING THE JOB AT THE NATIONAL
Physical Laboratory (NPL), I thought I was settled for life. Other deaf
people looked at me enviously for having such a well-paid and secure
job. None of my friends who had received training at the All India
Photography Training Institute for the Deaf (PID) had a job like mine.
Kesh, as a teacher at the PID, made half what I did. Raj Kishore made
even less. I should have been happy with and proud of my job. And I
was for a while. The restlessness took over during my second year at
the NPL. I felt I needed another job—with more responsibility and a
better salary.

I shared my thought with Bhai Narain, who thought I was crazy, but
also did not discourage me. He had faith in me and was sure I would
end up finding a "better" job. However, he also warned me that I should
not let my NPL job "go to my head."

My job hunt turned up some interesting possibilities, such as working
for a private corporation as a clerk. These companies, especially banks,
paid very well. They also paid bonuses at the end of the fiscal year. Several
friends of Bhai Narain who worked in private corporations and banks
told me that they made more than 600 rupees a month. That was twice
what I made.

Raj Kishore's father was the general manager of a national bank.
Two of his brothers worked there too. Both of them, despite having no
college education, rode motorcycles, a sign of prosperity in those times.
I asked Raj Kishore if I could talk to his brother.

"Why?" he asked. He was still working in the Goyle Studio for 110
rupees a month.

"I want to work in your father's bank," I told him.

He could not believe me. He told me he wished he could get the job I had; however, he did arrange for me to visit his home and speak with his younger brother with whom he lived.

Raj Kishore's younger brother told me without any hesitation that, if I could type, their father could help me get a job as a typist or a clerk. He also assured me that accountants there had plenty of upward mobility. "What about the bonus?" I asked. He pointed toward his Vespa scooter and smiled. The annual bonus was hefty!

The very next day, Bhai Narain and I walked to a roadside typing school that bore an ambitious name—the National Commercial College. The "college" was a one-room affair containing about ten Underwood and Remington manual typewriters sitting atop small desks with stools in front of them. The owner-teacher and Bhai Narain talked for a few minutes, and I was enrolled verbally after Bhai Narain counted out 30 rupees for one month's tuition. After Bhai Narain left, I straddled a stool and began to hammer on the keys, eager to learn the QWERTY system.

However, my enthusiasm for learning to type was short-lived. When I learned about a college for the deaf in America, my attendance at the National Commercial College became erratic.

Hester Bennet had given me the address for Gallaudet College, so I sent along a short application and waited. After three months passed with no response, I sent another letter. This met with the same fate as the first. After waiting for another three months, I gave up. Then I had an idea. I asked Jijaji B. K. Sharma to obtain contact information for the college from Mr. Nigam, who had visited the United States a year earlier for the World Games of the Deaf. I did not want to talk to Nigam myself; he would have discouraged me from trying to get into Gallaudet.

Jijaji was successful in getting a name. Nigam told him to write to Dr. Leonard Elstad, the president of Gallaudet College. Nigam claimed to be a good friend of Dr. Elstad's. In the opening line of my letter, I claimed to be a friend of Mr. B. G. Nigam, the general secretary of the AIFD, and expressed my desire to further my education. This worked! Only a month later, I received a letter and an application form from the registrar and was told that an admissions test would be arranged for me through the U.S. embassy in New Delhi.

And I had thought name-dropping helped only in India! I began corresponding with Hester Bennet also. She visited Mr. Greenberg, the registrar, on my behalf and asked him about my application. He told her that Gallaudet did not admit Indian students, as their experience with another student from India had not been very good. That guy had dropped out after repeating three years as a preparatory student. She assured him that I spoke very good English. I will never know whether it was Hester Bennet's personal contact with Mr. Greenberg or Dr. Elstad's recommendation that got a response to my letter. I did not check. I was too thrilled to finally hear from Gallaudet to care how it happened.

A month later, I got a letter from the American Embassy, asking me to come to their educational wing and take the Gallaudet College admissions test. I got very nervous thinking about how difficult the test would be. I did not even know on what I would be tested. I expressed my fears to Kesh who laughed. "You are very smart," he said. "I am sure this test will be easy for you." I felt better. I was grateful for my friend's opinion. Kesh could not read or write and did not know what this test was about, but he was so sure that I would pass, I believed him.

On the appointed day, I went to the address given in the letter. I met an Indian lady who was very nice to me and wrote explanations to me very clearly. Then she gave me the test and left me alone.

The first part was the mathematics test, and I got stumped on the first problem. It was a simple problem, but I got confused when I saw the four possible correct answers right next to it. I was supposed to pick the right answer. I had solved this type of problem in the fourth or fifth grade and did not understand why they wanted me to solve it for a college entrance examination. What was worse, they had given me the answer! I didn't even have to show the work that led to the answer!

The problems, however, began to get more difficult with each question. Algebra and geometry followed. At that point, I had not done algebra problems or solved geometry theorems for about ten years. Somehow, I managed to remember the formulas and finished the two-hour test in about thirty minutes. The lady told me to go over it again, and I did so just to please her.

The English part of the test was even easier for me. The answers were included in this section as well! I liked this American system of testing.

Indian tests require a lot of writing; for the American tests, I just needed to circle the correct answer. It did not make sense to me.

After finishing, I began to nervously wait for the results. I knew it would take several months. Meanwhile, my marriage date was fixed for February 26, 1967, only six months away. I wondered what would happen first: Would I get married or be admitted to Gallaudet College?

36
Marriage

THREE YEARS EARLIER, WHEN I HAD DECIDED
that I was going to remain a bachelor for all my life, a wise cousin from
Delhi told me: "All of us want to avoid getting married, and all of us
get married!" He was right. Some of us are more vocal in our refusal;
some more submissive. Two of my childhood companions, Vishwa and
Madan Gopal, married when they were seventeen years old and had
become fathers when they were eighteen. Madan Gopal had four kids,
and he was only two years older than me. At twenty-five, I was, in the
opinion of the people from my village, past the marriage age.

Babuji married for the first time when he was nine years old. His wife
died before the marriage was consummated. When he married a second
time, he was nineteen and Bhabhi was eleven. She was formally brought
to our home when she was fifteen to start her married life, which meant
cooking, cleaning, bringing water from the well, and bearing children,
not necessarily in that order.

The preparations for my marriage started several months in advance.
I was not involved in them. Babuji took care of the food and *janate*, or
wedding party, arrangements. The janate was the group of people who
would accompany me to Lohara for the wedding ceremony and then
bring my bride and me back to Gagret. Bhabhi and both my sisters
worked on jewelry and clothes for Nikki and all the relatives who were
coming to attend the wedding.

Weddings were major events in villages where little else happened.
Besides the annual fair, weddings were the only game in town. I remember
how all us kids looked forward to a wedding. It meant no school for
four or five days and all the cousins gathered in one house for a week.
Weddings meant new clothes, plenty of food, and all the sweetmeats you

could eat! For children, weddings were the ultimate in fun. They were like going to a theme park for a whole week.

Bhai Narain, ever the great planner without money, wanted to do everything in great style. He even had plans to send Nikki and me on a honeymoon, emulating rich people in the West. Babuji had asked him for the money to purchase all the clothes for me and Nikki. This cost several months of our combined salaries. Bhai Narain went into the purchasing frenzy with a vengeance. I wanted to keep everything simple and did not want to borrow even one rupee; however, no one listened to me. Relatives who lived in Delhi visited 21/6 in Kishan Ganj on a weekly basis to examine the purchased cloth materials, give their opinions on them, and have deep discussion about each piece over tea and samosas.

While all these preparations were occurring in Gagret and Delhi, I continued to work, leaving home at 7 a.m. and returning home after 10 p.m. I had, however, stopped playing cricket on Sunday mornings. This allowed me to have more time at home, at least on Sundays. Other than that, it was life as usual—busy but full of fun.

The invitations were sent out to all the relatives. No one declined, which meant they were all coming. I gave invitations to all my friends, and three of them decided to come; travel to Gagret was expensive. One of my friends, Govind Uppal, my former classmate and later my student, was working as a freelance photographer. He was coming to the wedding as the official photographer. He was paying his own way, and nothing was discussed about payment for his services. The other two—Balraj and Prem—were not exactly my close friends, but they could afford the trip and were very curious about my little village in the foothills of the Himalayas.

A week before the wedding, Bhai Narain, his whole family, and I traveled to Gagret. Half of the relatives had already arrived, and the house was full. Wedding ceremonies started with *ubtan*—the formal bathing of the groom for the wedding. Before the ubtan ceremony, the groom—and the bride in her own home—are not allowed to bathe or change clothes. It was February and still cold in Gagret, therefore, not bathing was no problem; however, wearing soiled clothes for three days had started to announce my arrival in any room well in advance. I was used to wearing soiled clothes when I was a farmer; but I had been a city slicker for almost six years now, and it now bothered me. I was especially embarrassed when my three friends dressed in their clean clothes arrived. As the groom, I was the most ungroomed person there.

The ubtan is prepared with flour, turmeric, and mustard oil. To begin the ritual, the groom sits on a settee wearing a *dhoti* (a loincloth). All the ladies sing wedding bath songs and slowly apply ubtan to the groom's body. As the mixture dries, it was rubbed hard until all the excess came off. At the end, they bathed me by pouring hot water on my head and rubbing the ubtan off. I felt really clean after that; it was similar to visiting a spa. The only difference was it was free and done by my loving mother, sisters, aunts, and other cousins. These ritual baths went on for three days.

The day before the wedding, everyone from the village was invited to our home for a feast. The hired cook and his assistants prepared several kinds of vegetables, dals, and *puris* (puffy fried wheat cakes) for the occasion. People sat on mats spread on the floor and were served food on plates and bowls made of banyan tree leaves. All the cousins and neighborhood men acted as hosts and ladled out the food. It was the opposite of a cafeteria line—the food bearers moved down the line of squatting people.

The wedding lunch lasted from noon to 3 p.m. The unwritten rule is that no one coming to the house—invited or uninvited—goes hungry. A lot of people brought their own utensils and containers and, instead of eating with us, carried food back home. If any item on the menu ran out, it had to be cooked again, and fast.

Finally, the wedding day arrived! Just before noon, I sat in the middle of a large dhurrie spread out in the courtyard. All my relatives and the village women sat around singing wedding songs. Of course, we did not use an interpreter; no one, including myself, knew about professional interpreters at that time. I had heard those songs being sung at weddings when I was a kid and had, without even trying, memorized each of them. These songs were just background music or noise; no one paid attention to them.

Bholu, our barber, helped me put on my new suit. He tied a turban around my head and added *sehra* to the front of the turban. The sehra is a decorative headdress made of tinsel with a crown at the top and about ten long golden tassels hanging all the way to one's stomach. After that, I was dressed as a groom!

With deaf friends and cousins before departing for Lohara for my wedding ceremony. From left, Govind Uppal, Surinder (my cousin), me, Prem, Balray. In front on the right is my cousin Beena (Uncle Ram Prasad's daughter).

People began taking turns giving me gifts, which were mainly cloth material with some cash stuck in half a coconut. One by one, they came and placed the gifts in my outstretched hands. They would also wave a coin over my head to ward off bad luck and then give the coin to Bholu. Some of them also put a tinsel or flower garland around my head. Then Bhabhi would take the bundle from my arms and put it on the growing pile of gifts while Bhai Narain wrote down who gave what. This list was later used to choose reciprocal gifts for future weddings.

I did not even glance at the gifts; they were useless to me. Some would later be given to visiting relatives, and the leftovers would be kept to give to other people at their weddings.

The gift-giving ceremony took more than an hour, and my back was aching from sitting on the ground. The weight of all the garlands around my neck did not help. The monotony of the ceremony started to get to me. I remembered reading in an article that everyone at a wedding has fun, except the bride and the groom. That was an understatement, I thought.

With the gift ceremony over, we had our lunch, which was a smaller version of the wedding feast of the previous day. Only the neighbors, close friends, and relatives who participated in the gift ceremony eat with us. People took turns at serving and being served.

The janate left for Lohara after lunch. As is customary, the janate is composed of relatives from near and far, neighbors, most of the village people, and friends. The bride's family usually informs the groom's father how many people to bring. Babuji had, on his own, decided to take only about forty people. My elder brothers' wedding janates had had eighty-plus people. (They were married into well-off families.)

Until my marriage, only men formed the wedding janates; however, times had changed, and Babuji decided that Pramila, my cousin, would join the wedding as well. She was the only female member of the janate.

I was put in a canopied palanquin carried by four *kahars*, or coolies. Both my brothers had been transported in this fashion all the way to their in-law's villages. This was an especially difficult task since Bhai Narain weighed more than 200 pounds and Ajjowal, Bharjai Krishna's village, was about sixteen miles from Gagret. His marriage had taken place in the month of June with its three-digit temperatures. Everyone agreed that this was murder on the kahars, even if they were hardy hill people.

Sham's kahars fared better. Bharjai Ram Kumari's village was only eight miles away, and Sham weighed about 150 pounds. The wedding took place in the cool month of December. My wedding was very different. The palanquin was used only for ceremonial purposes and only until we were about a mile outside the village. The parade was led by a band composed of two drums, a trombone, a trumpet, and a clarinet. The band people were farmers from another village who moonlighted by playing at weddings. They were amateurs and, according to cousin Mahesh, were making an insufferable noise. Tilku, my old classmate and now Babuji's friend and drinking buddy, was there with his two trucks. The to-and-fro transportation of the whole wedding party to Nikki's village was his gift to us. I sat with Pramila and Tilku in the cab of the truck. Babuji and uncle Bhardwaj, Pramila's daddy, sat in the cab of the other truck, driven by Tilku's assistant. Every member of the wedding

party had brought his own bedding—dhurrie and a quilt tied with twine—
and these beddings were loaded into the trucks. Then the members of
the wedding party climbed into the beds of both trucks.

"I should not sit here," I told Tilku. "I was supposed to be your
cleander."

Tilku gave his usual robust laugh and slapped me on my back and
pinched it hard, crumbling my garlands. We both laughed. Only seven
years ago, I had contemplated becoming a cleander!

The trip from Gagret to Kinnu—about ten miles—was fine. The six-
foot-wide ribbon of windy road that we traveled on was paved. A "road"
ran from Kinnu to Lohara as well but it was nothing more than rutty
bullock cart path. Babuji asked Tilku to drop all of us off at Kinnu so
we could continue on foot, but Tilku had other plans—he wanted to
drive the wedding party all the way to Lohara!

Our truck swerved right and left as Tilku maneuvered, avoiding trees
on both sides of the road. I guessed that the people riding in the bed of
the truck were being whipped by overhanging branches. After topping a
100-foot grade, the truck slowly grunted down to the bottom of a ravine
where a shallow stream flowed. Driving on the soggy sand didn't look
easy, but Tilku still managed it. The other truck, however, got stuck.

Tilku stopped and walked briskly back to the second truck. He pulled
his assistant out of the cab roughly, as if the situation were his fault.
Everyone hopped out of both trucks and began to roll the one that was
stuck back and forth to free it. The younger people could not miss this
opportunity to have some fun. The combined pushing of twenty-plus
people finally got the truck out. However, it soon got stuck again after
only traveling a few yards. Tilku was driving his new Mercedes-Benz
truck. His assistant had an older one which had less power and traction.
Following the unwritten rule that all bosses adhere to, Tilku blamed
the driver for his ineptitude and yelled at him in front of the whole
wedding party.

Babuji convinced Tilku to just drop us right there, as we only had a
mile left to reach Lohara. The younger members of the wedding party
unloaded the bedrolls, and, after considerable maneuvering, the trucks
managed to turn around and slowly wobble back toward Kinnu. The
wedding ceremony had yet to start. Getting there seemed to be all the fun!

37

Wedding Ceremonies in Lohara

AS THE SUN WAS SETTING, WE MADE QUICK
work of the last leg of our journey and arrived at the inn in Lohara on
time. The inn was a small house with mud walls and a grass roof. It
consisted of one large room surrounded by verandahs on three sides. My
in-laws had gathered spare cots from all over the village, and about forty
of them were lying there in the room in several piles. Bhai Narain had
a few young boys help him spread the large dhurrie we had brought from
Gagret over the floor in one corner. This became the groom's area. I sat
on a large cushion with another cushion behind my back and wished I
was somewhere else. I was bored stiff by all these ceremonies.

Everyone was having fun. The kids were running around in the gather-
ing darkness, exploring the trees and fields in this new village. The temperature dropped by the minute. Lohara is only seven miles from Gagret as
the crow flies and about twelve miles via the road and the oxcart tracks.
It is also about 500 feet higher in elevation, which made it fairly colder
than Gagret.

Babuji and his close friends gathered together on a few cots placed
in a circle and opened a bottle of country liquor. Young people who were
learning to drink took bottles into the bushes. Weddings were a great
occasion for drinking, a very antisocial behavior. I talked with Mahesh,
who could spell fluently and also sign some, and then fell asleep.

At 2 a.m., Mahesh and Bhai Narain woke me up from a dreamless
sleep. My in-laws had sent their barber to invite us to the wedding
ceremony. I got up, put on my clothes, and picked up my turban along
with the elaborate sehra around it. When I noticed Mahesh and Bhaiji
laughing at me, I stopped fumbling with the turban. I had forgotten that
this was to be Bholu the barber's job. Mahesh was amused that I did not
know or remember such intricacies of getting married. We kids were

With my brothers Sham (left) and Narain in Lohara during a lull in the
wedding ceremonies.

supposed to learn about such things by watching grooms while we were
growing up.

Nevertheless, I took my turban off and handed it to Bholu, who, with
a grim face, put it back on my head and adjusted it properly. Then Bhai
Narain stood up and performed the "egg" ceremony by whirling a rupee
around my head and giving it to Bholu. Through this ceremony, all of
my bad luck was passed on to Bholu, who did not mind as his was a
lucrative job.

"You were trying to save a rupee, right?" Mahesh taunted.

"Of course," I humored him. "I was going to give half to you."

I was put in another canopied palanquin, and the four kahars lifted
me. The entire wedding party was still asleep on cots on the verandahs.
The Lohara barber had brought a petromax lantern with him. He led
the way with the petromax on his head followed by the band, my palanquin, and another kahar carrying clothes and jewelry for the bride.
Mahesh and Bhai Narain made up the rear.

From left: Uncle D. C. Bhardwaj, Jija Rashan Lal Joshi, me, Jija B. K. Sharma, and Jija Mathra Das.

My future in-laws' house was about half a mile away. When we arrived, we were all offered a dhurrie on which to sit. The wedding ceremony would take place within a 6-x-6-foot area marked with lines drawn with wheat flour that had four bamboo posts in four corners. A square of red cloth suspended by strings tied to the bamboo posts was suspended in the middle of this structure. Two settees for the bride and the groom were set on one side. Two priests—one from Gagret and one from Lohara—sat on mats on one side. The third side was for the parents of the bride.

In the middle of this structure, the Lohara priest had built a square platform of sand about two inches high. On this platform, he drew a diagram made of crisscrossing lines, which looked kind of like a solar system with positions marked according to ancient Hindu scriptures.

A few minutes after our arrival, I was asked to take a bath. A settee was set in the courtyard next to the ceremony area. I stood on it and slowly undressed, giving my clothes to Bholu. I put on a dhoti before slipping my underwear down my legs. A bucket of hot water was produced, and I saw about thirty women in the shadows looking at me surreptitiously through their veils. Nikki, my future bride, was nowhere to be seen. I knew from experience that brides are hidden in the innermost room of the house.

I poured a few jugs of hot water on my head and used my hands to scrub myself off. Getting wet made me colder. A small boy, Nikki's brother, held a towel in his outstretched hands. I took it, quickly dried myself, and put on a shirt and a dhoti the in-laws had supplied by custom. I was not to wear my western clothes. A woolen shawl helped keep me warm.

After that, I sat down on the settee reserved for the groom. Mahesh came over and sat next to me. He was going to help explain whatever the priests told me to do. In this capacity, he was serving as my first "interpreter." Mahesh being Mahesh kept an ongoing commentary on what was occurring and also managed to slip in a couple of jokes. I had difficulty suppressing my laughter. He found out that my father-in-law's name was Mast Ram. When we were younger, we had read some pornographic stories written by a Mast Ram. Mahesh signed and spelled to me, wondering if we had been reading books by my esteemed father-in-law. This broke me up. My father-in-law-to-be, a very serious man, told our priest that the groom should not laugh during the ceremony. Our priest told him that laughter was OK. Nothing further was said about my laughing; but after that, I succeeded in remaining stoic despite Mahesh's ongoing efforts to make me laugh.

For about an hour, both priests chanted, and I remained sitting there. Then my future wife was brought in. She was dressed from head to toe in red and was carried as a bundle by one of her cousins. She was placed on the settee next to me. All I could see of her were her hands dyed in henna and her wrists decorated with about 100 red bracelets. About ten coconut halves and several seashells were tied with red strings to her hands. I took a sidelong glance at my future wife—a bundle in red.

I wondered about this bundle in red. Would she be a good wife? Would she be able to learn signs and communicate with me, or would she just write on her palm like the other members of my family? I told myself that arranged marriages seemed to work, some better than others. It would work for me too, I told myself, and I focused on the task at hand.

The ceremony went on and on. Around 6 a.m., Babuji, Pramila, Surinder, and some others came in and sat next to Bhai Narain on the durrie. They talked, smoked from a hookah, and drank tea.

For more than four hours, I threw pinches of rice, sugar, vermillion, and water on various interactions of the lines on the mound in front of me. These offering were to satisfy the various planets and gods, thus ensuring a happy married life for us. The priest would point to a spot on the diagram, and Mahesh would tell me to put those ingredients wherever was indicated. Soon it became a routine, and Mahesh did not have to interpret. He got up and joined Pramila and Surinder on the dhurrie. They were talking and laughing. I wished I could join them.

Nikki and I both had to do the rice-sugar-vermillion exercise for the next hour. After that, a fire was lit on the sand platform, and we poured on it a mixture of ghee every few seconds as instructed. The ceremony kept dragging on and on.

At about 9 a.m., seven hours later, we were both asked to stand up. Slowly amid all the chanting and women singing, we took seven *pheras* or circles around the fire.* Each of these circles—about ten feet in circumference—took more than fifteen minutes. After that, the ceremony was over. I walked to the dhurrie and, after drinking a glass of tea, I was hauled in the palanquin back to the inn, leaving my future wife with her friends and family.

After eating lunch, which was served in the same courtyard where the ceremony had taken place, we returned to the inn again. The kids played, photographs were taken, and I talked with my friends Uppal, Balraj, and Prem. They were city kids and wanted to know how my wife looked. They did not believe that I had yet to see her.

In the afternoon, after a short ceremony in my in-law's house, I was in the palanquin again. Nikki was put in a similar palanquin, except it was covered with heavy red cloth. My city friends wanted to see my bride, and now they were seeing her—in a covered palanquin! She was still covered in red clothes from head to toe.

---

*Each of these circles ended with a blessing or vow. The first was for abundance of food, the second for the couple to complement to each other, the third for prosperity, the fourth for eternal happiness, the fifth for being blessed with children, the sixth for living in harmony, and the last for being friends with each other.

We were marched to Tilku's trucks, which were waiting for us. Nikki and I were transferred to the cab of one truck accompanied by the barber's wife. Half an hour later, when everyone and their beddings were loaded, we slowly drove to Kinnu. At Kinnu, Nirmala, the barber's wife, and I were transferred to a waiting car, courtesy of a business associate of Babuji. I thought this would impress my future wife.

More ceremonies continued in Gagret that night and the following day. The next day, I took Nikki in a bus back to Lohara. I had yet to see her face. I sat in the guest room all day. I did not see my bride or even her shadow. After a day in Lohara, I brought her back to Gagret on a bus.

That night, my new wife and I were to sleep in a large room on the second floor, which was used only for drying grains. Nirmala was brought to me by one of my sisters-in-law and made to sit on the bed. She still had her veil on and looked like a bundle of red cloth. My sister-in-law smiled, winked at me, and was gone.

I was alone with my wife! She sat there and held a corner of her veil in her fingers. She still had red henna on her hands, and her wrist and fingers were decorated by new jewelry, gifts from my parents. I did not know what to do. What did she look like? How did she behave? Will she like me? Will she be a good wife? A thousand questions crossed my mind.

Suddenly, I thought about her fears. She did not know me. She was married to a strange man, nine years her senior. A deaf man! She did not know anything about deafness or communicating with them. She, I thought, must be worried and more scared than me. The red bundle of clothes with a single hand sticking out was trembling. God, I thought, she is more scared and worried than me. Is it not my duty to make her feel comfortable?

Slowly, I lifted her veil and looked at her. She had her eyes closed and did not move. I put a finger under her chin and raised her face. She did not resist but did not open her eyes either. I looked at her terrified but extremely beautiful face and felt sorry for her. Caressing her face, I asked, "How are you?"

38

Back in Delhi

MY "HONEYMOON" WAS A TWO-DAY VISIT TO
Dehra Gopipur where Sham worked as a sub-inspector of cooperative
societies. The village was about twenty miles from Gagret and situated
right on the Beas river. We were chaperoned by my two sisters-in-law—
Bharjai Krishna and Ram Kumari, Sham's wife. The trip was not a
honeymoon per se, but it was a nice family vacation.

Custom dictated that Nikki would not join me in Delhi for a couple
of months. After the honeymoon, I left her in Gagret and joined Bhai
Narain and his family for the train ride back to Delhi. My work leave
was running out.

We arrived at 21/6 in the evening. While checking the accumulated
mail, Bhai Narain held up an envelope to get my attention. It was from
Gallaudet. I jumped up and, with my heart pounding, tore the letter open
and began to read it. The second line made me yell in joy.

I was accepted to Gallaudet College!

We all sat there stunned. In the excitement of getting married, I had
forgotten about Gallaudet. This letter brought me back to the reality of
my goals for higher education. I was going to Gallaudet! Bhai Narain
put a damper on my excitement.

"This is just admission. What about expenses? They did not offer
you anything." He scanned the letter.

Money was an issue. At that time, the annual expenses of an American
college were between $3,000 and $10,000. Even $3,000 was a bit over
two years' combined salary for both Narain and me. Even if we lived
very frugally, it would have taken about twenty to thirty years for us to
save for one year of tuition and other expenses.

"American universities and colleges offer scholarships to needy students," said the ever-optimistic Bhai Narain. There was hope, I thought.

The next morning, I wrote a letter requesting a tuition waiver and a part-time job to support myself while attending Gallaudet. After that, I got busy with my jobs, working in the DDA and teaching at the night school. I made sure that everyone knew that I was accepted to Gallaudet. If I did not receive the scholarship and could not go, I would still be able to say that I had passed the examination and was accepted to an American college.

The word spread like wildfire among all the deaf people. Soon, people began to greet me with, "When are you going to America?" In the beginning, I enjoyed it. None of my friends or relatives had ever gone to America. Going there would not be very different from my going to the moon!

Within a month, I got a letter from Richard Phillips, the dean of students at Gallaudet. He enclosed an application form for grant-in-aid, instructing me to fill it out and return it. He also warned me that they did not have jobs for students, especially during their first year, and advised me to contact my country's government for additional support.

Asking for support from the Indian government was simply out of the question. Bhai Narain made some inquires and was laughed at. The only support the government would offer, he was told, was "50 rupees a month for the deaf and dumb." That would be less than $7!

A month later, I got another letter. I was to receive full support for tuition, room, and board. I was overjoyed. The only hassle was books, pocket allowance, and travel to America. I decided to forgo a pocket allowance. "Books," Mr. Phillips had written, "would cost about $250 per year." That was six months of my salary! Also, a one-way ticket to Washington, D.C., according to Jijaji B. K. Sharma, cost about 4,500 rupees. That was equivalent to fifteen months' salary. I realized I needed to look for help.

During all this time, I had been corresponding with Hester Bennet. She was also unable to get help from Gallaudet. She kept trying and was successful in getting a $250 donation from Byron B. Burnes, a teacher at the California School for the Deaf and also the president of the National Association of the Deaf. The problem of books was resolved.

Rupam Goswami was a student of mine when I taught at the PID. Rupam's grandmother was a member of parliament. When Rupam heard about my money problem, he asked me to visit his grandmother. She was a nice lady and was surprised to learn that I could not lipread despite my "normal" speech. I hoped she did not hold that against me. Rupam interpreted, and I was told to go see her friend who was a minister of state in the federal government for the Ministry of Social Welfare. She was kind enough to make the appointment for me.

Despite my misconceptions about government officials who wield power, the minister was a very nice lady. Not only was I ushered into her office as soon as I arrived, but I was also offered a seat and a cup of tea. When she realized I could not lipread, she began to write her questions on a piece of paper.

"You are deaf, not dumb." She was referring to my speech.

I did not know what to say.

"What will you study there?" she asked.

"Education, madam," I responded. "How to teach the deaf and dumb people." I used her parlance.

"How long will it take?" she wrote.

"Six years, madam," I replied with reverence.

She asked more questions: How was I going to support myself? Why won't Gallaudet cover my travel expenses?

After she was satisfied, she asked the main question: "How much money do you need?"

I needed 4,500 rupees for the ticket and about 500 rupees for travel expenses. The Indian government offered only $50, or about 400 rupees, for people traveling abroad. While visiting hard-currency countries, Indians had to cover their own expenses. But 5,000 rupees was a lot of money. I was afraid that she would say "no" if I asked for that much.

"I only need 2,000 rupees, madam," I blurted out.

"Do you think that is enough?" She looked surprised.

"Yes, madam," I said, trying to be convincing. "I will use my own money for the rest of expenses." As soon as I said that, I knew I had made a major blunder; but the arrow was out of the bow.

She was impressed and told me to come back in a week's time to pick up the check.

I wanted to kick myself for being such a chicken. She was wrong; I *was* both deaf and dumb. During the entire trip from her office to 21/6, I kept cursing myself. I had rejected an offer for much-needed money, which was equal to ten months' salary.

To rectify this mistake, I asked for the balance from Uncle Bhardwaj. He was the president of the Ahmedabad Electricity Company and earned more than 4,000 rupees a month. I sent him a letter and was pleasantly surprised by an affirmative response. He said that I should visit Ahmedabad with my wife and pick up the check.

Everything finally fell into place. My passport was ready, and all I needed was my student visa, which would allow me to travel. Jijaji Sharma and I went to the U.S. embassy with my passport, the letters from Gallaudet showing my admission and offer of full financial aid, and a letter from Mr. Burns promising $250 for books.

Everything seemed to be perfect and in order. I was excited beyond description. Finally, I was going to attend college and earn a degree. The fact that this college was in the United States of America made my going even more important.

39

The Elusive Visa

AFTER EXAMINING ALL MY PAPERWORK, THE visa clerk asked, "Where is the P Form?" From the expression on the clerk's face, I knew all was not right.

Jijaji and I looked puzzled. "What is that?" he asked the clerk.

The clerk talked and Jijaji nodded his head in understanding, while I looked at them, feeling alternately bewildered and worried.

Finally, Jijaji picked up all the papers, put them in an envelope, and walked out of the office. I had no choice but to follow him. I kept asking him what was wrong, and he kept telling me to wait until we reached home. All this could not be explained in a jostling bus with people staring at us.

The P Form was an assurance that I would have full financial support in the currency of the host country. India had no foreign exchange reserve at that time, and its exports were horribly below its imports. Thus, the government did not allow Indian subjects to travel abroad without making sure the necessary foreign exchange was available. The U.S. embassy could not issue me a visa unless I produced the 'P' Form issued by the Reserve Bank of India.

That did not sound so bad. After all, I already had the required amount of money. All I had to do was to demonstrate to the Reserve Bank of India that I had the money, and I would be on my way. This was occurring in late August; I had received a letter from Mr. Philips telling me to arrive at Gallaudet by September 6 for student orientation. I did not know what that was, but I wanted to follow his instructions.

Again, Bhai Narain made inquires on my behalf. He learned the whereabouts of the office that issued P Forms. We went there early one morning with all the necessary paperwork in hand. The clerks there told us that we had to go to another office for specific application forms. That office was a few miles away; however. When we arrived at the second office, we were told that they did not have the application forms handy and that we should return the following day.

The forms were not handy the next day either. I felt like crying, but Bhai Narain got very angry. He was a big man and could express himself very well. His eyes got red and he began yelling at the clerks. I got worried that his anger might cost us my visa, but somehow it worked. The application form materialized from somewhere within a minute, and we walked out leaving the scared clerks sitting there.

Outside, Bhai Narain explained by writing on his palm that those lazy bums had wanted a few hundred rupees in bribe. People who needed a P form were usually going abroad for business or pleasure. For wealthy people, shelling out a few hundred rupees was nothing, and those clerks were used to getting that *baksheesh*, or tip, as they called it. But for us, that money was difficult to get. I was glad that Bhai Narain's ferociousness made the clerks forget their "tip."

We filled out the form in a teashop and went to the office where we had gone originally and started on another wild goose chase. We arrived there only to find that Mr. Erady, the director of the department that issued the P form, was not there and would not return until the next day.

The following day, after several hours of lounging in the hot and steamy corridors, we were finally ushered into Mr. Erady's cool office. He was a very brisk and businessman-like gentleman.

Mr. Erady glanced at our paperwork for only a second and then handed it back. Bhai Narain continued to plead with him as we were escorted out the door.

The P Form was denied because the $250 donation from Mr. Burnes for books was "from a private party." The Indian government, which meant Mr. Erady, recognized only government or major university grants, not private donations. We were back to square one again!

We spent the next ten days pounding the pavement in various government offices known as the Secretariat area. Everyone we knew had a friend, relative, or friend's friend who was "in a very high position." At this point, I felt like a drowning man trying to grab at straws. Bhai Narain and I visited each of these "high position" people. Some of them refused to see us; others simply expressed their sympathy by telling us that this was not under their jurisdiction.

In Delhi with Nikki, 1967.

Bhai Narain had used up all his vacation time for my wedding and was taking leave without pay to help me. I told him to return to work, and I would visit the offices on my own. My boss had already granted me unofficial leave to pursue the visa. For him, my getting the visa and going to America was much more important than my working at INSDOC.

Of course, I could not go around alone; I needed an interpreter. At that time, our tenant Saini, who had become a member of the family, stepped in. He had a motorcycle and gave me rides whenever I needed one. Other times, Jijaji Sharma would escort me. This had become a community project.

As time went on, hopes began to die. Even Bhai Narain was beginning to lose his optimism. I would come home and lie on the sofa and think about my bad luck. I was so absorbed in my own plight that I did not think about my bride. Nirmala did not understand this at all. She had come to Delhi to live with my family because I was supposed to leave for the United States. She knew I was going somewhere far away and was not going to return for a long time. She did not want me to go.

During my last visit to Lohara, her mother had pleaded with me not to leave her daughter alone for such a long time. She told me I had a wonderful job and did not need to study anymore. By then, Nirmala had become conversant in writing on her palm. She acted as "interpreter." I did not like this argument and scoffed at the idea of my present job being "a wonderful job." Wonderful jobs are like new clothes; they become expendable and a shame to wear with time.

There was a time when having a government job was a dream come true for me. My goals were set much higher now. Going to America, where no one else in my family had ever gone, was a huge step forward for me, and I could not compare my present job to what lay ahead for me once I obtained a college education.

One afternoon, when I was lying on the sofa, quietly moping over my misfortune, Nirmala came and sat down at my feet. She asked me what was wrong. I was far too self-involved at that point to respond to her. She went away with tears in her eyes. I felt awful after that, but she was sitting with Bharjai Krishna and I could not talk to her in front of her. Husbands and wives did not talk in front of their elders. The question of showing affection—even holding hands—did not even arise.

My friend Kesh finally came to the rescue, introducing me to a friend's friend—a judge. After dealing with so many high-and-mighty people, I was skeptical at first. But as I said, my options were running out at that point.

I met the judge at his home, and he was a very nice and quiet man. He listened to my story and looked at my papers. His son, Kesh's friend, knew some signs and interpreted for us. Then he copied down Mr. Erady's phone number and told me to go home and call him the next day. As we'd hoped, the next day, the judge told Bhai Narain and me to visit Mr. Erady again. We hurriedly dressed and took a three-wheeled scooter rickshaw as there was no time to wait for a bus. We arrived at Mr. Erady's office within half an hour and were ushered in immediately.

He told us that he was now accepting the P Form. A short phone call from the judge had done the trick.

That afternoon, I went with Jijaji to buy the ticket to Washington, D.C. My plane would be leaving in two days. Bhaiji sent a telegram to Babuji, who along with Bhabhi and Sham, arrived in Delhi the next day. The little quarter at 21/6 was full of people.

At a farewell dinner with friends, September 12, 1967, the night before I flew to the United States. From left: Nirmala, Madan, O. N. Sharma, Harish Chugh.

On the morning of September 13, we rode a few taxis to Palam Airport in New Delhi. All my friends and relatives were already there— more than eighty people to see me off. Everyone kept putting garlands around my neck; soon I could not see above them.

As I prepared to leave, I looked at all my loved ones: the cousins I had grown up with, my parents, my siblings, my friends from childhood and present, my coworkers, the deaf people I had become so close with, and a host of other people who had come to see me off. They were all proud of me and genuinely happy for me. I watched my mother comfort Nirmala, who was sobbing under her veil. All I could see was her shaking body. I was leaving my young bride of six months with my family.

My smile froze, and before I knew it, I was crying uncontrollably. The frustrations of the past few weeks, the fear of what lay ahead in a strange country where I did not know a single soul, and the tragic feeling

At the airport before flying off to Washington, D.C., to attend Gallaudet.
Front row: Krishan Dev (Bharjai Krishna's brother), Bhabhi, me, Babaji (with
nephew Shashipal in front), Bhai Shiv Narain, my friend Govind Uppal, Uncle
Ram Prasad of Kanpur. Other friends and relatives are in the back row.

of leaving all these people with whom I had spent the past twenty-six
years all combined into a huge lump in my throat.

I embraced my family, shook hands with my friends, touched the feet
of Babuji and the elders to obtain their blessings. I looked at the veiled
Nikki, her body shaking from sobs, and moved on. I wished I could
touch her and say a few words, but talking to one's wife in public is
unacceptable in India. I could not say a proper goodbye to the person
who was hurting most—the newly married wife I was leaving alone for
six years.

Finally, my plane began to board. Jijaji led me to the waiting Air
India Boeing 707.

I was on my way to Gallaudet College and America!

EPILOGUE
Life in America

TWO DAYS LATER, AFTER AN OVERNIGHT layover in London, I arrived in America.

It was a crisp fall day in 1967 when the TWA plane I had boarded in London landed at Dulles Airport in Virginia. The excitement of coming to a new country and attending a college excited me greatly, and I had not slept since leaving New Delhi. I had a splitting headache and my eyes hurt. The bright fall sun made them water. I lined up behind the other passengers for customs and immigration checks. I was not sure what lay ahead, and to avoid making any mistakes, I looked around for any signs for instruction on how to go through immigration. There were none. A lady with a clipboard caught my attention. She would look at her clipboard and shout something I could not hear while scanning the passengers in the line. I decided to go read for myself what she was telling us. Looking at her clipboard, I saw she was holding a passenger list. My name was circled in red ink with the word "DEAF" written next to it. I tapped the woman and pointed at my name. She looked relieved. Apparently, she had been yelling my name in the hope that the deaf guy would hear her.

She was of great help. After learning that I could not lipread, she used pencil and paper to tell me that she would help me through the immigration and customs process. I did not have to stand in the line. She took me to a closed counter and spoke with a supervisor, who looked through my passport and stamped it with a smile. I thought about the immigration personnel I had dealt with in New Delhi; the efficiency, friendliness, and may-I-help-you attitude I found in America were simply overwhelming.

Then she took me to the baggage claim area. I was amazed at the luggage carousel. Bags of all shapes and sizes were going around and around, and people were picking up their bags. We waited, but my little bag never appeared. When the carousel stopped, I knew my bag was still somewhere between India and the United States. With the clipboard lady's help, I filled out the required forms, picked up my tote bag and small attaché case, and walked over to the airport bus, which would take me to Washington, D.C.

Up until then, I had envisioned America as being populated by cowboys trotting on their sorrels and pintos through the purple sage and mesquite. This impression had been informed by movies starring Gary Cooper, John Wayne, and other cowboys who rode fast horses, shot guns, cleaned up towns of black-hatted bad guys, and rode into the sunset for yet another adventure. The lush Virginia countryside along the Dulles Access Road was very different than the America I had expected. Imagine my disappointment at not seeing any cowboys or horses! I did have, however, more important things to worry about and decided to forget the missing cowboys and horses for now.

I had $43 in my pocket, two pairs of clothes, and a pair of shoes. That was it. I did not know anyone in the whole country and did not even have a letter of introduction. I was convinced at that point that I would never recover my other bag containing the majority of my clothes.

The bus dropped me in D.C. at 12th Street, N.W., and I then faced the task of finding my way to Gallaudet. I tried to talk to people like I always did in India, but found no one who understood me. My heavy Gagret accent made my speech unintelligible to the Americans. A huge black porter was helpful. He asked me to write down my questions and he wrote back answers. In India, hearing people had always written to me and I had always responded with my voice because I was understood there. I never had to write to express myself. This was a new experience. Hearing people in America did not understand my speech. I had never heard English spoken, especially by an American; therefore, I had no idea, and still do not, how Americans sound when they speak.

Neither the porter nor a cab driver knew where Gallaudet College was. I gave them the address, and the cab driver shook his head and drove away after looking at it. The helpful porter made getting a cab for me his personal mission. He waved for another and talked to the cab driver, who opened the back door for me.

I had practiced the American Manual Alphabet on the airplane and felt very comfortable with my speed. I was confident that I would be able to communicate with American deaf people easily. The cab entered the

Gallaudet campus, and we stopped outside a building called College Hall. I saw about thirty students milling around, signing to each other with the speed of lightning. The driver asked me where I wanted to get off. I told him this place would be fine. After the cab left, I stood with my Air India handbag at my feet and gaped at the students who were signing so fast. I could not understand even one word. I decided to keep my knowledge of the American Manual Alphabet a secret.

The students ignored me totally, and I wondered if I was invisible. In India, the arrival of a stranger is a big event. A student from another country would have been surrounded by people and questioned about where he was from and what he was doing. I knew I needed to get some assistance.

My first two attempts to get someone's attention were a total failure. The first thing I learned about Gallaudet students was that they have little or no patience with someone who does not sign. Finally, I did succeed in getting the attention of two pretty girls who passed close to me. They were very helpful. One of them asked if I was from India by pointing at my Air India bag. Then the second girl asked me something I could not understand. She then wrote on her notebook, "Are you a freshman or prep?" I did not know which one I was. Worse still, I did not know what a prep or a freshman was. Our attempt at conversation got the attention of a bespectacled male student. The three consulted with each other, and then the male student motioned for me to follow him. I waived to the two girls and followed my benefactor.

He wrote on paper that his name was Godsay, and that he was from Florida. "Where are you from?" He wrote. I pointed at the Air India bag, and he nodded his head in understanding.

We walked to Fowler Hall, which was the dorm for boys in the preparatory department. I learned that students who were weak in English or mathematics spent 1 year in such departments. My guide introduced me to a short but muscular man. They exchanged words with their fingers and hands flying to and fro. I still could not understand what was being said. When they were done, the muscular man handed me a key along with a pillowcase and two bed sheets. Godsay led me to a room—his own—on the fourth floor and helped me make one of the beds. I had never seen, much less used, a mattress before and was grateful for his help. Later, he showed me where the bathroom was, and I changed into

my sleeping suit, slowly got into the bed, and passed out. I slept for
12 hours.

The next morning when I woke up, Godsay was in the room, sitting
in a chair. He smiled when he saw I was awake and signed, "Eat." I was
indeed hungry. I took a hurried shower and dressed in my suit and the
tie. Godsay, who was dressed in a T-shirt and shorts, did not say anything.
He was a very understanding guy.

My visit to the Gallaudet cafeteria was a revelation. The stainless
steel equipment and floors were so clean, they amazed me. However,
what really got my attention was the number of machines that dispensed
Coke, three kinds of fruit juices, and milk. You could fill your glass with
all the milk or any other drink you wanted. In India, you were given
measured amounts of everything, and you didn't ask for seconds. I had
read in history books how rivers of milk used to flow in ancient India;
however, I had not read that there were countries like America where
these rivers were still flowing. I knew the United States was a wealthy
nation, but reading about prosperity is not enough. You have to experience prosperity to really understand it; just as you have to experience
poverty to understand it.

While eating my first American breakfast, I watched the other students,
still trying and failing to understand what they were saying. A student
caught my attention as he poured himself four glasses of milk and one
of orange juice. His tray also held a stack of some round stuff, which I
later learned were pancakes, bacon, and a heap of hash brown potatoes.
I was hungry, but I was sure that I could not eat half of what he had
and then drink four glasses of milk on top of it. The guy was big, and I
was curious to see how he was going to finish his enormous breakfast.
The real shocker came when I saw him eat half his breakfast and drink
only one glass of milk. The other three glasses of cold milk went down
the drain! I thought of all the little kids clamoring for milk back home
in India and felt guilty as I looked at my breakfast tray.

My friend from Florida was a very patient guy and fingerspelled words
slowly for me or wrote on paper to explain things. After breakfast, he
showed me around the campus, introducing me to the students he knew.
I had met many Americans in India; they were all "Americans." Here,
however, they were not from America; they were from Florida, California,

New York, and other states! Of course, I was from India; nobody asked about Himachal Pradesh or Punjab.

While passing a large field filled with players involved in some sort of game, Godsay asked me if I was interested in watching football. Now, football back in India, as well as the rest of the world, is what the Americans call soccer. I loved playing and watching football, so I said "yes," and he led me to the bleachers. Americans had always looked big to me, but the players dressed in their football gear looked huge. I made a mental note to never get any of them irritated at me. I wondered why they had all that gear, and then I saw that the "football" was oddly shaped. I also wondered how they would be able to run while wearing all that stuff.

There was something odd about this game. First, the players would huddle and discuss something. Then the two sides would line up facing each other with one of both hands on their knees. Suddenly, everyone would be falling on each other or running in all directions except for where the football was. Then they would stop only to huddle and line up all over again. They continued doing that for a while, and I got bored. I figured they were trying to start the game, but something was going wrong.

After waiting patiently for some action for about 10 minutes, I asked my friend, "When will they start to play?" As I mentioned before, he was a very understanding guy; however, my question must have pushed him to the brink. He shook his head and wrote, "They are playing." His face, however, clearly said, "Boy, are you dumb."

After this very brief educational tour of campus, Godsey took me back to our room. Then we walked to Ely Hall, the dormitory for freshmen. He introduced me to the two hearing dormitory supervisors, shook my hand, and left. I was sorry to see him go. He was a real nice guy.

Upon learning I could not sign at all, the two dormitory supervisors had a brief discussion and then one of them filled out a form, had me sign it, and gave me a key. He wrote on a piece of paper, "Go to room number 308." I took the key, walked up the stairs, and found the room that was to be my home for 1 year. As I entered, a tall young man who was reading a book jumped up. He looked at me coldly and then left the room without saying anything. He was not friendly like Godsey. Well, I told myself, Indian people are all different from each other; the Americans are different too. I stood in the middle of the room wondering what to do. A few minutes later, my new roommate returned. He shook my hand and began to talk. When he found I could neither lipread nor hear, he wrote on a piece of paper, "I am Dan from Indiana." I wrote back, "I am Madan from India." We both laughed. The "Dan" in "Madan" and "India" in "Indian" helped break the ice.

I knew English before coming to America. I had read Zane Gray, Louis L'Amour, Max Brand, Ian Fleming, Jane Austen, and Thomas Hardy. Although I understood it, I was not prepared for "American" English and had some problems.

Thanks to the time I spent getting the notorious "P" Form, I was 2 weeks late arriving at Gallaudet. I missed the required orientation and had to learn about Gallaudet by asking people and bumbling around the campus. I did not know about the course work, the semester system (India follows the British full-year term) and credit hours earned, or the number of credit hours required to graduate. This was all new to me.

The worst part of being a new guy in a new place was my inability to communicate in American Sign Language. All I knew was the alphabet, and my speed at spelling could have put even the most patient person to sleep. Everyone signed at Gallaudet, and those who did not were either hard of hearing, skilled lipreaders, or both. I did not fit into any of these categories. I was enrolled in a sign language class and was picking up signs fast. I could sign fairly well after about 2 weeks, but I could not read anyone at all because of the speed. Whenever someone approached me, I would sign slowly, "I do not know signs." The reactions to this statement varied from a gentle pat on my back to the rolling of eyes and an expression, which clearly said, "What are you doing at Gallaudet?" Gallaudet students, I learned, had little or no patience with someone who did not sign.

The wave after wave of cultural shock that I faced during my first year would literally fill a book. I am including just a few of my experiences here.

This was in 1967, a little before long hair became fashionable. A month after I arrived at Gallaudet, I needed a haircut and asked around where I could get one. Someone told me about a student who gave 50-cent haircuts and "was not really that bad a barber." I wrote my name on the signup sheet posted on the dorm bulletin board; it said that this person would cut hair in the first-floor restroom of my dormitory. The next day at the appointed time, I waited for my barber in the dormitory lounge. He did not show up. After waiting for more than an hour, I thought maybe I was on the wrong floor. Therefore, I asked a passing student, by pointing to the signup sheet, where I might find the restroom. He told me to go straight ahead, turn right at the end of the corridor, and enter the second door. I followed his directions and found myself in the bathroom. I did not consider the student's trick very funny. I decided not to ask anyone again, fearing that the next guy might send me to another bathroom. That night, I asked Dan where the restroom was. He looked puzzled and asked, "Didn't you just come from there?" That's when the light dawned on me. "You mean a bathroom is called a restroom here?" I asked. I had thought that a "restroom" was where you rested— a drawing room. Well, I guessed, people can rest in strange places.

As time went on, I learned more American English. Americans do not sell garages or yards when they advertise garage or yard sales. An African friend went to a professional photographer for a new photograph of himself since his counselor had recommended that he "present his best picture" at an upcoming job interview. I had already learned that Americans played "football" with their hands (and no foul was called) and rarely touched it with a foot. Doughnuts (usually) do not have any kind of nuts in them. Americans do not live in their living rooms. When a boy and a girl take their car to "park" behind a building, they usually have some other purpose in mind. The list is endless.

I also had to get used to the differences in attitudes. In India, you can ask an acquaintance how he paid for a certain item, what his salary is, and whether he is happy with his wife. Such questions reflect your concern for the individual. In America, my polite inquiries about people's personal affairs generated shock and annoyance. The nicest response to my questions was "none of your business." Sometimes, people would also interject some other words before the word *business*. I acquired a pretty good vocabulary of four-letter words while checking on my new friends' general welfare.

However, I was very thankful for this "mind your own business" attitude in my PE class. In my ignorance, I had elected to take "football" for PE, hoping to play soccer. I was never very athletic, and during class, I would confuse offense with defense and mistakenly try to manhandle the player lined up against me when I was supposed to be defending. I could not throw the ball; it would just wobble to the ground a few yards away. Each time I made a mistake, I expected the other students to laugh at me. I would look around with an embarrassed smile only to find that they were politely ignoring my mistakes.

In a similar situation, students at an Indian college would have laughed their heads off and made the life of such a bungling idiot miserable. I was grateful for the mature attitudes of these 18- and 19-year-old boys.

In India, you do not thank or apologize to someone unless you really are thankful or are sorry. The perfunctory "excuse me," "thank you," or "please" puzzled me. When someone sitting at the same table for a meal would leave, he or she would make a big deal of their departure with an "excuse me." When they did that, I was left wondering what mistake they had made. The continuing "thank you" also baffled me. People must have thought I was very rude, since I only thanked people when I really meant it and not just for passing a potato dish to me.

I also had to re-think what sort of clothes I wore around campus. One Sunday morning, I was reading the newspaper in the dorm lounge. A student wearing nothing but cutoff jeans interrupted my reading and advised me that I had better go up and change as girls might be coming to the lounge later. I did not understand what was wrong with my paisley sleeping suit; however, I knew he was serious. I went upstairs and told my roommate about my experience. Instead of sympathizing, he said with a frown, "Don't tell me you were in the lounge in your pajamas."

In India, two male friends or cousins can walk hand-in-hand, and friends and relatives hug each other upon meeting all the time. A new friend at Gallaudet once called me "queer" and slapped my hand away because I left it on his arm for longer than 2 seconds. Queer in my dictionary meant strange. Later, my roommate Dan, who was my unofficial cultural tutor, explained what queer meant. I was careful not to touch any other boy after that.

These were some of my first experiences in America. A day did not go by without me learning something new. Some of these things were funny, some were crude, and some were totally embarrassing. However, in a few months, I felt at home at Gallaudet. I made friends, learned sign language, took classes, won awards, and moved on.

I received my bachelor and master's degrees in education from Gallaudet and then applied for teaching jobs in India through the Indian embassy in Washington, D.C. I didn't get one answer to the 122 applications I mailed through the Indian Embassy. I was wondering what to do when some of my friends advised me to teach in America for a couple of years and get some real-life experience that I could take back home to India. So, I did.

Each of my years at Gallaudet, I kept telling myself that I would soon return to India to work with my old friends and share what I had learned in America. My "going back to India" slowly became a joke among my friends. At the end of my third year in America, I knew I was not going back home. And the great American dream kicked in.

My friends kept advising me to work for a few years as a teacher in the United States to gain experience before returning to India. They also said that I would have my summers free to do research there. That made sense, and I accepted a teaching job at Kendall Demonstration Elementary School for the Deaf on the Gallaudet campus. My wife Nirmala joined me a month later in October 1973. The idea was that we would live here for a while, save up money, and then go back to India as soon as I got a job offer.

This did not happen. My own resolve about starting a school in India was weakening. I was so used to the American way of life that returning to my roots and leading a life of abject poverty, by American standards, scared me. My efforts to apply for jobs in India tapered off slowly.

Since then, I have done things and achieved milestones that I had never even dreamed about. I have worked as a teacher, administrative assistant, supervisor, associate principal, assistant superintendent, and superintendent in several schools for the deaf. In 1977, I started working in India during summers and researching Indian Sign Language with the help of American scholars. With the help of some American linguists, I authored four dictionaries of Indian Sign Language. I also wrote a number of professional articles and book chapters, and I made presentations at national and international conferences covering deaf education, administration, and Indian Sign Language to name a few.

Dheeraj, our son, was born in 1974; and Neerja, our daughter, arrived 3 years later. We bought a house in Maryland and began to lead an all-American life.

Perhaps my son Dheeraj was right when he said, "Daddy, you were lucky to become deaf." Deafness did open new doors for me, and I used them to arrive where I am now. I cannot wait to start writing about my American adventure—the people I met and friends I made. The experiences I had as a teacher, an administrator, and a person would fill a book—the one I am working on now.